Learning Through Inquiry:

Weaving Science with Thinking and Literature

Learning Through Inquiry:

Weaving Science with Thinking and Literature

by

Caryn M. King

Grand Valley State University

and

Stephen R. Mattox

Grand Valley State University

Christopher-Gordon Publishers, Inc.
Norwood, Massachusetts

Copyright Acknowledgments

Every effort has been made to contact copyright holders for permission to reproduce borrowed material where necessary. We apologize for any oversights and would be happy to rectify them in future printings.

Extracts from "Making Sense of Online Text" by Julie Coiro, *Educational Leadership, 63* (2), 30-35, used with permission.

Moon Phase Diagram and Moon Phase Activity Sheet reprinted with permission from *Astro Adventures II*, by Dennis Schatz and Paul Allan, copyright © 2003 by Pacific Science Center. Astro Adventures available from Pacific Science Center Education Division, 200 Second Avenue North, Seattle, WA 98109 (206-443-2001).

Christopher~Gordon Publishers, Inc.
Bridging Theory and Practice

1502 Providence Highway, Suite 12
Norwood, MA 02062

800-934-8322 • 781-762-5577
www.Christopher-Gordon.com

Printed in the United State of America
10 9 8 7 6 5 4 3 2 1   10 09 08 07

ISBN 13: 978-1-933760-08-7
Library of Congress Catalogue Number: 2006940274

Table of Contents

Acknowledgements

This book would not be possible without the generous contributions of experts and classroom teachers who have lent their valuable expertise.

First, we want to thank our colleague and good friend, David Whitehead, from the University of Waikato in Hamilton, New Zealand. David's work with thinking tools has become a most crucial aspect of this book. Thinking tools are used in our units because we wanted a way to help children turn their scientific observations into higher order thinking and have a means to articulate it. Thinking tools are different from thinking skills, which are actually unconscious, automatic processes. Instead, thinking tools provide learners with labels that describe particular types of thinking (i.e., predict, question, summarize, visualize). By making learners more aware of their own thinking processes, and by giving them words to describe their thinking, both receptive and productive language modes are enhanced. These tools originate in David's recent book, *Top Tools for Teaching Thinking* (Whitehead, 2004) and are the basis for chapter 2, Literacy and Thinking Tools for Science Teachers, which David wrote.

We want to acknowledge classroom teachers Ginger Vanderbeek, Janet Norman, and Susan Gray for their creative ideas and willingness to experiment with ways to involve children in the inquiry process. These women have greatly influenced the content of our life science and physical science chapters. Both Ginger and Janet have worked closely with Grand Valley State University's (GVSU) Regional Math and Science Center to improve elementary science instruction. We were very fortunate when Mary Ann Sheline and Karen Meyers of the Center connected us with Janet and Ginger. It has been a fruitful collaboration, and we want to thank Ginger, Janet, Mary Ann, and Karen.

Several additional colleagues at Grand Valley State University have contributed to this book in a variety of ways. Larry Fegel, of GVSU's Geology Department, collaborated with Steve to create the units in the Earth science chapters. Larry, who works with GVSU preservice teachers, has taught for over 30 years in K–12 schools. He continues to teach children at the Discovery Outdoor Learning Center in Holland, Michigan.

Other content experts at Grand Valley State University have been instrumental, and we were fortunate to work with colleagues from various disciplines who are involved in our preservice teacher program. For instance, Chris Dobson, a biologist, reviewed and approved units and books for the life science chapters; and Keith Oliver, a physicist, did the same for the physical science chapters. Each of them have their own young children, so when reviewing books, they were careful to recommend books they felt were appropriate for children and use in elementary classrooms.

Our list would not be complete without recognizing Elaine Collins, Dean of the College of Education, Fred Antczak, Dean of the College of Liberal Arts and Sciences, and Kevin Cole, Geology Department Chairperson, for supporting our ongoing work. Their encouragement has been instrumental in creating an atmosphere within GVSU that fosters interdepartmental, interdisciplinary collaborations. Their support contributes to the creation of a vibrant college culture that fosters inquiry and learning.

Finally, we wish to thank our colleagues at Christopher-Gordon, especially Jennifer Bengtson and Sue Canavan. Their insights, encouragement, and assistance along the way have been invaluable. We could not have done this without you!

Preface

Learning Through Inquiry: Weaving Science with Thinking and Literature is designed to provide you, the upper elementary teacher, with a resource to integrate science, literacy, and children's literature in a unique way. We realize there are many Internet resources available to those who teach science and literacy. However, activities found on the Web typically do not integrate these content areas. What makes this book unique is the fact that our chapters act as a scaffold for novice, or even reluctant, teachers who may not be comfortable teaching, much less integrating science and literacy. By providing you with detailed examples of how such integration might occur, we think you will be better prepared to offer your students instruction that is meaningful, memorable, and grounded in best practices.

Using a consistent format, we demonstrate how to engage your third through fifth graders with hands-on activities and quality children's literature. We demonstrate how to teach valuable thinking tools that will help your students remember information and to be critical, creative, and reflective thinkers. These units involve students in the scientific processes of engagement, exploration, explanation, elaboration, and evaluation, which are also the processes literate individuals use. Plus, both language arts and science standards are taught within the same series of lessons, enabling you to make the most of your planning and instructional time. The first three chapters serve as an introduction. Chapter 1 defines content literacy and science literacy and describes national content standards. This is followed by an explanation of best practices for teaching both science and literacy. The second chapter defines thinking tools, not thinking skills, and offers examples of how these tools can be used when teaching science. Chapter 3 provides the rationale for using children's literature in the science classroom and offers a step-by-step process and checklist for selecting good trade books.

The remaining chapters focus on: states of matter; force and motion; light; properties of earth materials; erosion; characteristics of the Earth, Moon, and Sun; heredity; and animal adaptations. We chose aspects of each topic that have high utility because they are commonly listed in state and local science curriculum guides. In addition, the topics we selected are ones we felt were underrepresented in other science materials on the market or were not taught well. Thus, our units are designed to have maximum impact. Each content chapter uses the following format:

- · an Introduction that uses examples from everyday life to show why this topic is important to study;
- · a Big Idea, which summarizes the core concept of the chapter;
- · a Key Science Question, which helps focus students' attention on the core concept;
- · the national science standard addressed in the chapter;
- · the national language arts standard addressed in the chapter;
- · the estimated time needed to teach the entire unit;
- · an advanced organizer to show an overview of the chapter;
- · a Teacher Background section, which provides factual information explaining the core concept;
- · a list of materials needed to teach the unit;
- · a suggested procedure to follow, including classroom management tips; and,
- · a Teacher Resources section containing a bibliography of associated trade books, Web sites, videos, and reproducible student pages.

We hope that you and your colleagues use this book as the basis for discussion, experimentation, and professional development. All activities are designed to use various materials and children's books, which you will need to gather prior to teaching each unit. Try out the lessons, then come together to share your experiences, insights, and materials. We encourage all of you to familiarize yourselves with the introductory chapters (i.e., chapters 1, 2, and 3). If you are a new teacher or are squeamish about teaching science, start by observing a more experienced teacher who is using this book. Or, if that isn't possible, begin experimenting with the ideas in chapters 4 and 5. These chapters are straightforward and use the 5E framework in a sequential way. Once you feel more comfortable with the format, continue working through the book and try the physical science chapters next (i.e., chapters 6, 7, and 8), followed by the last three chapters on Earth science. More comfortable, experienced teachers can begin anywhere in the book, but keep in mind that some of the literacy activities highlighted in later chapters are built on activities used in previous chapters. We feel confident that this process will provide you with insights, and we invite you to develop your own lessons that integrate science and literacy. Likewise, we invite your students to develop a love for learning science as a result of engaging in the activities in this book. Thus, our book is not a means to an end, it is a beginning.

This book is a result of collaboration of the best kind—one involving many talented individuals who truly care about effective teaching and learning. In an information age such as this one, we feel it is critical to teach our students to think for themselves, especially so they can locate and understand new information as well as answer questions about their changing world. Plus, when we encourage our students to think, learning is a natural result, which makes our jobs as teachers that much more rewarding. So this book is for you: the dedicated teacher who believes all students can learn, inspires them to be inquisitive thinkers, and needs a resource to get started. Good luck!

C. M. K.

S. R. M.

Chapter 1

Content Literacy and
Best Practices

Introduction

Do you remember your first attempts at reading and writing? What were they? I recently shared one of my creations with Steve when we were meeting about this book. My mom kept it all of these years and gave it to me recently when she was cleaning out the attic. She told me I wrote this "story" when I was almost 5 years old, and at the time, I told her it was about autumn.

My "story" went something like this:

We picked apples. It was sunny. My mom made me wear my jacket.
The leaves were orange. They are pretty. We will make a pie.

Despite the fact the sentences are simple, the verb tenses irregular, and the letters looked more like squiggles on the page, the piece reveals a personal observation about the season. These elements, knowledge of scientific content and an application of that knowledge, are two elements of science literacy. Even though the writing did not contain perfectly formed letters and actual words, the lines represented an important message that I wanted to record and share. Thank goodness my mother realized my first attempts at literacy were valuable. In fact, they should be acknowledged and celebrated, especially since they are the foundation for future learning.

What Is Content Literacy?
What Is Science Literacy?

As more research is done on literacy and what it means to be literate, our definition of literacy has expanded beyond merely the ability to read and write. Today's technological world demands sophisticated thinking and reasoning, in addition to skilled reading and writing. The average individual has constant, immediate access to large amounts of information, and visual images conveying messages flood our environment. To make sense of our world, we must sort through this information, analyze it, evaluate it, synthesize it, and act on it. Being literate in the 21st century is far more complex and multidimensional than in the past.

So what does *content literacy* imply? Content literacy has its roots in the near past when the term "content area reading" was used to describe the ways in which teachers helped students better comprehend their subject-area texts (e.g., social studies, math, science). However, technology alone has forced us to expand our notion of "text" to include electronic as well as visual media. We now acknowledge the cultural demands our society places on literate individuals, and we recognize that literacy also involves the context in which learning occurs. Vacca (2002) refers to content literacy as the ability to use reading, writing, talking, listening, and viewing to learn subject matter in a given discipline. We concur with this definition, but we want to point out that content literacy also requires elements of critical thinking and decision making. Not only is content literacy the ability to use reading, writing, talking, listening, and viewing to learn subject matter, it is also the ability to question assumptions, explore perspectives, and incorporate new knowledge with existing knowledge. Content literacy demands that we develop critical perspectives based on our experiences *and* the content to be learned, putting us in a position to be successful in today's competitive, technological society.

When thinking about what it means to be literate in the science classroom, we should consider the ways in which scientists use language. Scientists use oral language to talk to other scientists, as well as present and debate ideas. They engage in listening when they consider the ideas of other scientists, the public, or their students. They practice viewing when reading diagrams, charts, or when making careful observations about scientific phenomena. Scientists read journals and reports, which often inform their own research, and they write to communicate, record, and document scientific observations. Science literacy, therefore, involves the types of critical thinking, cognitive and metacognitive abilities, and habits of mind necessary to conduct the work of the scientist. As Ford, Yore, and Anthony (1997) point out, it involves constructing an understanding of scientific disciplines, identifying the big ideas or unifying concepts of those disciplines, and then communicating those understandings to persuade others to take informed action. Science literacy begins in the classroom, but it deepens over a lifetime. The attitudes and values established toward science early in a child's life will likely shape his or her development of science literacy as an adult (National Research Council, 1996).

What Are Content Standards?

When children enter school, they learn about math, social studies, science, art, and music. These subject areas are also referred to as content areas, and most states and national organizations have established "content" standards, which detail what students are supposed to know in a given area. Content standards also specify at what grade level we expect our students to know certain concepts. But content standards are more than a list of student expectations. They represent not only the criteria to judge the quality of student knowledge, but also the criteria to determine the quality of instructional programs and teaching. Moreover, content standards can be used to assess our progress toward a national vision of teaching and learning (National Research Council, 1996).

For our purposes, two content areas are highlighted in this book: science and language arts. As part of the educational reform movement that began in the 1990s, learned societies such as the National Academy of Sciences, the International Reading Association, and the National Council of Teachers of English, among others, were charged with establishing national goals and content expectations for their respective disciplines. As a result, each discipline compiled its own set of national standards. The next section will explain the content standards applicable to this book.

Science Standards

In 1996, the Governing Board of the National Research Council, whose members were drawn from the councils of the National Academy of Sciences, the National Academy of Engineering, and the Institute of Medicine, published a document entitled, *National Science Education Standards*. This document specifies broad goals for school science programs so that students studying science would:

- experience the richness and excitement of knowing about and understanding the natural world;

- use appropriate scientific processes and principles in making personal decisions;

- engage intelligently in public discourse and debate about matters of scientific and technological concern; and

- increase their economic productivity through the use of the knowledge, understanding, and skills of the scientifically literate person in their careers. (p. 1)

By identifying these goals, the authors attempted to clarify their vision of a scientifically literate society, and the standards identified the understandings and ways of thinking that are critical for living in a world shaped by science and technology. Taken collectively, the goals recommended that schools implementing the national science standards develop programs to encourage students to learn science by "actively engaging in inquiries that are interesting and important to them" (p. 1), practices in which scientists commonly engage.

The *National Science Education Standards* document (1996) outlines what students should know, understand, and be able to do in science. The standards are described as a set of outcomes, divided into eight categories, designed for a range of grade levels, such as K–4, 5–8, and 9–12. It's important to note they are not a prescribed curriculum (National Research Council, 1996, 2000). In fact, you most likely have your own science curriculum. But, we are certain that if you were to compare your curriculum to the national standards, you would notice parallels. Since we are writing for a national audience, we chose to frame our units around these broad, national goals.

In this book, we focused on four content standards: (1) science as inquiry; (2) physical science; (3) life science; and (4) Earth and space science. The units focus on the K–4 range and touch upon the 5–8 range. We chose to target Grades 3–5 because these grades are most often housed in the elementary school, whereas sixth through eighth grades are most often in middle schools. You should be aware that in order to fully meet the 5–8 standards, additional instruction would be necessary. The next section of this chapter specifies aspects of each content standard that are addressed within later chapters in our book.

Science as Inquiry

This content standard specifies that "as a result of activities . . . all students should develop abilities necessary to do scientific inquiry, and an understanding about scientific inquiry" (National Research Council, 1996, p. 121). This means children should experience science in a way that engages them in active construction of ideas and knowledge within their developmental capabilities. Activities should encourage students to ask questions about objects, organisms, and events in their environment. With your guidance, students should plan and conduct simple investigations using equipment and tools to gather data. Inquiring classrooms encourage students to use data to construct and justify reasonable explanations, as well as communicate, critique, and analyze their work and the work of others. Obviously, this is not something that can be achieved with a lock-step approach, and we feel Bybee's (1997) 5E framework, which will be explained later, is especially suitable. Even though the units in this book are set up in a sequential manner, we encourage you to consider them as guidelines for generating student interest and inquiry. Moreover, these units do not fully address all aspects of each content standard, which further encourages you to spend additional time in further study, based on your students' interests and needs.

Physical Science

This content standard specifies that "as a result of the activities . . . all students should develop an understanding of properties of objects and materials; position and motion of objects; light, heat, electricity, and magnetism" (National Research Council, 1996, p. 123). The unit you will read about in chapter 6, entitled What Matters About the States of Matter?, focuses on one aspect of this standard: the properties of objects and materials. The goal of the unit is to help students realize that materials can exist in different states—solid, liquid, and gas. Through experimentation and observation, this unit encourages students to define the states of matter and draw conclusions about their properties. The unit in chapter 7, Roll It, focuses on the second component of this standard: position and motion of objects. The goal of this unit is to have students demonstrate real-world situations involving the forces of push or pull and determine how force affects the motion of an object. Once again, this is accomplished by student-led inquiry. Finally, the unit in chapter 8, Light Blockers, focuses on shadows and light, which is one aspect of the standard's final component. Using various light sources and materials, students make observations about light.

Life Science

This content standard specifies "as a result of activities . . . all students should develop an understanding of: the characteristics of organisms, life cycles of organisms, and organisms and environments" (National Research Council, 1996, p. 127). It lends itself well to the elementary classroom, since most children are naturally curious about the plants and animals that surround them. In the unit Nature and Nurture, which appears in chapter 4, students develop an understanding of the role that both nature (inherited traits) and nurture (environmental factors) play in determining an individual's characteristics. The unit helps students understand why we are alike in some ways yet different in others. As a follow-up, students are encouraged to answer the question "How are animals adapted to survive in nature?" in the unit in chapter 5, entitled Birdie Buffet. By analyzing the physical characteristics that birds need for survival, students create and justify their own example of adaptation. We have purposely omitted a unit on life cycles because there are many good resources for teaching this topic, and the teachers we spoke with when we planned this book told us it is one science topic they are comfortable teaching.

Earth and Space Science

The final content standard our book addresses states "as a result of their activities . . . all students should develop an understanding of properties of earth materials; objects in the sky; and changes in earth and sky" (National Research Council, 1996, p. 130). Three units are devoted to this standard. For instance, chapter 9, The Earth Beneath Our Feet, engages children in sorting and classifying earth materials and discovering the types of materials that make up our Earth. The Away We Go! unit in chapter 10 focuses on how water, wind, and ice cause changes on Earth. As a result, students will develop an understanding of agents of change in the Earth's surface. Finally, the unit in chapter 11, The Earth in the Solar System, encourages students to observe the sun, moon, stars, and Earth in order to identify their properties and actions.

Language Arts Standards

Like the national science standards, the *Standards for the English Language Arts* were published in 1996 as a result of a 4-year collaboration between the National Council of Teachers of English (NCTE) and the International Reading Association (IRA). The members of the committee responsible for this document were chosen for their specialized competence and with regard to philosophical balance. Thus, the English language arts standards are grounded in what we know about language and language learning, as well as reflect our nation's commitment to educating *all* students (IRA & NCTE, 1996, p. vii). This document does its best to reflect the many different voices of teachers, parents, legislators, administrators, researchers, and policy analysts who were involved in the project since its inception. It is an attempt to offer a coherent vision of the essential goals of English language arts instruction that are not restricted to one set of standards per subject area. For this reason, you will notice that the standards are very broad and incorporate all aspects of the language arts: reading, writing, listening, speaking, viewing, and visually representing. And, in addition to detailing the content knowledge we want children to know *about* language, these standards also define what we expect children to be able to *do* with language.

An interactive model placing the learner at the center is the basis for the *English Language Arts Standards* (IRA & NCTE, 1996). The learner is at the heart of the model because the standards are grounded in the experiences and activities of humans engaging in literate activities. Intersecting with the learner is the *content* dimension, which addresses what students should know and be able to do with the

English language arts. Also intersecting with the learner is the *purpose* dimension, which addresses the question of why we use language. The *development* dimension is the third and final intersection with the learner and focuses on how learners develop competencies in the language arts. All three—content, purpose and development—are viewed not as entities in and of themselves, but as dimensions of language learning. Surrounding these dimensions of learning is the *context* of learning. Context is superimposed over all of the dimensions because "all language learning takes place in, responds to, shapes, and is in turn shaped by particular social and cultural contexts" (p. 13).

As mentioned previously, the language arts standards represent a vision of the essential goals of English language arts instruction just as the national science standards articulate the central goal of science literacy. Therefore, the standards are meant to be suggestive, not exhaustive—a starting point for ongoing discussion about best practice. For this reason, the authors of the *Standards for the English Language Arts* are careful to point out that the standards should not be atomized into isolated components of instruction. Rather, the view that "virtually any instructional activity is likely to address multiple standards simultaneously" (p. 24) provides the perfect scenario for integrating language arts and science. The vision guiding the language arts standards is that all students must have the opportunities and resources to develop the language skills they need to pursue life's goals and to participate fully as informed productive members of society. This vision parallels that of the American Association for the Advancement of Science (AAAS), whose definition of science literacy involves "those understandings and ways of thinking that are essential for all citizens living in a world shaped by science and technology" (1990, p. xiii). Language arts and science, therefore, are a natural bridge to helping students develop the skills, attitudes, and knowledge necessary to complete the vision.

The 12 content standards for the English language arts are found in Figure 1:1. These standards assume that literacy begins long before children enter school, and its development continues within the school walls and within the larger community. Despite the fact the standards are presented as a list, they should be viewed as a whole.

---

1. Students read a wide range of print and nonprint texts to build an understanding of texts, of themselves, and of the cultures of the United States and the world; to acquire new information to respond to the needs and demands of society and the workplace; and for personal fulfillment. Among these texts are fiction and nonfiction, as well as classic and contemporary works.

2. Students read a wide range of literature from many periods in many genres to build an understanding of the many dimensions (e.g., philosophical, ethical, aesthetic) of human experience.

Figure 1:1   IRA/NCTE standards for the English language arts.

3. Students apply a wide range of strategies to comprehend, interpret, evaluate, and appreciate texts. They draw on their prior experience, their interactions with other readers and writers, their knowledge of word meaning and of other texts, their word identification strategies, and their understandings of textual features (e.g., sound-letter correspondence, sentence structure, context, graphics).

4. Students adjust their use of spoken, written, and visual language (e.g., conventions, style, vocabulary) to communicate effectively with a variety of audiences and for different purposes.

5. Students employ a wide range of strategies as they write and use different writing process elements appropriately to communicate with different audiences for a variety of purposes.

6. Students apply knowledge of language structure, language conventions (e.g., spelling and punctuation), media techniques, figurative language, and genre to create, critique, and discuss print and nonprint texts.

7. Students conduct research on issues and interests by generating ideas and questions, and by posing problems. They gather, evaluate, and synthesize data from a variety of sources (e.g., print and nonprint texts, artifacts, people) to communicate their discoveries in ways that suit their purposes and audience.

8. Students use a variety of technological and informational resources (e.g., libraries, databases, computer networks, video) to gather and synthesize information and to create and communicate knowledge.

9. Students develop an understanding of, and respect for, diversity in language use, patterns, and dialects across cultures, ethnic groups, geographic regions, and social roles.

10. Students whose first language is not English make use of their first language to develop competency in the English language arts and to develop understanding of content across the curriculum.

11. Students participate as knowledgeable, reflective, creative, and critical members of a variety of literacy communities.

12. Students use spoken, written, and visual language to accomplish their own purposes (e.g., for learning, enjoyment, persuasion, and the exchange of information).

Figure 1:1   IRA/NCTE standards for the English language arts. *(Continued)*

What Are Best Practices for Teaching Science?

Since 1990, when the AAAS first envisioned "science literacy" and its importance, calls for changes in the way science is taught have been made. Today, as a result of the work of the AAAS and the recommendations made in the *National Science Education Standards* document (National Research Council, 1996), more and more science teachers are using a hands-on, inquiry-based teaching-learning model. Inquiry-based learning is grounded in constructivism, which encourages learning by doing. It is a learning experience that enhances students' abilities to think critically. In an inquiring classroom, students engage in in-depth investigations with objects, materials, phenomena, and ideas, and they draw meaning and understanding from those experiences. This approach requires students to be-come active participants in their learning, instead of remaining passive learners. When engaged in hands-on learning, students can directly observe, question, dis-cuss, and better understand fundamental scientific principles. Today's use of tech-nology in the classroom is especially advantageous because real-world applications of scientific principles can be further explored, fostering relevant, long-lasting interest in science.

One of the most commonly used instructional frameworks for inquiry-based learning is known as the 5E framework (Bybee, 1997; National Research Council, 2000). The 5Es represent specific aspects of the inquiry process, and a complete unit ideally contains all five aspects: Engagement, Exploration, Explanation, Elabo-ration, and Evaluation. The intended outcome of using the 5E framework is the desire to structure learning experiences that provide students with the opportuni-ties to *read* like scientists, *think* like scientists, and *act* like scientists. In doing so, we promote science literacy. The units you will read about in this book follow the 5E format and incorporate the 5E philosophy. Figure 1:2 and the accompanying ex-planation may be helpful in conceptualizing how the 5E framework can be used in your classroom.

A 5E unit begins with the Engage phase, which initiates the learning task. The activity used should make connections between past and present learning experi-ences, identify students' misconceptions, anticipate activities, and focus students' thinking toward the learning outcomes. Its purpose is to get students' attention and arouse curiosity about the topic to be studied, often resulting in dis-equilibrium and cognitive dis-sonance. There are two components to this phase: (1) elicit students' prior knowledge and (2) engage them. In order to accomplish this, the engage-ment activity should be novel and relevant to the students. Acting out a problematic situ-ation, asking a question, and defining a problem are all ways to engage students and focus them on the learning task. This phase is short and simple. This is not a time when you explain concepts, provide definitions,

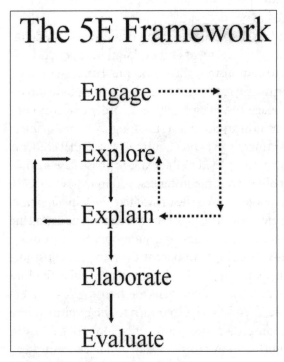

Figure 1:2 The 5E framework.

answer questions, or lecture. Those teacher behaviors are inconsistent with the 5E philosophy.

The next phase of the 5E unit is the Explore phase. At this point, students have the opportunity to engage in meaningful inquiry. This phase provides them with a common base of experiences within which concepts, processes, and skills are identified and developed. The activities selected for this phase of the unit should be concrete, foster discovery, and be meaningful to the student. At times, the activities are teacher guided; at other times, they are student initiated. During this phase, direct instruction is limited and you should encourage collaboration among students, much like a community of scientists working together to solve a problem. Your role is to act as a coach or facilitator by observing and listening to students as they interact. Ask probing questions to redirect students' investigations, when necessary, and provide enough time for students to work through any problems they may encounter. The goal is to model scientific thinking processes, and helping students to realize these processes are not always linear.

Some of you may be uncomfortable with this type of approach. However, the traditional roles of the teacher and student are often reversed when implementing the 5E framework. Thus, it is important that you do not provide answers or explanations during the Explore phase, since one of the goals of inquiry-based learning is to allow students to work though their cognitive dissonance and seek solutions to their own questions, just as scientists do in real life. At the same time, it is important that you set up the Explore phase in a way that provides students with the support and resources they need to be successful.

The Explain phase typically follows the Explore phase. This phase focuses students' attention on a particular aspect of their engagement and exploration experiences. It provides opportunities for students to demonstrate their conceptual understandings, skills, or behaviors. This phase is primarily teacher directed, since this phase directs students to specific aspects of the Engage and Explore phases in order to clarify concepts, correct misconceptions, and introduce scientific terminology. Feel free to interject an explanation of the scientific principle in a direct, formal way so that students realize the significance of the activities completed in the Explore phase. Use formal, scientific vocabulary in your explanation. In some instances, you may wish to use a video or an explanation found on a reputable Web site to facilitate the Explain phase. The goal is to enable students to organize and articulate their thoughts concerning the Explore activities. Fellow students listen critically and add additional explanations.

Often, during the Explain phase, it becomes apparent that students, just like scientists at times, may not be able to articulate the significance of their Explore experiences. If this lack of knowledge is likely to prevent them from deep understanding of a key scientific principle, then it is wise to return to the Explore phase for additional experimentation, reading, discussion, and reflection. That is why in Figure 1:2, you see the arrows pointing away from Explain and back toward Explore. This process reflects actual scientific inquiry.

You will also notice the dotted lines in Figure 1:2. We placed them in the figure because, as we have said before, inquiry-based teaching and learning are not necessarily linear. Even though in a traditional 5E unit you would begin with Engagement, followed by Exploration, and continuing with Explanation, Elaboration, and Evaluation, there may be situations when this sequence is not the most appropriate. There may be a time when you realize during the Engage phase that students have well-developed prior knowledge. For instance, they may know a lot about the food, energy, and environmental needs of plants. In this case, you may want to go directly to the Explain phase to determine the depth of their knowledge. Once you are satisfied they truly understand this concept, then you may decide to focus on a different aspect of the life science standard in the Explore phase. In this example, you may set up some experiments to lead students to explain the functions of selected seed plant parts. Thus, you may alter the 5E sequence based on your evaluation of student prior knowledge and interest.

Three things should be kept in mind. First, careful planning is needed, but be willing to change those plans to respond to student knowledge and interests, while also knowing the goals of your science program and activities that are consistent with those goals. Second, you need to be aware of the developmental needs of your students and plan accordingly. It makes little sense to create plans based on what students already know, or to engage them in activities that are too abstract or conceptually difficult for them. Finally, you need to have the appropriate resources for students to engage in developmentally relevant inquiry activities. When these three items are addressed, 5E units can be successfully implemented.

During the Elaborate phase of the unit, students' conceptual understanding and skills are challenged. Through new experiences, students develop deeper and broader understandings, acquire more information, and develop adequate skills. The activities used in this phase must provide further time and experience in order to reflect on learning. Group discussion and cooperative learning are key elements of the Elaborate phase, since peer learning is valued in an inquiring classroom. Students use previous information to ask questions, propose solutions, make decisions, or design experiments. They test solutions in different contexts. They read and write articles, books, and reports. You expect them to use appropriate vocabulary, definitions, and explanations as they apply concepts and skills in new situations. They are reminded of alternative explanations and you encourage discussion. The classroom is organized as a scientific community so that students have the opportunity to explain their understanding to one another and receive feedback from their peers, just as scientists often do in real life. Internalization of concepts, processes, and skills is the primary goal of this phase.

The final phase of the 5E framework is the Evaluate phase. This phase encourages students to assess their understandings and abilities and provides opportunities for you to evaluate student progress. This can be done in a variety of ways by asking open-ended questions, such as "Why do you think...?" or "What evidence do you have?" or "What do you know about the problem?" Look for evidence that students have changed their thinking by observing them as they apply new concepts and skills. The information gained in this phase can be used for formative and/or summative evaluation. Although evaluation is possible at each and every stage of the 5E framework, the most significant measure of understanding is the ability to transfer the knowledge to new and different situations. This is best accomplished in the Evaluate phase.

The fluid nature of the 5E framework is closely aligned with the actual processes used by scientists. As such, the methods of scientific inquiry are effective means by which students hypothesize, experiment, and test solutions. The activities included in the following chapters are intended to encourage inquiry through reading, writing, and discussion to process and make sense of what occurred. In doing so, we are attempting to create classrooms that are congruent with the discipline of science and reflect on the scientific genre.

What Are Best Practices
for Teaching Literacy?

Students typically encounter texts and other reading materials as they participate in various phases of the 5E framework. However, many children have difficulty understanding the texts typically used in the science classroom. Sometimes the problem is created by the text itself when authors use specialized vocabulary without adequate definitions (McRae & de Sa, 1997), or they present too many abstract concepts for young readers to grasp. Other problems, such as limited knowledge of English, poor instruction, and few adults available to serve as good reading models, may also exist. As one solution, we are advocating the use of literacy strategies that have roots in a process-based theory of reading comprehension. We believe in the efficacy of process-based comprehension instruction because it is designed to overcome the difficulties readers typically have with text. Moreover, all of the literacy strategies we are suggesting have been tested empirically (Collins Block, Schaller, Joy, & Giane, 2002).

Process-based comprehension instruction teaches the reader the thought processes needed at strategic points in the text so that personal connections are made and the text becomes memorable (Pearson & Duke, 2002). The strategies used in our units focus on understanding and comprehending information, synthesizing that understanding with prior knowledge and experience, and communicating new knowledge with others. Thus, a natural connection exists between these comprehension processes and the scientific processes students experience in the Engage, Explain, and Explore phases of the 5E framework. By implementing the suggested comprehension strategies, teachers better prepare readers to experience science literacy. The remainder of this chapter will share general characteristics for effective process-based comprehension instruction, as well as describe their application to the 5E framework.

Process-Based Comprehension Instruction

We begin with a short summary of skilled comprehension, since it is helpful to understand what skilled readers do when they read. If you are reading this text, most likely, you are an adept reader. As such, we are often unaware of the processes we use automatically when reading. The tools we use as good readers have become so habitual that they have become transparent to us, yet if we consciously think about them, they can serve as valuable templates when teaching comprehension. So what do we know about skilled reading?

We know that competent readers establish a link between their prior knowledge and their interpretation of a text (Anderson & Pearson, 1984). This prior knowledge guides them in the reading process. For instance, competent readers know it is important to have a purpose when reading. It might be to find information, verify a prediction, or even answer a question. Prior knowledge also helps the reader connect bits and pieces of information within the text in order to form a gist of the text, as well as draw conclusions. Effective readers are thoughtful and strategic (Baker & Brown, 1984). They recognize when something doesn't make sense, and they use "fix up" strategies so that the text does make sense to them. They realize that different kinds of texts need to be approached differently, depending on their purpose for reading and type of text. Finally, good readers are productive (Paris, Wasik, & Turner, 1991). They think about texts before, during, and after reading, and they understand that reading is hard work.

The processes used by skilled readers are complementary to the processes and skills of inquiry (Klentschy & Molina-De La Torre, 2004). For instance, when a reader makes a prediction about a text, this mental process is similar to the scientist who hypothesizes about what will happen during an experiment. Good readers, like scientists, observe and remember details. This helps the reader make inferences about what was read, and helps the scientist use observation and evidence to formulate hypotheses. Skilled readers notice the sequence of events and understand their significance, which parallels the scientist, who practices logic and analysis. Finally, competent readers and scientists both draw conclusions. Readers use their prior knowledge and information from the text to do this, and scientists combine data from various sources to reach logical conclusions.

Not all classrooms, however, produce skilled readers, and thoughtful teachers understand there are benefits associated with teaching comprehension strategies to both good and struggling readers alike. Comprehension strategies are procedures that guide students as they practice reading and writing (National Reading Panel, 2000). They are based on what we know about the mental processes used by skilled readers. Effective teachers tell their students what strategy they will be learning, why it is important to learn, and where and when it can be used. They understand that both comprehension and comprehension instruction involve the careful coordination and use of a variety of strategies, especially when a comprehension problem occurs. Savvy teachers understand that teaching process-based strategies is not the same thing as teaching skills. Explanations cannot be scripted, proceduralized, or packaged (Duffy, 1993), but they should be very explicit. Flexibility and consistency are key when teaching both comprehension and inquiry in the science classroom.

Effective comprehension strategy instruction involves explicit teacher scaffolding (Pressley, 2002). For instance, we should begin by explaining what the strategy is, including the purpose for using the strategy. Then, it is important to model the strategy using a think aloud. By verbalizing our own thought processes during the think aloud, we set a good example for inexperienced readers to follow. It is important to literally show your students how a skilled reader thinks about and processes text. At this point, discuss when it would be appropriate to use the strategy. Talk about different kinds of text and compare that with the purpose for using the strategy. Help students draw conclusions about where and when certain strategies are beneficial to use. After modeling, continue to scaffold by providing many opportunities for guided practice. During this phase, readers need your feedback about their use of the strategies, and be sure to link a strategy taught on one day with a strategy taught on another day to build the understanding that good readers choose from a menu of strategies as they read (Reutzel, Smith, & Fawson, 2005). Follow up with even more practice and discussion among peers about their use of the strategies. By modeling, offering feedback, and supporting students as they are learning and practicing the strategies, thoughtful teachers create an environment in which readers are encouraged to develop the confidence to use the strategies independently.

It's important to remember that process-based comprehension instruction should be explicit yet not overly teacher dominated or prescriptive. When instruction is dominated by the teacher, students do not learn how to apply the strategies without prompting. Likewise, when instruction is too open ended, or is not explicit, students do not develop tools to think strategically as they read (Collins Block et al., 2002). Just as the science teacher must make judgments about the proper amount of direction to give students during inquiry-based lessons, the literacy teacher also must decide how, when, and where to coach students when teaching comprehension. It is a challenge!

Multiple Strategy Instruction

At this point, we have used the term "strategies" when discussing comprehension instruction, and this was done on purpose. According to the National Reading

Panel (2000), there is scientific support for "multiple strategy instruction" (p. 46). In other words, readers benefit from instruction that uses a repertoire of reading comprehension strategies, especially when teacher modeling, followed by student practice and teacher coaching, is used. Pressley and colleagues (1992) coined this type of instruction as transactional strategies instruction.

We may think that comprehension instruction is most beneficial for students in upper elementary grades, but Duke and Pearson (2002) argue that even children in primary grades can benefit as well. They recommend teachers focus on a combination of the following strategies: (1) predicting, (2) constructing visual images, (3) clarifying information, (4) text structure analysis, and (5) summarizing. There is evidence to suggest that when teaching a "set" or "family" of cognitive strategies within a collaborative, interactive, engaging routine, children as young as 8 years can make gains in both comprehension and acquisition of science content knowledge in as little as 5 months (Reutzel, Smith, & Fawson, 2005). Obviously, using transactional strategy instruction with informational text in the science classroom holds promise.

It is important to reiterate that the science units described later in this book are written in a linear manner, but effective comprehension instruction requires that you constantly make decisions on what strategy to use, when to use it, and who is most likely to benefit. There is no recipe. We suggest you initially begin by teaching individual strategies, such as those listed below. Remember to give explicit explanations about the what, why, how, when, and where of each strategy and model its use. After your students have had ample time practicing the strategy, then consider combining the strategies in a single lesson. Reutzel et al. (2005) recommend that novice teachers begin with explicit single-strategy instruction and work up to coordinating a "set" of strategies during instruction. Being explicit, however, is the key to being effective. Reutzel et al. (2005) also found that using a minimum of six of the following strategies produced the best results with young readers.

- activating background knowledge
- observing text structure
- making predictions
- setting goals
- asking questions
- using visual imagery
- monitoring/clarifying
- summarizing

Although this list may appear quite simplistic, it does represent the process-based strategies research has shown to be effective with young and older readers alike. As we mentioned earlier in our description of best practices for teaching science, when teaching comprehension in the context of our units, be willing to change those plans to respond to the developmental needs of your students or the demands of the text.

In the next section, we will describe how these process-based comprehension strategies can be taught within the context of teaching science. You will see these strategies again when you read our science units, and we encourage you to use them frequently, in multiple contexts, and with a variety of texts.

Content Literacy Instruction

Because context plays such a significant role in learning language, our discussion of best practices for enhancing literacy will be framed in the context of learning science through inquiry. As such, our goals for enhancing content literacy within the science classroom parallel those outlined in the national science standards (1996). We want our students to experience the richness and excitement of knowing about and understanding the natural world. We want them to engage intelligently in discourse and debate about matters of scientific concern, and use their knowledge in ways that are critical for success in today's technological world. To help our students achieve these goals, we need to engage them in discovery, challenge their thinking, and provide opportunities for them to verbalize their learning.

The 5E instructional framework is a tool that not only enhances the scientist in our students, but if we think about each component, we realize each component also provides many opportunities for teaching multiple literacy strategies. For instance, during the Engage phase, students make connections between past and present learning and experiences, or make predictions about what they are about to learn. Both involve activating and eliciting students' prior knowledge, and both are specific comprehension strategies recommended prior to reading. When we focus on these comprehension strategies in the context of science, they provide opportunities for students to practice the strategies in a content area other than the language arts and in an activity other than reading. When the strategies are used again prior to reading science materials, students are in a better position to understand that this is a high-utility strategy useful in learning across the curriculum.

Likewise, during the Explore phase, we want to encourage students to set goals and make predictions, both of which are valuable comprehension strategies, and both of which parallel the scientific process of formulating hypotheses prior to experimentation. During this phase of the 5E lesson, you act as a coach and guide your students by asking them probing questions. In doing so, you have the perfect opportunity to model the kinds of questions and thought processes skilled readers—and scientists—might have about the content. Again, an opportunity to practice process-based comprehension strategies in the context of inquiry-based science is provided.

More opportunities within the Explain phase also exist. Monitoring our understanding is a critical component of comprehension and science learning. It is important to realize when something doesn't make sense to us, as well as have an idea of how to "fix" our thinking or understanding. During the Explain phase of 5E, we can model this awareness by using open-ended questions to guide discussion and monitor our students' understanding. When we purposely articulate how to go about the monitoring process, our students are provided with yet another example of how skilled thinkers, like scientists, try to make sense of something as they are experimenting or, in the case of our students, learning. We can continue to model these thinking strategies and apply them to reading science texts. For instance, if something doesn't make sense, we can go back and reread the sentence. We can slow down our reading rate. We can model how to skip over the difficult word, or use context clues, pictures, or captions to help us determine its meaning. The important thing to remember here is that our students must be made aware of the strategies skilled readers use to make sense of science texts, as well as know what to do when something doesn't make sense. Most of us do a good job of teaching children how to monitor their comprehension when reading stories, but don't always apply this to the content classroom.

It is during the Elaborate phase that opportunities abound for both critical thinking and critical reading, two important aspects of content literacy. During this phase, we want students to have new experiences, delve deeper into the content they are studying, and refine their conceptual understandings. One strategy we have not explained in great detail is observing text structure. When we observe text structure, we first notice how information is linguistically presented in the text. Since the books we are recommending you use in our science units are informational, the concepts will be presented in one or more of the following ways: description, sequence, comparison and contrast, cause and effect, problem and solution. Unlike stories, which are written to entertain, the primary purpose of informational text is to inform the reader, and this is one reason why it is difficult for our students to understand. It is important for you to teach your students about text structure, because skilled readers use it to help differentiate the important information from less important information (Meyer & Poon, 2004). This is a precursor to being able to think about information critically.

One of the most helpful ways to teach text structure is through a graphic organizer. Many process-based comprehension strategies can be modeled, discussed, and practiced when completing the graphic organizer with your students. Some of these include asking questions, using visual imagery, clarifying information, and summarizing information. Once the basic organizer has been completed, it also provides a framework for adding new knowledge gained during the Elaborate phase of 5E. For this reason, many of our science units make use of graphic organizers.

Conclusion

There is no question that language is used to learn content, but it is not always emphasized in content areas, such as science, math, or social studies. In fact, the majority of public discourse about literacy, of late, has focused on beginning reading instruction and how to teach children to read well before third grade (National Reading Panel, 2000). One reason is the emphasis the federal government has placed on beginning reading achievement (No Child Left Behind, 2001). Another reason can be traced to traditional teacher education programs for elementary teachers. Within these programs, when reading methods courses are required, most focus on teaching children how to read. Less emphasis is placed on teaching children how we use reading to learn content. Those courses are typically designed for teachers entering secondary classrooms, even though elementary children are also expected to learn content from reading and other literacy activities. With so much emphasis on beginning reading, the assumption is that once children learn to read, they will be able to use reading to learn, but developmentally speaking, this assumption is faulty (Vacca, 2002).

Yore and colleagues (2004) have identified several processes in which a science-savvy reader engages. They include "activating prior knowledge of the specific topic, genre, and evidence; analyzing and synthesizing new information; evaluating new information with respect to criteria for scientific evidence; and integrating the text-based message with prior conceptions" (pp. 348–349). Notice the critical stance of many of the processes described (e.g., analyzing, synthesizing, evaluating, integrating). These processes are especially key when teaching comprehension within the context of the science classroom because they not only produce critical readers, but they also exemplify the *science as inquiry* aspect of the national science standards (National Research Council, 1996). The specific comprehension strategies recommended in this book are a starting point, designed to help learners develop the knowledge, skills, and dispositions of the scientist. For more information about helping your students read, write, and think like scientists, read *Science Workshop* (Saul, Reardon, Pearce, Dieckman, & Neutze, 2002).

The intent of our book is to encourage you to expose your students to process-based strategies and thinking tools that will help them use language to learn science. We believe content literacy is a neglected aspect of the curriculum, and by focusing on it, we do our students a service not only in terms of helping them become more literate, but also learning science content. Our approach is not prescriptive, however. Just as we are encouraging children to stretch in their thinking about science concepts, we are also asking you, the teacher, to stretch your thinking about your own teaching and learning.

Chapter 2

Literacy and Thinking Tools for Science Teachers

by David Whitehead, University of Waikato

Introduction

Josephine, a third grader, carefully draws two intersecting circles on a piece of paper and labels her Venn diagram "Birds." She then lists, on scrap paper, words that describe Chirpy, her pet parakeet, in one column, and in a separate column, words that describe bald eagles that she identified in a text she is reading. Happy with her lists, Josephine writes the words that describe Chirpy only in one circle, and words that describe bald eagles only in the other circle. Some words describe both birds, so she writes these words in the space where the circles intersect. She then shares her completed Venn diagram with her teacher, who encourages Josephine to talk about similarities and differences between the two birds. Josephine is reminded to add words to her Venn diagram over the next few weeks as she learns more about the two birds. The teacher then models how the completed Venn diagram might be used to write a compare and contrast–structured paragraph.

The next time Josephine reads and makes notes or prepares to write a similarly structured paragraph, she might again use a Venn diagram literacy and thinking tool, which is a tool she can now name, use confidently, and state when it might be used. Wisely, Josephine's teacher designs a science unit assessment item that requires

Josephine to use a Venn diagram tool prior to writing a paragraph. This assessment item will indicate Josephine's understandings of birds and her ability to use this literacy and thinking tool to learn science and think like a scientist.

Literacy and thinking tools, such as Venn diagrams, are construction tools for the mind. Just as carpenters use tools to construct a piece of furniture, literate thinkers learning science can use tools to construct new scientific understandings. Like tools used by a carpenter, some literacy and thinking tools are purpose-built for science education; Josephine used a Venn diagram tool because she wanted to compare her pet bird to a bald eagle. Just as a screwdriver is built to slot into the head of a screw and rotate it, you can use literacy and thinking tools for subject- and text-specific purposes.

Frequently, a carpenter will use two or more tools together—hammer and chisel—to fit a lock-set. Likewise, you can help students achieve sophisticated scientific understanding by using literacy and thinking tools in combination. For example, Josephine may have used a Brainstorm tool (see chapter 9, The Earth Beneath Our Feet) to think about the attributes of birds, and then grouped and labeled those attribute groups, prior to constructing multiple Venn diagrams.

Just as carpenters use a range of screwdrivers depending on the type of screw they want to move, you can help students use a range of more or less sophisticated tools to help them gather information, process, or reflect on what they know. Carpenters also use more or less technologically sophisticated screwdrivers, depending on their technical ability and task demands. Similarly, literacy and thinking tools can be, in a developmental sense, more or less challenging.

In this chapter, we examine some characteristics of literacy and thinking tools (Whitehead, 2001, 2004). A list of these tools, together with the chapters associated with their use, is provided in Table 2:1.

The Wider Context

Consistent with the content, purpose, and developmental dimensions of the International Reading Association and the National Council of Teachers of English (IRA/NCTE) *Standards for the English Language Arts* (1996), the tools described in this chapter provide students with a means of comprehending, interpreting, evaluating, and appreciating scientific texts. They are designed to achieve our intentions as authors of this book to build a scientifically literate society, and to help literate thinkers live in a world shaped by science and technology, through the use of hands-on inquiry-based lessons. Likewise, in terms of the *National Science Education Standards* (1996), these tools are designed to support Standard A: Science as Inquiry, designed to help students develop the abilities necessary to conduct scientific inquiry. Finally, the literacy and thinking tools are designed to fit seamlessly into the 5E framework outlined in chapter 1 and used in subsequent chapters.

The Characteristics of Literacy and Thinking Tools

We begin with the premise that just as carpenters cannot turn a screw into a piece of timber with their fingers, students cannot turn their minds to higher order scientific thinking without the help of tools that give power to their minds. And just as carpenters know when to use a screwdriver, a literate thinker needs to know when to use different types of tools. Of course, tools are not always used for the tasks they were designed for; plenty of people have taken the top off a can of paint with a screwdriver, that is, used it as a lever rather than a screwdriver. Likewise, the creative use of literacy and thinking tools in science is to be encouraged.

The selection of tools described in this chapter is based on a set of seven theoretically embedded criteria. Ideally, literacy and thinking tools should be:

1. Teaching and/or learning focused

2. Text-linked

3. Subject-specific

4. Smart

5. Brain-friendly

6. Developmentally appropriate

7. Assessment-linked

Each of these criteria is described and illustrated below with examples of the tools used in association with the science units outlined in the following chapters (see Table 2:1).

Teaching and/or Learning Focused

The difference between literacy and thinking teaching tools and learning tools is, like the Chinese proverb: "Give a family a fish and they will eat for a day; give them a fishing line and they will eat for a lifetime." Teaching tools are like fish, but learning tools are like fishing lines. For example, you might teach students how to design questions around titles and subheadings prior to reading a science text. And you might model how students can ask these questions while reading to enhance their recall and comprehension. This is a learning tool because it is transferable, and because it equips students with an independent means of inquiry.

Some teaching tools, such as Think-Pair-Share (used in chapter 4 as an introduction to the study of traits) and Summarize-Pair-Share (used in chapter 8 to assist students to understand shadows and form generalizations), allow you to engage students in quality instructional dialogues. However, simplistic teaching

Table 2:1   Links between Selection Criteria, Literacy and Thinking Tools, and Chapter Use

Selection Criteria	Linked Literacy and Thinking Tools	Used in Chapter
Teaching (teacher) focused	*Concept Cartoon*	5
	K-W-H-L	4
	Summarize-Pair-Share	8
	Think-Pair-Share	4
Learning (learner) focused	*Question Maker*	4
	Venn Diagram	11
Text-linked	*Concept Frame*	7
Subject-specific	*Multi-Flow*	10
Smart	*Brainstorm*	9
Brain-friendly	*Moving Visual Imagery*	6, 8
	Concept Frame	7
	Short- and Long-Term Consequences	10
Developmentally appropriate	*Concept Frame*	7
Assessment-linked	*Meaning Grid*	11

tools, such as matching a list of scientific words to their definitions, evoke very little in the way of dialogue. In contrast, more complex teaching tools, such as the Concept Cartoon tool (see chapter 5), allow you to evoke high-quality instructional dialogue that will help students explore the scientific hypotheses and theories in their heads.

Thus, a fundamental difference between teaching- and learning-focused tools is that some are, and will always be, literacy and thinking teaching tools, while others are designed as learning tools. Both teaching and learning tools can be designed to achieve deliberate and purposeful outcomes with science text, but only learning tools are designed to help students achieve strategic outcomes with science texts, independently. We, therefore, favor the use of learning tools. Learning tools equip students for lifelong learning.

The Concept Cartoon Teaching Tool

The Concept Cartoon tool (Goodwin, 2000; Naylor & Keogh, 2000) is a cartoon-styled drawing that illustrates students' conceptions, or misconceptions, of science (see Figure 2:1). This tool, used in chapter 5, Birdie Buffet, has a problematic, scientific dimension designed to evoke constructive instructional dialogue. The ideas beginning with BUT… expressed in the Concept Cartoon callouts can come from either a teacher, who understands some common misconceptions students might have about the topic, or from students, with the teacher taking a "back seat." The visual format and minimal written text of the Concept Cartoon tool, together with its potential to help students express diverse and complex scientific viewpoints, make it an effective teaching tool.

To use the Concept Cartoon tool, you will need to initially provide the *Observation* ("Some birds have beaks curved at the end"). Students then provide more observations about birds with curved beaks, such as "they are carnivores" or "they are fish eaters." Finally, as a result of this discussion with you, the class generates a *Big Scientific Idea*, which in Figure 2:1 is: "Birds with curved beaks at the end might starve if rats and mice and fish die out."

This *Big Scientific Idea* is then transferred to a Concept Cartoon, and then your students suggest what might be written in the callouts beginning with BUT. These BUT statements form the basis of discussion around the challenge question "What Do You Think?" printed at the bottom of the Concept Cartoon.

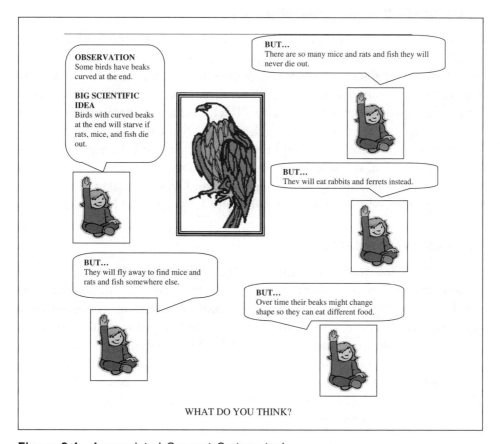

Figure 2:1 A completed Concept Cartoon tool.

Through discussion around your initial science *Observation*, then through the instructional dialogue that enabled students to make the intellectual leap to a *Big Scientific Idea*, you are able to help students talk themselves to meaning—to clarify and elaborate their scientific understandings. Inevitably, this requires that you adopt a more constructive, rather than transmissive, approach to the teaching of science.

Although we are thinking about teaching and learning tools separately, some tools, such as the K-W-H-L tool used in chapter 4, Nurture and Nature, and the Venn Diagram tool used by Josephine, can be introduced as a teaching tool then become a tool learners use independently. The *K* in this tool represents what students Know about a topic; the *W* represents what students Want to learn about a topic; the *H* represents How the students will find information on a topic; and the *L* represents what students have Learned (Ogle, 1986). You can use this tool, initially as a teaching tool with the whole class, but it has the potential to be used, independently, as a learning tool. Like the K-W-H-L, the Question Maker (chapter 4) and Multi-Flow (chapter 10) tools may be used initially as a teaching tool, but are designed to be, primarily, learning tools.

The Question Maker Learning Tool

Perhaps the most significant learning tool you can equip students with is one that empowers them to ask questions. Like the K-W-H-L, the Question Maker tool (see chapter 4) enables students to independently construct questions about any science topic. The Question Maker lets you and your students identify what is not known and what is needed to be known. The tool also provides learners with an independent means of designing research questions that serve as purposes for reading, talking, and writing, as well as initiating or expanding a scientific investigation. To this extent, it is a learning tool rather than a teaching tool. Figure 2:2 outlines how you might help your students use the Question Maker tool with the topic of heredity, which is addressed in chapter 4, Nurture and Nature.

The Multi-Flow Learning Tool

The Multi-Flow tool (see chapter 10, Away We Go!) is also a learning tool because after students gain some mastery with it, they can apply the tool independently while reading, or prior to writing a scientific explanation. The Multi-Flow tool evokes cause-and-effect thinking typical of science. To use a Multi-Flow tool, you might first ask your students to read and discuss a text that explains something and that uses a cause-and-effect text structure. Then, ask your students to list causes and effects relating to the topic and write them in the boxes of the Multi-Flow tool. Finally, the completed tool can be used to structure a written explanation about the topic or a new topic.

Step 1: You state: "The topic is, for example: 'Inheriting Eye Color.'"

Step 2: You ask your students: "What Level One Questions can we ask about this topic?"

(N.B.: Level One Questions begin with: What..? When..? Why..? Where..? How..?)

Level One Questions for this topic might be:

- What color eyes can you inherit?
- Why do some children have brown eyes when their parents don't have brown eyes?

Step 3: You ask your students: "What Level Two Questions can we ask about this topic?"

(N.B.: Level Two Questions add modifiers to Level One Questions)

- What   if…
- When   might
- Why   should
- Where   could
- How   would

Level Two Questions for this topic might be:

- What if we could choose our baby's eye color?
- How would we find out whether it is healthier to have a particular color of eye?

Step 4: You ask students to group their questions around a common theme, and write a single question that covers this group of related questions. These questions are now available to steer the inquiry process. Students discard questions they choose not to research.

Figure 2:2 A Question Maker learning tool.

Text-Linked

The text-linked criterion acknowledges a relationship between the type of thinking evoked when reading and writing scientific texts, and specific literacy and thinking tools. If a tool evokes the same type of thinking as is required to read, write, or discuss a particular text, then it is probably best used when students read, write, or discuss that type of scientific text. Recall that the Multi-Flow tool (see Figure 2:3) evokes causal thinking—students list the causes and effects associated with the process of erosion. Therefore, it can be used as a catalyst for your students' writing when the purpose of their text is to explain erosion. Given that both the Multi-Flow tool and a written explanation evoke similar types of thinking, they are best used together. (See Appendix A for an annotated writing sample about erosion that is based on the information generated from the Multi-Flow in Figure 2:3.)

You can also gain the benefits of the text-tool link by using the Concept Frame tool (see Figure 2:4) to help students organize information they gather, as well as help them write more descriptive scientific texts. This tool evokes attribute

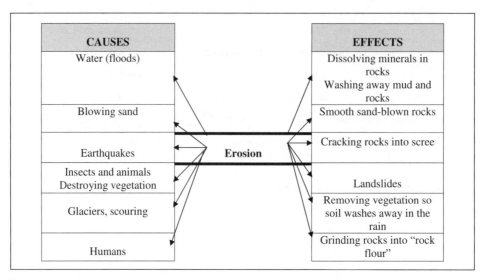

Figure 2:3 A simple Multi-Flow learning tool about erosion.

A bird is...	A bird can...
1. An animal that can fly	1. Fly
2. An avian	2. Squawks
3. An animal with feathers	3. Eat grain
	4. Glide
	5. Eat nectar
Examples of birds are...	**A bird has a...**
1. Eagle	1. Feathers
2. Hummingbird	2. Beak
3. Parakeet	3. Wings
4. Emu	
5. Kiwi	

Figure 2:4 A simple Concept Frame tool about birds.

thinking—students list/describe the attributes of (or things about) an object, event, or idea. Then, they use their lists/descriptions to write about that object (i.e., crystals), event (i.e., respiration), or idea (i.e., evolution). Given that both the Concept Frame tool and descriptive writing evoke similar types of thinking, it makes sense to use them together. Chapter 7, Roll It, uses the Concept Frame tool to help students organize information they gather about force and motion and then write a description to show what they know.

Different parts of the simple Concept Frame illustrated in Figure 2:4 reflect some of the typical features of descriptive writing associated with the activities in chapter 5, Birdie Buffet. One feature, usually found toward the beginning of this type of writing, classifies the topic that the students are asked to describe. You can help students write this part of their text by telling them to use information from the top-left unshaded cell of the Concept Frame. Then, tell them to use information in the other shaded cells to write the body of their text. This information can be written as a simple sentence, or as more complex sentences and paragraphs that reflect deeper understandings. You could use Figure 2:4 together with the short annotated writing sample about birds provided in Appendix B to model this text-tool link when working with the Birdie Buffet unit in chapter 5.

Subject-Specific Criterion

While some literacy and thinking tools, such as Thinking Maps (Hyerle, 1996), suit most subjects, some tools are better suited to science. As we have seen, there is probably more use for a Multi-Flow tool (see Figure 2.3) in science than in most other subjects because cause-and-effect thinking is central to science. This tool is designed to help students understand causal dimensions typical of scientific concepts.

A generic aspect of the subject-specific criterion is that some tools will operate at the word level, to help students decode and comprehend the vocabulary of science, while other tools will help students comprehend whole texts independently. Tools operating at lower levels (i.e., decoding and vocabulary comprehension) tend to be teaching tools, while tools that operate on whole texts tend to be learner tools with a reflective dimension.

Smart Criterion

The literacy and thinking tools described in this chapter are consistent with the teaching and learning, text-linked, and subject-specific criteria. In addition, all the tools can be used to help students read or write, as well as listen or talk, about science. Tools with these complementary characteristics are consistent with the smart criteria. Just as a builder's screwdriver can be used to either screw in or unscrew a fixture, so, too, tools consistent with the "smart" criterion can be used to help students use the receptive and productive modes of spoken language (listening and speaking) and the receptive and productive modes of written language (reading and writing).

The simple Brainstorm tool (see Figure 2:5) used generatively in chapter 9, The Earth Beneath Our Feet, is a smart tool. To use this tool, you will need to first ask your students to construct the "Words about erosion" list as they "receive" (read, listen, or view) information about erosion, and call upon their prior knowledge of the topic. You can then ask them to construct groups and labels for those words as a means of further processing that information, prior to their producing a written or oral text about erosion. Based on Figure 2:5, you might expect students to produce at least a paragraph based on Label One: "Agents of erosion" and at least one paragraph based on Label Two: "Effects of erosion." The Brainstorm tool is consistent with the smart criterion because students can use it productively (as a prewriting and pretalking tool) and receptively (as a note-taking tool).

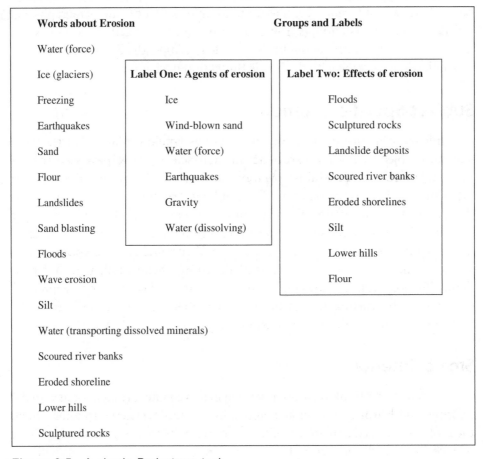

Figure 2:5 A simple Brainstorm tool.

Brain-Friendly Criterion

Literacy and thinking tools are consistent with the "brain-friendly" criterion when they align with how the brain learns naturally (Wolfe, 2001). Acknowledging a tool as brain-friendly requires an understanding of how the brain learns. At a general level, we know the brain processes verbal language (words, mathematical and scientific symbols, and formula), and nonverbal language (e.g., images or pictures in the head) in two separate, but connected, neural systems. These systems provide your students with different ways of knowing. For example, the verbal system provides one way of knowing about light waves (stating in a sentence: "Light waves come from the sun"), and the nonverbal system provides another way of knowing about light waves (forming a visual image in their head of light waves coming from the sun) (Farah, 1989; Farah & McClelland, 1991). Moving my arms like a light wave to demonstrate what happens when they reflect off a mirror provides me with a further, kinesthetic way of knowing about light.

Some literacy and thinking tools, such as the Concept Frame tool used in chapter 7, Roll It, are more verbal; others, such as the Moving Imagery tool used in chapter 6, What Matters about the State of Matter, and chapter 8, Light Blockers, are more nonverbal. The Short- and Long-Term Consequences tool used in chapter 10, Away We Go!, evokes both nonverbal responses as students "see" into the future and verbal responses as they represent in words what they "saw." This use of a "dual coding" tool broadens students' perspective for science. This section explains why visual imagery tools are consistent with the brain-friendly criterion.

Moving and Melting Visual Imagery Tools

Picture in your head what happens as water turns into steam. Visual imagery (making pictures in your head) and visual imagery thinking (doing something with the pictures you made in your head) are crucial to learning science. This is because explanations of how and why things occur often rely on understanding things unavailable to direct inspection—sometimes because they are hidden, sometimes they are too small to see, and sometimes they would take more than a lifetime to observe. The picture in your head about water turning into steam requires you to make a "melting" image rather than a "still" image, like a photograph, because you are imagining matter changing state.

Now try this one: Picture in your head how a T-rex that died in a swamp slowly turned into a fossil! This requires you to see bone transforming into stone—again, you need a "melting" image because you are picturing a change of state. Likewise, in the absence of direct experience, your students need to rely on visual imagery to understand what might be happening to magma full of gas as it blasts out of a volcano (see chapter 9, The Earth Beneath Our Feet), or what is happening between two surfaces as force is absorbed (see chapter 7, Roll It). In chapter 8, Light

Blockers, students are invited to make moving visual images to help them clarify and elaborate their observations of shadows and the absorption and reflection of light. They are also invited to write about and sketch their images. In chapter 6, What Matters About the State of Matter, you can invite students to make moving visual images to help them understand gases, liquids, and solids at the molecular level. By drawing what they image, students begin to both understand things hidden from direct inspection and synthesize and comprehend what they can "see." So reading and writing science—indeed, understanding science—is not exclusively verbal; students of science also form meaningful visual images (Sadoski & Paivio, 2001).

Imagery-based literacy and thinking tools are consistent with the brain-friendly criterion because they activate specific areas of the brain that allow us to make images, move and melt images, and inspect images. For example, we know the area at the rear of the brain, that allows us to see with our eyes, also works when we "see" images in the brain. It is an area crucial for both visual perception and visual imagery (Kosslyn, Ganis, & Thompson, 2001). This rear area of the brain works in concert with areas on the left side of the brain, which make visual images meaningful, and areas on the right side of the brain that allow us to think about the extent of our images. Further, a "motor area" on the left side of the brain allows us to rotate our images (Tomasino, Borroni, Isaja, Rumiati, & Farah, 2005). All of these areas work under the direction of the front part of the brain that acts like an executive decision maker.

Visual imagery tools are consistent with the brain-friendly criterion because we know that our "picture-in-the-head" knowledge is stored in the brain close to the areas that work when we see or handle objects directly (Martin, Haxby, Lalonde, Wiggs, & Ungerleider, 1995). Thus, direct concrete experience is an essential prerequisite for the use of Visual Imagery tools. Direct experience provides students with the raw materials for imagery thinking.

There is an important difference between making visual images and using them. When you ask students to use images to help them understand science, they engage in visual imagery thinking. Use implies thinking, and use implies doing things with our visual images—moving them or moving our point of view in relation to an image, or melting them, zooming in, and scanning across them. For example, picture in your head what happens at the surface of the water in a boiling jug, now zoom in for a close-up view, and then position yourself just under the surface of the water. Changing perspective—doing something with our images—offers insight into this scientific process.

In a practical sense, during a science lesson, you might ask students to make a still image (a picture in their head that does not move) of an object or event central to a lesson (the beak of a bird, light hitting an opaque object, the contact between a toy car and sandpaper). Then, you might ask students to engage in imagery thinking, to make their images move, to "see" the bird using the beak, to "see" the light hitting the object, and to "see" under the toy car as it rolls across the sandpaper. When you ask students to share the things they "saw," you move from using a nonverbal system in the brain to using a verbal system. And in doing so, you give your students the opportunity to express, and further clarify, what they know. When you ask students to make their images move, to explain what's happening from a different position (e.g., from inside the flower as the hummingbird feeds), you give them an opportunity to gain further understanding. As a lesson closure, you can even ask students whether their moving images affected their understanding of an object or event; whether the use of this literacy and thinking tool helped them learn science.

The justification for using brain-friendly literacy and thinking tools is that they are consistent with the criterion that states tools should reflect the way the brain learns naturally. The application of this criteria leads to deeper learning in science and to the design and selection of better literacy and thinking tools.

Developmentally Appropriate

You may have already noted that some of the literacy and thinking tools associated with the science units in this book have been designated as simple or complex. The design of tools at these two levels is consistent with the developmentally appropriate criterion. Multi-leveled tools are essential for differentiated instruction. The two levels are designed to align with students' intellectual development and experience. Simple tools are probably best suited to students in Grades 1–4, or those students using literacy and thinking tools for the first time. Complex tools are designed for students in Grade 5 and beyond, or for gifted students who will probably begin to use a range of tools in combination. What these two developmentally appropriate levels do not assume is that grade level should absolutely determine which tools students use. If students in Grade 3 are developmentally ready, they should use a complex, rather than a simple, tool.

Initially, you might use both simple and complex tools as "teacher" rather than "learner" tools. So, although developmentally appropriate tools provide challenge levels designed to guide science teachers in their planning, the levels should never deny students opportunities to think.

The two developmentally appropriate levels also reflect beliefs about students' attention spans and the types of text-related intellectual tasks they encounter in science classrooms. For example, you can use a tool such as a simple Concept Frame (see Figure 2:6) as a text-linked prewriting tool in a matter of minutes. This tool enables you to assess and record prior learning by collaborating with students as they use each sector of the completed frame to write or dictate simple sentences beginning with "A bird can…. A bird has…. A bird is…An example of a bird is…" This is an achievable challenge well within the capabilities of most Grade 1–4 students that can be completed with a minimum of teacher intervention (Chapman, 1999).

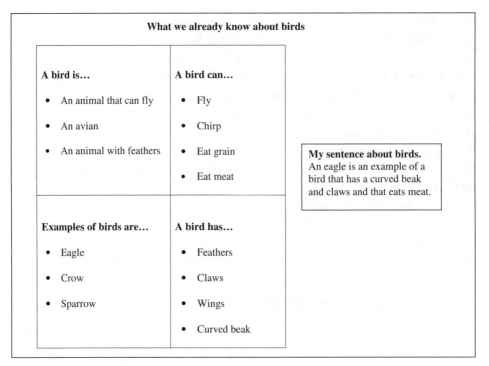

Figure 2:6 A simple Concept Frame tool about birds.

In contrast, students may find the complex Concept Frame tool (see Figure 2:7) slightly more challenging. Successful use of this tool requires persistence and a degree of independent learning behavior. This complex tool requires students to further attend to what they know by ordering information in each sector of the Concept Frame. This order will be reflected in the structure of their writing. They might also decide that some information doesn't align with what they want to write, and signal this with an X beside the word (see Figure 2:7).

A complex Concept Frame also requires students to generate additional ideas using the *Examples* words (see right-hand bottom sector in Figure 2:7) to construct questions. Based on this figure, you would direct students to begin with the name of a bird listed in the *Examples* sector, such as "eagle," and add a sector header word ("is," "are," "can," or "has") to "eagle" to construct their question. For example, "An eagle is…?", or "Eagles can…?", or "An eagle has…?" You would then record the words that answer the question in the appropriate sector of the Concept Frame. For example, "Eagles can… catch rabbits" so you would record the words "catch rabbits" in the "can" sector of the Concept Frame (see point 6, "Catch rabbits" under "Can" in Figure 2:7). A complex *Concept* Frame additionally requires students to group information. Figure 2:7 illustrates how you might help students make groups for "bad" things birds *can* do, and for *examples* of birds that are "meat eaters" and "grain eaters."

Is.../is a...		Are...	
Order Belongs to a group		*Order Things about them*	
3. Animals that fly		2. Pets	
2. An avian		1. Expensive to keep	
1. Animal with feathers	**BIRDS**	X Colorful	
X. A noisy thing		3. Meat eaters	
		4. *Threatened*	

Can	**Has.../has a.../have...**	**Examples**
Order Actions Groups	*Order Things they have*	*Order Groups*
4. Chirp	1. Feathers	2. Eagle ⎫ Meat
2 Fly	2. Claws	1. Crow ⎭ eaters
1. Eat grain	3. Wings	3. Sparrow ⎫ Grain
5. Spread bird flu ⎫ Bad	4. Curved beaks	4. Chaffinch ⎭ eaters
3. Dirty windows ⎭	6. Stubby beaks	
6. *Catch rabbits*		

Figure 2:7   A complex Concept Frame tool about birds.

In addition to increasing demand on students' attention, the two developmentally appropriate levels increase intellectual demand on students. For example, a simple Concept Frame provides students with just four cues that assist them to gather and record information. In terms of Bloom's taxonomy (Bloom, 1956), this evokes little more than recall and understanding. In contrast, a complex Concept Frame requires students to work with five sectors and to further process information in each sector. In terms of Bloom's taxonomy, this requires students to analyze and synthesize information. In taxonomic terms, literacy and thinking tools consistent with the developmentally appropriate criterion evoke higher order thinking.

Assessment-Linked

A final criterion is that, ideally, literacy and thinking tools associated with science programs can be used as assessment tools. The forms of assessment you use in science have a powerful influence on the kinds of learning your students do and the kinds of teaching your students encounter. In a high-stakes testing environment, teachers tend, quite naturally, to teach to content-focused testable standards. In a high-stakes testing environment, the measures used are usually norm-linked and summative rather than diagnostic and formative (Calkins, Montgomery, Santman, & Falk, 1998). The assessment of prior knowledge and the growth of students' understanding assessed using formative measures tend to play second fiddle. Literacy and thinking tools consistent with the assessment-linked criterion can be used for both formative and summative purposes.

The Formative Assessment of Scientific Knowledge

A Meaning Grid tool (see Figure 2:8) is ideal as a formative, science assessment tool because you can use it on several occasions during a series of lessons to measure students' growth in content knowledge. This tool is gradually introduced throughout chapter 11, The Earth in the Solar System. To use the grid as an assessment tool, you will first need to draw a grid with the objects or events you wish to assess listed across the top (see igneous, sedimentary, and metamorphic rocks in Figure 2:8). Then, together with your students, you will need to list two or more descriptors of each rock type down the left-side column of the grid (see "Made when hot rock cools").

Figure 2:8 illustrates that, part way through a study about rocks, students were unsure of some facts (see the question marks), and in some cases, just plain didn't know (see the blank sections of the grid). There is also a possibility that what they think they know (as indicated by dots, crosses, and checks) might be wrong, and that eventually, your intervention will be required.

The tool can also be used flexibly as a summative assessment measure. For example, you might provide students with the types of rocks listed across the top of the grid and descriptors of those rocks listed down the left side of the grid. The assessment would simply involve students using ✓, ✗, or • to indicate their understanding. A more rigorous assessment would involve students providing their own descriptors down the left side of the grid and then completing the grid with ✓, ✗, or • and adding summary statements beside and below the grid.

Testing Like We Teach

As the preceding description illustrates, there is nothing inherently wrong with the assessment of content knowledge, as long as you simultaneously assess *how* you taught the science. This presupposes that some of the assessment items in a science unit test are constructed in such a way that students recognize and treat them as familiar and representative of the actual learning experience—of how they learnt the science. Thus, the challenge signaled by the inclusion of literacy and thinking tools described in this book is for you to test both the science curriculum content together with students' ability to apply the literacy and thinking tools used to teach the content. In effect, this form of assessment is providing a measure of content knowledge *and* students' ability to inquire.

For example, you can use the Concept Frame tool illustrated in Figure 2:9 in association with the unit, The Earth Beneath our Feet (see chapter 9), to help students learn about rocks as an inquiry tool. This tool can also be used as a pretest item to gauge students' prior knowledge of the topic, as well as a summative post-test

Key:

✓ = We are sure

✗ = We are sure they are not

• = Some are/do and some are/do not

? = We are not sure

Blank square = We don't know yet

	Igneous rocks	Sedimentary rocks	Metamorphic rocks	**Comment**
Made when hot rock cools	✓	✗	?	
Made from broken pieces of rock	✗	•	✗	
Made when igneous, sedimentary, and metamorphic rocks are changed by heat and pressure	?	✗	✓	
Lots of tiny crystals	✓	?	✗	Most metamorphic rocks seem to be fine grained.
Contains fossils	✗	•	•	
Often have shiny surfaces	•	✗	✓	
Generally dark in color	✓	✗	•	Rocks come in all different colors.
Often in layers				
Used in carving	?		?	We need to find out which rocks you can carve.
Basalt	✓	✗		
Granite	✓	✗	✗	
Sandstone				
Limestone		?		
Marble			?	
Slate				

Comment

We think that some metamorphic and sedimentary rocks may contain fossils.

Figure 2:8 A Simple Meaning Grid tool used as a formative assessment tool.

item. Again, using this tool provides you with an opportunity to "test as you teach," to assess not only what you taught (about rocks), but also how you taught it. That's smart teaching, and that is the kind of assessment one would expect to see if literacy and thinking tools were used as an integral part of a science curriculum.

Conclusion

The use of literacy and thinking tools that are consistent with the criteria outlined above, and when used as an integral component of your science program, should be prized and valued. Their application leads to attractive scientific destinations. And the journey toward these understandings is, itself, extremely satisfying and motivating for both you and your students alike.

Instruction:	Define the meaning of a rock as accurately as you can by completing the Concept Frame.	

A rock is...	A rock can...
1	1
2	2
3	3
Examples of rock are...	A rock has...
1	1
2	2
3	3

Figure 2:9 A Simple Concept Frame tool used as a pre- and postassessment.

Chapter 3

Supplementing Science
with Nonfiction Literature

Introduction

Lately, there has been a lot of interest generated with regard to using literature in the classroom. Experts and teachers alike are touting the merits of exposing children to all types of literature, including informational text (Galda & Cullinan, 1991). And there is good reason. Literature can serve as a tool to help students learn about science, as well as encourage inquiry. By showing children how to apply language arts skills in ways that help them comprehend and compose their own science texts, we are promoting both literacy and science. When literature is used to validate observations, raise additional questions, and synthesize concepts, we are exposing children to the ways of thinking and understanding that are essential for all citizens living in a world shaped by science and technology (American Association for the Advancement of Science [AAAS], 1990). Using literature enhances science literacy because careful reading involves critical thinking and using logic to solve comprehension problems. These scientific habits of mind foster intellectual growth, especially when cultivated in a supportive classroom environment.

Time is another factor to consider when incorporating more literature across the curriculum. Since the passage of the No Child Left Behind legislation (2001), schools are under enormous pressure to make adequate yearly progress, as demonstrated by performance on standardized reading tests. As a result, the teaching of reading and language arts has received significant attention, time, and money—often at the expense of other content areas, such as science. One way to make time for science instruction is to make more efficient use of the school day. For instance, when teaching science, why not have students read more informational text (Duke, 2000)? They can learn valuable science content, as well as practice necessary comprehension strategies (Dreher, 2002). We are not suggesting a return to the past, where the science textbook *was* the science curriculum. We are, however, suggesting that teachers supplement their hands-on, inquiry-based science programs with literature. From our perspective, this is a win-win situation in terms of literacy development and learning science content.

Defining Informational Text

Before deciding specific titles to use, first consider what kinds of texts are appropriate in the science classroom. Opinions differ about what is meant by *informational text* (Saul & Diekman, 2005). We associate the term primarily with exposition. Exposition does not have a storyline and its purpose is to inform, explain, or describe a topic. Expository structures, such as cause-effect, problem-solution, compare-contrast, sequence, and description, are used to convey the content. Some high-quality informational books written for children include both narrative and expository features, such as the *Magic School Bus* series by Joanna Cole or *Wally and Deanna's Groundwater Adventure* by Leanne Appleby and Peter Russell (2001). They are known as "faction" because they blend fact and fiction. These books are appealing to children because they use characters and setting to describe scientific phenomenon. One criticism of faction texts is that some gloss over scientific concepts in order to develop a storyline or meet a readability formula (Ford, 2004; Saul, 2004). The checklist described in this chapter is more appropriate for reviewing books that are expository in nature. When selecting trade books to use in science classrooms, it is critical to choose titles that encourage readers to develop deep content understandings (Reardon, 1992). Books should link science content to the scientists who produce it. They should raise interesting questions in children's minds, and although rare, ideally they should model or explain the practice of scientific investigation and reasoning (Ford, 2004). In choosing books wisely, we help readers develop an authentic appreciation and deeper understanding of the nature of scientific inquiry.

Because all readers vary in their abilities, when we use a variety of informational texts, we are in a better position to meet individual needs. Carefully chosen texts can be used by teachers to model comprehension, as well as support readers during guided reading or independent reading time. When we introduce science topics with hands-on activities, children often have questions about the topic. Using literature is a viable way to help children satisfy their natural curiosity. By reading more about the topic, additional questions often arise, which promotes further inquiry. For many young readers, informational books are their favorites because they capture readers' curiosity and attention (Caswell & Duke, 1998), thus engaging them in deeper learning and fostering scientific habits of mind. Trade books help promote a scientific world view in which readers develop and understand concepts, something that is not always possible when using only hands-on approaches or science textbooks.

It is essential to "remember that texts are used differently in *inquiry* science than they are in more traditional science and literacy instruction" (Ford, 2004, p. 277). Children need to experience science in ways that engage them in active construction of ideas and knowledge within their developmental capabilities. The right books can provide the necessary support. The key is to select books that serve as tools for inquiry. It's also important to have a variety of texts available, just as actual scientists use a variety of texts in their daily work.

Locating and Analyzing Literature

One problem, though, with using informational literature is finding appropriate texts. Luckily, many options exist, especially with respect to locating titles that teach common science concepts. Some schools across the country use FOSS science kits, which address national standards with engaging, inquiry-based science activities (see http://www.fossweb.com/), and most FOSS modules include a list of resources that often include books for teachers, children, and parents. This is one source.

For years, the National Science Teachers Association (NSTA) has annually published a list of notable trade books that can be found at http://www.nsta.org/ostbc. The journal, *Science and Children,* which is published by NSTA, also lists good science trade books in each issue. Another print publication with a subscription-based, online option is provided by the AAAS. At their Web site, http://www.sbfonline.com/, subscribers can read reviews of books, videos, and software.

An excellent online subscription-based resource is the Search It! Science Web site developed by Wendy Saul (available at http://searchit.heinemann.com/). For a minimal fee, subscribers can search this database of over 4,000 titles to locate appropriate books for classroom use. However, before committing to a subscription, users may log on as a guest and try out the site. The Web site is very user-friendly, and subscribers find books by using multiple search criteria, such as: subject, topic, kind of book, title/series, key words, author, grade level, and teaching concerns. Once the search has been completed, a list of books appears. Each description includes bibliographical information, a photo of the book's cover, a summary, whether or not the book is still in print, and cost. Additional helpful links include: a Wonder Questions section, which presents questions that others have asked and lists books that can answer those questions; a Brainstorm section; and, a Quirky Subjects section. Search It! Science is a great resource.

Some print sources help you evaluate the accuracy of books, and these include: *The Horn Book Guide to Children's and Young Adult Books, Book Review Digest,* and *Book Review Index.* Most public libraries have these resources. There are even recommendations for picture books. One of the oldest awards for nonfiction picture books is the Orbis Pictus Award given by the National Council of Teachers of English (NCTE). For a list of winning picture book titles, see http://www.ncte.org/elem/awards/orbispictus.

One challenge with using literature in the classroom is selecting the best titles for children in a particular classroom. Not only is this process time consuming, but with the curriculum as demanding as it is, it is important to select trade books that both engage readers and address multiple content standards. One way to identify books that are best for your classroom is to systematically evaluate them. To help you do this, we have developed a checklist that we think you will find helpful. In fact, we have used the checklist to evaluate the titles we are recommending in this book. Our checklist is made up of six sections, and the aspects of text we recommend analyzing include: accuracy, organization and layout, cohesion of ideas, treatment of specialized vocabulary, reader appeal, and scientific viewpoint.

Accuracy

The first component to consider is accuracy. Often, we do not take the time to think about this aspect of text; we assume that if the information is on the page, it is accurate. Yet, that is not always the case. New scientific discoveries are made regularly, and when using trade books in science classrooms, it is critical to use trade books that have current, up-to-date, accurate information (Donovan & Smolkin, 2002). In addition, many children have misconceptions about science concepts (Bar, 1989; Baxter, 1989; Freyberg, 1985; Ryan & Aikenhead, 1992), so it is imperative that we select high-quality literature that does not reinforce such misconceptions. To check for accuracy, we ask these questions as we complete the checklist:

- Is information on the author's experience and expertise provided?
- Are photo credits given?
- Is the information current?
- Is the information accurate?

TITLE: _____

AUTHOR: _____ ISBN: _____

PUBLISHER & DATE: _____

TOPIC: _____

STANDARDS ADDRESSED: _____

TOTAL SCORE: ___/15_ RECOMMEND? _____ FOR WHOM? _____

3 = meets all or most criteria   2 = meets some criteria   1 = meets few criteria

Check all that apply, or write N/A if not applicable. Then, choose overall score for each category and write score on blank.

_____ **Accuracy**
         Information about author expertise/experience is given
         Information about photo credits is given
         Information is current and accurate
Notes:

_____ **Organization and Layout**
table of contents	chapter headings	section headings
index	glossary	charts and graphs
maps	page numbers	Web sites
Notes:

_____ **Cohesion of Ideas**
         Major ideas are logically connected throughout text
         Sentence-level ideas are logically connected to each other
         Text respects reader's probable background knowledge/experience
         Appropriate conceptual load
         Good model of expository writing
Notes:

_____ **Specialized Vocabulary**
         Defined as it is introduced
         Defined in pictures, captions, labels, or clarified visually
         Defined in glossary
Notes:

_____ **Reader Interest**
         Has aesthetic appeal
         Has colorful illustrations or photos
         Uses appropriate font and page size for intended reader
         Has positive role models with respect to gender and ethnicity
Notes:

Scientific Viewpoint: Do not give this item a numeric score. Note which is the primary, and if appropriate, the secondary focus.

_____ Science as facts
_____ Science as observation
_____ Science as measuring/experimenting
_____ Biographical/scientist's work

Annotation:

_____
_____
_____
_____

Figure 3:1   A checklist for evaluating nonfiction trade books. (Full size form available at www.Christopher-Gordon.com/authors/KingMattox-shtml)

To illustrate how we would evaluate each component on the checklist, we will model our thinking using *Earth Alive* by Sandra Markle (1991). We note the following things about the accuracy of this book. First, we are aware that Sandra Markle has written several trade books for children on a variety of science topics. Although that does not guarantee accurate content, it is an indication that others in the field value her work. In fact, this statement by Gerald H. Krockover, Professor of Earth and Atmospheric Science Education at Purdue University, appears on the inside cover of the book: "An excellent book, extremely accurate in portraying Earth as the dynamic entity it is." When examining the first page of the text, Markle includes a personal note thanking Professor Krockover for his expertise, so we conclude it is likely the two consulted one another as Markle wrote *Earth Alive*. Second, this text describes changes in the Earth's crust and illustrates those changes with beautiful color photographs. Since the photos take on a significant role in *Earth Alive* by explaining concepts visually, we would expect the text to contain captions to explain the photos, as well as give photo credits. Markle has done both. Third, *Earth Alive* was originally published in 1991, and some might question the timeliness of its information. So we looked at other, more recent books on this topic and noticed they contained similar information. This finding, coupled with the fact that *Earth Alive* is still in print, leads us to believe the information is current. We would be more careful evaluating the accuracy of information in books on genetics, for instance, since this is a field where new discoveries are being made daily. Given our evaluation, *Earth Alive* earned a 3 for accuracy because it met all of the criteria on our checklist.

Organization and Layout

The second item on our checklist is organization and layout. This section examines if the text is arranged in a way that makes it easy to use in the classroom. For example, consider these items:

- Is there a table of contents that gives an overview of the book's contents?

- Do chapter and section headings provide information about the important concepts?

- Is an index provided? Does it aid the reader in finding specific information?

- Is a glossary provided? Does it clarify the meaning of important vocabulary?

- Are visual aids, such as charts, graphs, maps, and illustrations, used to assist the reader's comprehension?

- Are page numbers included?

Returning to Markle's *Earth Alive,* we can make the following observations. No, there is no table of contents nor are there chapters in this 39-page text. However, there are natural divisions between topics, and those divisions are fairly obvious. For instance, on page 9, after Markle concludes her description of sinkholes, half of the page is left blank. On the following page, a photo of a house buried in volcanic ash takes up most of the page and the caption reads: "This home in Iceland wasn't swallowed up by a sinkhole. But its owners surely didn't bury it themselves under all that black stuff. Is it mud? Or maybe the Icelanders' coal supply?" (Markle, 1991, p. 10). This indicates a new topic is about to begin on page 11, and this pattern is repeated throughout the text. The questions also prompt the reader to begin engaging in inquiry, a relevant practice in today's science classrooms.

Earth Alive does have a detailed index with over 90 entries. Such detail makes it easy for readers to quickly locate a topic of personal interest so that, for instance, information can be found to help answer a question. *Earth Alive* does not have a glossary, but it is important to keep in mind that not all books need to have a glossary, since its purpose is to clarify technical vocabulary. In the case of *Earth Alive,* Markle addresses technical vocabulary using description, photos, and analogies embedded in the text when readers first encounter them. This is advantageous to comprehension, since vocabulary is best learned within a rich context (Blachowicz & Fisher, 2002). Thus, in this instance, we feel a glossary is not needed. Later in this chapter, we will more specifically describe how vocabulary is addressed in *Earth Alive.*

Beautiful color photographs are the visual aids that Markle has chosen for *Earth Alive.* There are no maps, charts, or graphs. However, in this particular book, there doesn't need to be. Topics are explained completely, and we are not convinced that such visual aids would enhance the content more than the photographs do in this particular text. It is important to use flexible judgment when evaluating the appropriateness of visual aids. Some informational text contains small amounts of information and lots of visuals, in which case visuals greatly aid the reader since little text is provided. This is not the case, however, in *Earth Alive.*

Our last criterion in this category deals with page numbers. Having page numbers is an important feature of texts, especially when they are used with groups of children for instructional purposes. Page numbers facilitate giving directions and locating information. *Earth Alive* has large page numbers. Based on our observations, *Earth Alive* received a 2 for organization and layout since it met some of our criteria in this category.

Cohesion of Ideas

The third section of our checklist is cohesion of ideas. In cohesive text, ideas are developed using a text structure that is logically ordered from beginning to end. A single focus is maintained throughout the entire chapter or section of text. Typically, the text structure authors use to explain information involve one of the following: sequence, cause-effect, compare-contrast, problem-solution, and description. In cohesive text, this structure is consistently developed with significant supporting details, evidence, and discussion. Unity of the whole text occurs when all ideas logically belong together to develop the thesis, and there is little extraneous information. Both unity and coherence are vital within individual paragraphs, as well as throughout the text. When a text is cohesive and unified, it facilitates comprehension because few inferences are needed in order for the reader to get the gist. Thus, cohesive text is conducive to allowing the reader to learn more content (Armbruster, 1984; Britton & Gulgoz, 1991).

Unfortunately, many textbooks and trade books are not cohesive in nature, which places a cognitive burden upon the reader, especially less able readers (Beck, McKeown, Hamilton, & Kucan, 1998). Consequently, they often do not read their science textbooks even when assigned to do so (Guzzetti, Hynd, Williams, & Skeels, 1995). One simple consideration teachers can make is whether or not the text respects the reader's prior knowledge. It is helpful to try to think like the intended reader when analyzing text. We can ask ourselves questions such as, "Is it likely that my students know enough to make the necessary connections to get the gist?" and "Does the author assume they have more prior knowledge than they do?" Having a reasonable conceptual load is important as well.

To help us analyze cohesion, we ask ourselves the following questions:

- Are major concepts logically connected throughout the text?
- Are sentence-level ideas logically connected to each other?
- Does the author assume the reader has more prior knowledge than is likely?
- Are abstract concepts introduced one at a time?
- Are abstract concepts accompanied by a sufficient number of concrete, relevant examples?
- In general, is this text a good model of expository writing?

To determine if the major concepts of *Earth Alive* are presented in a logical way, we examined the manner in which topics are introduced. First, Markle introduces the entire book by asking the reader to imagine his or her neighborhood on a typical morning. Markle asks readers to think about what they see and hear, leading them to observe that their neighborhood is an active place where "everything seems to be doing something or making some sound—everything but the Earth itself" (p. 5). A large photograph of a huge sinkhole follows Markle's introduction on the next page. Again, Markle encourages readers to observe the photo and draw conclusions, immediately engaging them in the text. This photo is followed by five paragraphs of explanation and two more photos to illustrate the content. On page 10, which marks the introduction of volcanoes, Markle again inserts a photograph and asks readers to make observations about what they see. She reminds them the photo is not an example of a sinkhole, thus contrasting the new topic with the topic just discussed. This process repeats throughout *Earth Alive*. Markle's use of second person and a conversational tone encourage children to think along with the author, much like a think aloud does. Because each topic is introduced in a similar manner and in relation to previously described topics, the major concepts within the text are logically connected.

Paragraph-level cohesion is also critical for comprehension, especially for young and less able readers. Therefore, it is important for authors to write in a way that clearly links each and every sentence in a logical progression so the number of inferences required for comprehension is reduced. The following example is a representative paragraph found in *Earth Alive*:

> Mineral residues aren't the only deposits that shape the Earth's surface. Snow and ice can build up into a huge body of ice. You may not be surprised to read that glaciers, like this one on Mount Spurr, Alaska, are hundreds of feet across, several thousand feet thick, and many miles long. But did you know that glaciers travel? (p. 24)

In this example, the first sentence explicitly relates to the topic of the previous paragraph, mineral deposits. The second sentence clarifies another feature that shapes the Earth's surface, specifically glaciers. The third sentence respects what the reader is likely to know about glaciers (i.e., glaciers are hundreds of feet across, thousands of feet thick, etc.), and the last sentence introduces a feature of glaciers that readers may not be aware of. Thus, Markle's writing style facilitates comprehension within paragraphs by making connections for the reader, acknowledging what the reader is likely to know about the topic, and then guiding the reader to consider new information about it. In addition, she naturally sets a purpose for reading—to learn about how glaciers travel.

To determine whether or not this text is a good example of expository writing, we made the following observations about *Earth Alive*. Each section begins with a question for the reader to answer and a brief reference to the previous section. Each new topic is described in depth, photographs are used to clarify and illustrate the descriptions, and references to the photographs are made in the text. Explicit connections to previous descriptions are made throughout the text, resulting in a very cohesive text and a good model of expository writing. Having good examples of well-written informational text in the science classroom is significant especially when teaching children how to write their own science texts. In addition, it is more likely that children will pick up and read well-written text, especially if they can comprehend it on their own. Because of these features, *Earth Alive* rated a 3 for cohesion.

Specialized Vocabulary

The fourth section of our checklist is specialized vocabulary. By necessity, informational text contains technical vocabulary, and young readers often struggle with such vocabulary. Typically, nonfiction texts define vocabulary in one of three ways: (1) as it is introduced; (2) with pictures, in captions, or with labels; or (3) in a glossary. In each of these cases, to maximize comprehension, the vocabulary must to be explained in a way the reader can understand *and* at a lower level of abstraction than the word being defined (Beck & McKeown, 1991). Too often, the definition of technical vocabulary is as abstract as the target word being defined. Therefore, to guide our thinking about specialized vocabulary, we ask:

- Is the vocabulary defined as it is introduced?
- Is vocabulary defined in pictures, captions, labels, or clarified visually?
- Is vocabulary defined in a glossary?
- Is the target vocabulary defined at a lower level of abstraction than the vocabulary word itself?

Sandra Markle is fairly consistent when introducing technical vocabulary in *Earth Alive*. This example shows how she carefully defines the term, "magma":

A volcanic eruption, like a sinkhole, starts underground. Deep inside, the Earth is so hot that solid rock melts. This molten rock, called *magma*, can remain underground and cool off and harden into new rocks. Or, trapped gasses may begin to build up pressure. Then the *magma* will rise to the surface through cracks in the Earth's crust. If overlying rock does not block it, the *magma* will ooze out onto the surface like toothpaste being squeezed out of a tube. (p. 12)

The strength of this example is that the definition of magma (i.e., molten rock) is conceptually described at a lower level of abstraction than the target word, magma. By using toothpaste as the example in the analogy, Markle provides an analogy that most young readers will understand.

Because not all magma oozes onto the surface, Markle's next paragraph describes the explosive quality of magma, further clarifying the target concept. Again, she uses a relevant analogy of soup boiling in a lidded pot to describe how pressure builds up and can become great enough to cause an explosion. By providing both scenarios associated with magma, Markle provides a thorough, accurate description of the target vocabulary.

Two paragraphs later, Markle introduces *lava*, which is the term used when magma reaches the Earth's surface. She does this, however, after she provides significant supporting details about magma and its characteristics. Her descriptions are complemented by a variety of photos illustrating a volcanic eruption, pumice, and obsidian. Each photograph has an accompanying explanation to draw the readers' attention to the significance of the photo and how it relates to the description in the text. Markle's treatment of specialized vocabulary is one of the best we have seen in trade books. Even though *Earth Alive* does not have a glossary, we felt it deserved a 3 for specialized vocabulary since other aspects of this category, which are directly related to comprehension, were so well done.

Reader Interest

The fifth section of our checklist is reader interest. We consider this aspect to be critical since reader attitude and engagement, comprehension, and the amount of reading done are all affected by reader interest (Guthrie & Ozgungor, 2002; Matthewson, 1985). Quite simply, we want to know if the text grabs and holds the reader's attention. So, we ask:

- Is the text visually attractive?
- Does the text include colorful illustrations or photos?
- Is the format appropriate with regard to print and page size?
- Are positive gender and racial/ethnic role models shown?
- Will the reader want to read this text?

We rated *Earth Alive* a 2 with regard to reader interest. The colorful photographs within the book have aesthetic appeal and serve a valuable purpose. The large font and page numbers are appropriate for young readers. The amount of description devoted to specific topics (e.g., five to six paragraphs per topic) is not overwhelming for the intended reader yet provides ample explanation of target concepts. It's true there are no people shown in the text, and we are not convinced that children will pick up this book independently and want to read it. *Earth Alive* is, however, an excellent book to use for instructional purposes. Far too many materials intended for classroom use are not cohesively written nor do they address technical vocabulary with the young reader in mind, and *Earth Alive* scores very high in both of these significant categories. Therefore, it rated a 2 in this category.

Scientific Viewpoint

The final category our checklist considers is the text's scientific viewpoint. We use the term "viewpoint" to describe the image the book portrays about science. Borrowing on the work of Ford (2004), our checklist includes the following four categories: Science as Facts; Science as Measuring/Experimentation; Science as Observation; and Science as Biography. You will notice on the checklist that these items do not receive a numeric score.

The majority of trade books available today view science as facts (Ford, 2004), and *Earth Alive* is one example. Markle describes the major features of the Earth's surface, its natural changes, and different types of earth materials. *Earth Alive* does not mention scientists, their lives, or the methods they use to determine facts about our changing Earth. Thus, this book portrays a "science as facts" viewpoint. "Science as facts" books may be helpful for learning science content, but they are not as helpful in teaching children about the nature of inquiry. Therefore, it is essential that when we use books in the science classroom, we use them as one aspect of an inquiry-based curriculum.

Books that focus on the lives of scientists fall into the Biographical/Scientist's Work category for obvious reasons. Supplementing the science curriculum with books about scientists provides rich examples of actual people who discover scientific ideas and are good role models for children. With teacher guidance, these texts can be used as springboards for learning more about science concepts and the process of scientific inquiry.

Books that fall into the category, Science as Observation, encourage children to independently engage in observing the natural world. *Earth Alive* contains some elements of "science as observation" as noted in section introductions. As new topics are introduced, Markle encourages the reader to observe their natural world. On the checklist, we would note that "science as facts" is the primary viewpoint, and "science as observation" is less pronounced even though it is significant in a scientific sense.

Some books focus on scientific activity and are collections of experiments with brief explanations. These books represent the "science as measurement/experimentation" viewpoint because they focus on the methods used to discover basic scientific principles, such as force and motion. Having such books available in a hands-on science classroom is essential, since they address the science as inquiry standard emphasized in the national standards documents (National Research Council, 1996). Determining a book's viewpoint can be helpful when reviewing several books on the same topic because it is wise to select books with a variety of viewpoints.

Annotations

After completing our initial analysis, we find it helpful to write a short annotation. Usually, we list the major concepts that the book addresses and ideas on how we might use this book in the classroom. This can range from independent reading, a teacher read aloud, a reference book, or a model of good writing. Then, we note any unusual or outstanding features and include a note about for whom we think the book is most appropriate. This is either an individual child or a group of children. The annotation is especially handy when reviewing many books on the same topic.

Conclusions

There is value in supplementing a hands-on science curriculum with expository literature. Students benefit, especially those who prefer to read and write nonfiction. When we create situations in our classrooms that encourage children to ask questions, experiment, and read, they gain a deeper understanding of science concepts and scientific inquiry. They realize that reading is a natural component of inquiry and can validate observations, raise more questions, or even cast doubt. When literature is carefully integrated with science, our students gain valuable practice in critical thinking, problem solving, and comprehending complex texts. However, knowing which texts to use can be a daunting task for busy teachers.

In this chapter, we have provided sources that identify highly recommended literature. But, as Ford (2004) points out, life science topics comprise 64% of all trade books receiving outstanding ratings by the experts. Since national science standards, as well as most state-level curricula, also include physical and Earth science, teachers need a means to help them select the most appropriate texts in those areas. The checklist described in this chapter is one tool to use. By analyzing a text's accuracy, organization, writing style, and viewpoint, you are in a better position to select the best books for science instruction. This process does not take very long and offers a systematic way of evaluating texts for your classroom.

TITLE: _Earth Alive!_

AUTHOR: _Sandra Markle_   ISBN: _0-688-09360-4_

PUBLISHER & DATE: _1991, Lothrop, Lee, & Shepard Books_

TOPIC: _Changes in the Earth's crust_

STANDARDS ADDRESSED: _Earth and Space Science: Properties of Earth Materials_

TOTAL SCORE: _13/15_ RECOMMEND? _YES_ FOR WHOM? _Gr. 3-5_

3 = meets all or most criteria   2 = meets some criteria   1 = meets few criteria

Check all that apply, or write N/A if not applicable. Then, choose overall score for each category and write score on blank.

____3____ **Accuracy**
  Information about author expertise/experience is given _Markle has written several books; had a consultant for this book_
  Information about photo credits is given _Yes_
  Information is current and accurate _Yes, when compared with newer titles, this book still in print too_

Figure 3:2 A completed checklist for _**Earth Alive!**_.

___2___ **Organization and Layout**

table of contents NO   chapter headings NO   section headings NO
index Yes, detailed   glossary NO   charts and graphs NO
maps   NO   page numbers Yes   Web sites NO
Consistent, natural divisions between topics used: photo then explanation

___3___ **Cohesion of Ideas**
Major ideas are logically connected throughout text
Throughout text, invites readers to imagine, observe their world;
consistent manner of introducing topics, setting a purpose for reading

Sentence-level ideas are logically connected to each other
Yes. Makes connections for reader, acknowledges reader
background knowledge

Text respects reader's probable background knowledge/experience
Yes. Well done.

Appropriate conceptual load
Yes. Well done.

Good model of expository writing
Each section begins with ?, in depth explanation with photos follow,
mention of previous section made

___3___ **Specialized Vocabulary**
Defined as it is introduced Yes, in a context children will understand;
                 good analogies used
Defined in pictures, captions, labels, or clarified visually Yes, well done
Defined in glossary Not applicable

___2___ **Reader Interest**
Has aesthetic appeal Yes
Has colorful illustrations or photos Yes
Uses appropriate font and page size for intended reader Yes
Has positive role models with respect to gender and ethnicity no people pictured

Scientific Viewpoint: Do not give this item a numeric score. Note which is the primary, and if appropriate, the secondary focus.

___X___ Science as Facts primary focus
___X___ Science as Observation secondary focus
_____ Science as Measuring/Experimenting
_____ Biographical/Scientist's Work

Annotation:

This engaging book explains how sinkholes, volcanoes, glaciers, weather, and water affect the Earth's

crust. It makes excellent use of analogies that are relevant to children. The writing style encourages

readers to make predictions as well as connect content to their daily lives. Very well written.

Figure 3:2 A completed checklist for *Earth Alive!*. *(Continued)*

Chapter 4

Nature and Nurture

Introduction

Anyone who has attended a family reunion quickly realizes there are similarities and differences among family members. Some of these likenesses are obviously inherited, while others are learned. This concept may be difficult for some young children to grasp because it "appear[s] to be paradoxical: Siblings are like one another, but they are also different" (American Association for the Advancement of Science [AAAS], 2001, p. 82). The focus of this unit is to begin building an understanding of the difference between inherited and noninherited traits. Because few good trade books appropriate for children studying heredity exist, this unit emphasizes the use of electronic text.

We chose to emphasize electronic text because the abilities to read, write, and communicate have always been determined by the information and communication technologies of the day (Leu, Jr., 2002). Today, the technologies we use for reading, writing, and communicating involve the Internet, and they require sophisticated problem solving. These "new literacies" are subcomponents of a larger definition of online reading comprehension (Leu, Jr., Leu, & Coiro, 2004). Therefore, just as scientists use a variety of print and electronic materials in their daily work, we want to encourage you and your students to do the same. By doing so, you provide an opportunity for your students to practice these "new literacies."

Big Idea: There is variation among individuals of one kind within a population. Individuals of the same kind differ in their characteristics, and sometimes the differences give individuals an advantage in surviving and reproducing (AAAS, 2001, p. 83).

Key Science Question: Why are we alike in some ways and different in other ways?

National Science Standard: As a result of activities in Grades K–4, all students should develop understanding of the characteristics of organisms.

National Language Arts Standards: Students read a wide range of print and nonprint tests to build understanding of texts . . . Students apply a wide range of strategies to comprehend, interpret, evaluate, and appreciate texts . . . Students apply knowledge of . . . media techniques . . . to create critique, and discuss print and nonprint texts . . . Students conduct research. They gather, evaluate, and synthesize data from a variety of sources to communicate their discoveries . . . Students use a variety of technological and informational resources to gather and synthesize information and to create and communicate knowledge.

Thinking Tools: Question Maker tool

Action	Hands-On Activities	Literacy/Thinking Tools and Activities
Phase 1: Engage		
Discuss likes, dislikes, talents, abilities, and interests of students and their families.		Activate prior knowledge
Phase 2: Explore		
Generate list of personal traits and preferences. Categorize characteristics as nature, nurture, or both.	Survey 3 people about their traits.	Compare/contrast information; Pair-Share
Phase 3: Explain		
Compile and discuss trait data.		Compare/contrast information
Phase 4: Elaborate		
Play Web game. Identify important questions and/or problems related to nature and nurture. Using the Web and informational books, locate additional information, critically evaluate it, and synthesize it.		K-W-H-L Question Maker tool
Phase 5: Evaluate		
Role-play a geneticist and communicate new learning.		Writing

Figure 4:1 A framework for science literacy.

Teacher Background

People can be described in terms of their characteristics. Some characteristics, also called traits, are inherited and others result from interactions with the environment. Thousands of different characteristics make us who we are. Some traits, such as eye color, are determined mostly or entirely by genes. These kinds of traits are said to be due to nature. Other characteristics, or preferences, such as a favorite color, are determined by nurture. Nurture involves the environment in which we live as well as our upbringing. Most characteristics, however, develop through a combination of nature and nurture.

Parents pass traits to their offspring so there are often similar characteristics seen in both parent and offspring. Have you ever heard someone say, "He has his father's nose" or "She has her mother's eyes"? You may also have noticed that some siblings look alike. Their inherited traits are what make their physical appearance so similar. An inherited trait is a genetic characteristic or quality that is passed from parent to child. Inherited human traits include:

- The ability to curl the tongue
- Attached or unattached earlobes
- Dimples or freckles
- Naturally curly or straight hair
- Hitchhiker's or straight thumb
- Color-blindness or normal color vision
- Widow's peak or straight hairline
- Color of skin and hair

Scientists agree that both nature and nurture play an important role in who we are. In this unit, students begin to develop an understanding of the role played by nature and nurture in defining who we are and what it means to be human. Because the field of genetics is rapidly changing with new discoveries, this unit makes use of electronic text to help students answer their own questions. To make the most of Internet technologies, you will model four effective strategies necessary for inquiry: searching for information, navigating Web sites, critically evaluating them, and synthesizing information gained (source: http://extension.usu.edu/aitc/teachers/pdf/heredity/traits.pdf).

Estimated Time: 4 periods, approximately 60 minutes each

Phase 1: Engage

Ask students to share details about their family.

- How many brothers and sisters do you have?
- What do they look like?
- What do they like to do for fun?
- Describe your mom and dad. What do they look like? What do they like to do for fun?
- Are you like your brothers and sisters in any way? Are you different in any way?
- Are you like your parents in any way? Are you different from them in any way?

Next, have students turn to a partner and briefly discuss details about their family, including physical traits and personal traits, such as likes, dislikes, talents, abilities, and interests.

Phase 2: Explore

Materials Needed:

Nature and Nurture definition cards, one set for each group

Traits T-chart, one for each group

Large Traits T-chart on chart paper

Colored sticky notes, one color per group

Chart paper

A Traits Survey sheet, one for each student

Advanced Preparation:

Preview recommended Web sites for information pertaining to the Traits Survey so that you can answer questions that may arise.

Procedure:

1. Write the unit's key science question on the board: "Why are we alike in some ways and different in other ways?"
2. Use a Think-Pair-Share activity next.
   a. **Think.** Give the students 3 minutes to describe themselves in writing using words and/or drawings on a sheet of paper. This is a silent

activity. You may want to encourage students to list both preferences and traits.

   b. **Pair.** After 3 minutes, have students pair with a partner, share their
lists and drawings, and discuss similarities and differences with their
partners for 3 minutes.

   c. **Share.** Have one pair meet with another pair to form a group of 4.
Have quads generate a group list of traits and preferences. As a
whole class, share lists and generate a class list on the board, with
each group sharing one idea at a time to be added to the class list.

For the list to be manageable for the next activity, work toward a list of
10–15 items that are a good mix of both nature and nurture characteristics, but do not put the terms into nature/nurture categories at this time.

3. Distribute definition cards to each group. Also, write definitions on the
board. Read through the definitions and explain. Ask the class if they
need clarification or have questions.

4. Give one blank copy of a Traits T-chart to each group. Draw another T-
chart on chart paper. Select from the class list an obvious inherited trait,
such as skin color, and model the next activity.

5. Tell students that for each characteristic listed on the board, they are to
discuss if that characteristic is due to nature, nurture, or both, and write
it in the appropriate section of their group T-chart. Model this process
with "eye color." Read each definition and compare it with "eye color."
Think aloud your thought processes, and say something like: "According
to the definition card, **Nurture** is related to my upbringing, like where I
lived, ate, and did for fun. That *contrasts* with 'eye color' because the
color of my eyes doesn't have anything to do with that. I think I will look
at the definition of **Nature** and *compare* that. Nature means traits you
are born with. I think I was born with green eyes, so I would say 'eye
color' is due to Nature."

6. Model again with "athleticism." Begin by reading each definition. Think
aloud your thought processes, and say something like: "I'll start with
comparing 'athleticism' and nature. Nature means I've inherited this trait
from my parents. Neither of my parents are athletes, but they always
encouraged me to play sports. How does that *compare* with nurture?
Nurture means something related to my upbringing. Maybe my parents'
encouragement influenced me to play sports. But whenever I try a new
sport, I pick it up immediately and am rather good at it, so I must have
some natural talent, too. Hmmmm. I think this is an example of both
nature and nurture." Then, place "athleticism" on the line that separates
Nature and Nurture, and explain to the class why you are placing it

there. To the extent possible, you should use the terms "compare" and "contrast" when you model since compare/contrast is one way information can be organized in text. So, it is beneficial to provide a concrete example with the compare/contrast concept when you have the opportunity.

7. Hang the large Traits T-chart written on chart paper where all students can see it. Write "eye color" under the Nature section of the Traits T-chart.

8. Let groups of students decide where they think each characteristic on the class list goes on the T-chart. Encourage students to make predictions. Do not try to influence their answers. As students are working on this task, circulate and listen in on student conversations and debates. Questions you might ask groups are:

   • Can you give an example of something you were born with (i.e., a dimple in your chin)?

   • Is that trait something that can easily be changed? (No)

   • Where could you place that trait on the T-chart? Look at your definition cards. (Dimples would fit under nature.) Why? (Because you are born with them.)

   • Why did you place that trait under nature? (Nature means that you inherit the trait.)

   • If you are born with something, can you change it? (Most times, you cannot change it because being born with something means you inherited it from your parents. But you can change things like hair color by dying your hair, or if you have cosmetic surgery, you may look different as a result.)

   If students discuss a trait as being due to both nature and nurture, ask:

   • What aspects of this trait are due to nature?

   • What aspects of this trait are due to nurture?

   Encourage students to look at their definition cards and their T-charts. Encourage them to notice any similarities or differences between trait A and trait B. Next, ask:

   • Explain your thinking. What was your reasoning?

9. Once students have made a decision about the position of each trait on their group T-chart, bring the class back together for the next step. Give each group a different color packet of sticky notes. Explain that each group will now copy the traits listed on the board onto the sticky notes. Write one trait per sticky note.

10. Read off each trait listed on the board. As a trait is announced, have one group come to the front of the room and place this trait in the correct category (Nature or Nurture) on the large Traits T-chart. Continue with all traits so that each group contributes to the chart and you end up with a multicolored class Traits T-chart.

11. When all groups have placed their sticky notes, briefly discuss with the whole class, asking whether there were any disagreements with the placement of the traits. The group should be able to justify their placements. Encourage students to make use of their definition cards when explaining their reasoning.

12. Tell students that over the years, scientists have had this same discussion about which human characteristics are a result of nature and which are a result of nurture. They do not always agree, but there are some traits scientists do agree are inherited. Scientists always collect data when they are studying something. They use these data to help them interpret their observations and provide evidence, or justification of their conclusions. Tell students we are going to act like scientists and collect some data from our families on whether or not members of our family have these traits. Then, we will look at the data and play a game that will demonstrate what we have learned today.

13. Hand out the Traits Survey data collection sheet to each student. Explain to students that when scientists collect data, they keep it organized in some way. This chart will help us keep our data organized. Review the directions and column headings. Review any traits listed with which students may be unfamiliar.

Phase 3: Explain

Procedure:

1. Review data from the Traits Survey completed at home. Discuss the information students gathered on their surveys and compare it with the information gathered during the Explore phase. Ask questions such as:

   • Why do you think there are so many similarities or differences within your family? (There are similarities because some traits can be inherited and differences because some traits, such as a favorite food, are not inherited.)

   • Can you think of traits you may have inherited from your parents? From your grandparents? (Have students refer to their chart if they chose a parent or grandparent to complete the survey.) What traits do they have in common with you?

Explain that knowing this kind of information is important since certain diseases can be inherited from your parents or grandparents, such as diabetes, heart disease, or sickle-cell anemia. As we get older, it is important to tell our doctor of any close family member's chronic health problems, such as heart disease or high blood pressure. Conclude with the question:

- Predict which traits you may pass on to your children. (The entire list can be inherited traits, except allergies. Specific allergies are not inherited, per se, but the tendency for allergies is.)

Phase 4: Elaborate

Materials Needed:

Chart paper

Internet access in the computer lab

Internet access in the classroom with projector

Advanced Preparation:

1. Preview the Internet activity used in this lesson, A Nature and Nurture Walk in Mendel Park, at http://ology.amnh.org/genetics/naturewalk/index.html Bookmark this site on computers in the lab.

2. Familiarize yourself with the Question Maker tool, discussed in chapter 2 of this book.

3. Conduct an Internet search on one or two student-generated questions or a sample question. Capture the results of the search by using the Print Screen feature. Make copies of this screen for each student.

Procedure:

1. Take students to the computer lab. Then, go to the following Web site: http://ology.amnh.org/genetics/naturewalk/index.html

   Play the game, A Nature and Nurture Walk in Mendel Park, once in pairs.

2. Then, ask students to write at least two other questions that could be used in the online game. Each pair should develop one question that has a "nature" answer and one question that has a "nature and nurture" answer. Play the game again as a class, using student-generated questions.

3. Go to the Gene Scene link on the Web site and click on Genetic Journey. Have pairs complete the genetics investigation. When finished, ask students to compare their answers with others.

4. Stop at this point and create a K-W-H-L chart on chart paper. Remind students that the *K* represents what we Know about a topic; the *W* represents What we want to learn about a topic; the *H* represents How we will find information on our topic; and the *L* represents what we have Learned.

   a. **What we Know.** Ask students to reflect on what they now Know about the influence of nature and nurture on a person's traits and preferences. Record this information in the *K* column.

   b. **What we Want to know.** Ask students if they are curious about any other aspects of nature and nurture, and lead them to create an inquiry question using the Level 1 and Level 2 Question Maker tool from chapter 2 of this book. Solicit several questions from the class, and record them in the *W* column.

   c. **How will we find out?** To complete the *H* column, which stands for How will I find out?, the Internet will be used.

   This part of the unit is grounded in Leu, Leu, and Coiro's (2004) "new literacies perspective," which focuses on online reading as a problem-solving inquiry process. The components—locate, evaluate, synthesize, and communicate—form the basis of the next phase of the unit. Use the four-part sequence developed by Coiro (2005) to help you model and demonstrate how to make sense of online text. The four steps are: *search* for sites; *navigate* sites; *evaluate* sites; and *synthesize* information.

Search for Information:

5. Prior to conducting this part of the lesson, use your favorite search engine, such as Google or Dogpile, and look for answers to some of the questions the class generated in the *W* column. Or create a sample question, such as "Why are my eyes green?" Capture the first few entries of your search using the Print Screen button on your computer, which is next to the F12 key. Paste the screen into a word-processing document, such as Microsoft Word, and print out the results. Or, if you are a Macintosh user, simply use the built-in screen capture capabilities. Make copies for students.

6. Prepare some questions toward guiding students to examine the entries on your list. Or use these questions prepared by Coiro (2005):

   • "How many Web sites were found in this search? (Look at the top of the Search Results page for the total.)

   • Which sites feature information about _____?

   • Which site is likely to disappear in the next 3 months? (Look at the URL. If it is an "aol" site, chances are it is a personal Web page and is likely to change often.)" (p. 32).

The goal here is to have students stop, think, and make predictions about which sites will yield the most helpful information.

7. Most likely, your students will realize your search needs to be narrowed. To facilitate, ask questions such as:

    - Exactly what information do we need?

    - Are there words in the question (i.e., in the *W* column) that we might use to help us refine our search?

    Lead students toward identifying key words. If identifying key words is difficult for students, have books on the topic available, such as those in the Teacher Resources section. Prompt students to look at the table of contents, glossary, and index for possible key words. List possible key words on the board. Encourage students to read the sample question again. Ask:

    - Do you think we have all the key words we need now?

    Once you and your students are satisfied with the selection of key words, plug them into the search engine. Remind students to use quotation marks around phrases or terms that need to be kept together. Repeat the process.

Navigate Sites:

8. For this part of the lesson, model for students Coiro's (2005) seven steps for previewing a Web site. The goal here is to have students stop, think, and anticipate. Think aloud for your students, and show how you would make decisions about each site. If you determine a site is worthy of further exploration, bookmark it for future use.

    a. Read the title of the page and the title of the Web site in the margin at the top of the window.

    b. Scan the menu choices. Hold your mouse over the navigational or topical menus that often appear down the left frame or across the top of the window, but don't click yet. Get a big picture of the information available within the site.

    c. Make predictions about where each of the major links may lead, and anticipate a link's path through multiple levels of a Web site.

    d. Explore interactive features of dynamic images (i.e., animated images, or images that change as a viewer holds the mouse over them), pop-up menus, and scroll bars that may reveal additional levels of information contained within the site.

    e. Identify the creator of the Web site and when the site was last updated. You can often find this information by clicking on a button on the home page, labeled About This Site, but sometimes deeper exploration is needed to find the site's creator. Consider what this information indicates about the site.

    f.   Notice and try out any electronic supports the site has, such as an organizational site map or internal search engine.

    g.   Make a judgment about whether to explore the site further. If the site looks worthwhile, decide which areas of the site to explore first" (pp. 32–33).

Evaluate Sites:

9.   In order to critically evaluate the content of a site, teachers and their students need to think and check (Coiro, 2005). Remember that anyone can post information on the Internet, and some of this information is purposely misleading. Thus, Internet text must be carefully screened for accuracy and validity. Return to the Web sites previously bookmarked. Evaluate the information on the sites by asking questions such as:

- "Does this information make sense?

- Where else can I look?

- Who created the Web site and why?

- Who is the author?" (Coiro, 2005, p. 34).

It is important to model how to be a skeptic. Remind students that not all Internet sites provide reliable information. Lead them to realize that verifying the accuracy of information is important. They can do this by consulting other reliable sources, such as books, encyclopedias, and experts.

10. Have students practice verifying information by becoming "fact finders." Have bookmarked Web sites available, as well as books listed in the Teacher Resources section at the end of this unit. Ask questions such as:

- How does the information from the Web compare with the information in the books? Is it similar or different?

Be sure students take note of any inconsistencies. When facts can be corroborated, record them on the board. If information is conflicting, ask:

- What should we do when we cannot validate the information we found? What would a scientist do?

Lead students to understand the significance of validating findings with scientific observation and experimentation. Point out that for some topics, such as genetics, the Internet does contain the most up-to-date information on a topic, so the information in books might be outdated.

Synthesize Information:

11. Before recording what was learned in the *L* column, have students read again the sample question and the facts listed on the board. Ask:

    • Do we have all the information we need to answer our question?

    • Do we have all the information we need to have a valid answer to our question?

    If not, continue searching.

12. Next, model for students how to synthesize the information collected during the verification phase. Read words or phrases that could be grouped together. Ask:

    • Can you tell me what this means, using your own words?

    If students struggle, help them paraphrase by saying, "Are you trying to say _____?" With each interaction, encourage students to refine and clarify their word choices. As students compile the information and verbalize it, record it in the *L* column.

13. Remind students of the process used during this part of the unit. Review the steps completed. First, we identified an important question. Then, we searched for information and evaluated it. Finally, we put the information into our own words and synthesized it. Connect this process with those used by actual scientists. Point out that scientists also identify questions they think are important. Then, they collect data and make observations. Finally, they test their observations and attempt to verify what they observed. We did a similar thing when we turned to books and other sources to verify information we observed on the Internet.

Phase 5: Evaluate

Materials Needed:

    Letter Planning sheet, one for each student
    Blank Letter form, one for each student
    Blank paper, one sheet for each student

Procedure:

1. Remind students of the unit's key science question: "Why are we alike in some ways and different in other ways?" Students will role-play a geneticist. As a geneticist, they will write a letter to one of their relatives (either a parent or grandparent), explaining to them the reasons why they share certain characteristics but do not share others. Ask students:

- As geneticists, how should we handle this task?
- Encourage students to use the Letter Planning sheet and materials available to them, including their Traits T-chart, their Traits Survey, and their Nature and Nurture cards. When students have finished planning, ask them to write their letters on a blank sheet of paper.

2. Have students meet in pairs to proofread and edit their draft letters.

3. Students will write a final draft of the letter on the blank letter form. After letters are written, ask them:

- What does it feel like to have written a piece like this?
- Why would a scientist write something like this?
- What have you learned about being a geneticist?

Then, encourage them to actually give or send the letter to its intended recipient.

Teacher Resources

Trade Books

Balkwill, Fran. (1993). *Amazing schemes within your genes.* [Mic Rolph, Illus.] Minneapolis, MN: Carolrhoda Books, 32 pp.; ISBN: 0-87614-804-6 (paperback); $8.95.

> This book discussed the structure and functions of genes using colorful, multicultural illustrations. Chromosomes, DNA, adaptations, and mutations are described through examples, comparisons, and pictures. The text is interesting but runs the risk of being outdated, as new discoveries in genetics are occurring rapidly, and it is appropriate for advanced readers.

Balkwill, Fran, & Rolph, Mic. (2002). *Gene machines.* Woodbury, NY: Cold Spring Harbor Laboratory Press, 32 pp.; ISBN: 0-87969-611-7 (paperback); $8.95.

> *Gene Machines* is a humorous, colorful introduction to how genes work. The book begins by welcoming the reader to the family of inhabitants on planet Earth and explains that every human, plant, animal, and microscopic creature shares something in common: genes. Basic information about gene therapy and cloning is included. Beautiful, accurate illustrations help to explain abstract concepts.

Balkwill, Fran, & Rolph, Mic. (2002). *Have a nice DNA*. Woodbury, NY: Cold Spring Harbor Laboratory Press, 32 pp.; ISBN: 0-87969-610-9 (paperback); $8.95.

> The format of this book is similar to the other books by this pair of authors. It is written with children in mind, and it has colorful, multicultural illustrations. This book contains a more detailed explanation of DNA than either *Gene Machines* and *Amazing Schemes Within Your Genes* do, explaining the nature and function of DNA.

Walker, Richard. (2003). *Genes and DNA*. Boston: Kingfisher, 63 pp.; ISBN: 0-7534-5621-4 (hardcover); $11.95.

> This very interesting and comprehensive text explores many facets of genetics, including genes and inheritance, DNA, and genetic technology. A combination of colorful illustrations and photographs make concepts come alive for readers. Readers are encouraged to discover more though links to Web sites, books, places to visit, and career opportunities. This book is a great resource for the classroom.

Westberg Peters, Lisa. (2003). *Our family tree: An evolution story*. [Lauren Stringer, Illus.] New York: Harcourt, 45 pp.; ISBN: 0-15-201772-0 (hardcover); $17.00.

> Using fabulous illustrations and simple text, this book explains the roots of our family tree, dating back millions of years to the beginning of life on Earth. It describes what humans have inherited along the way to becoming modern-day human beings. This book can also be used with lessons on adaptation.

Winston, Robert. (2004). *What makes me me?* New York: Dorling Kindersley, 96 pp.; ISBN: 0-7566-0325-0 (hardcover); $15.99.

> This comprehensive text, written by a world-renowned scientist, would make an excellent reference book for the classroom or school library. Using expert yet readable explanations, this book introduces human biology by explaining both body and mind. Textual features include colorful photographs, sidebars with Frequently Asked Questions, a glossary, an index, and a test for readers to take.

Web Sites

Note. The authors realize that Web site addresses are not guaranteed to work, as they change, move, or are removed from the Internet. Therefore, the authors have included the sponsoring organization of the Web site in the event the link provided here does not work. Simply type in the name of the organization in your search engine, and it will direct you to a new URL.

The American Museum of Natural History Web site at:

http://www.ology.amnh.org/

OLogy, the Museum's Web site for kids ages 7 through 12, is based on the premise that "everyone wants to know something" and is designed as a place for kids to explore, ask questions, get answers, meet OLogists, play games, and see what other kids are interested in. Explore the Genetics and Biodiversity links for more information on nature and nurture.

http://ology.amnh.org/genetics/naturewalk/index.html

This link is also part of the American Museum of Natural History's Web site. This is the link for the A Nature and Nurture Walk in Mendel Park used in the Elaborate phase of the lesson.

http://ology.amnh.org/genetics/geneticjourney/index.html

This link is a part of the American Museum of Natural History's Web site. This link has students participating in a simple, four-item genetics survey, compares their responses with others, and explains the reasons why some people have various traits.

http://ology.amnh.org/genetics/youYou/youyou.html

This link is part of the American Museum of Natural History's Web site. This link provides information on what makes each of us unique. Designed for children, it describes, in a simple fashion, cells, chromosomes, and DNA.

The University of Arizona, Science Outreach at:

http://student.biology.arizona.edu/sciconn/heredity/
worksheet_heredity.html

This site provides information that is good for additional teacher background on simple genetics or heredity. Written in a hands-on worksheet format, it is designed for students to provide them with a general understanding of this topic.

The Utah Foundation for Agriculture in the Classroom at:

http://extension.usu.edu/aitc/teachers/elementary/heredity.html

The Utah Foundation for Agriculture in the Classroom is a nonprofit organization that receives financial support from interested individuals and organizations. Its mission is to improve agricultural literacy by developing programs that increase student awareness about agriculture and instill in students an appreciation for our food and fiber system. This site contains seven different lesson plans on the topic of heredity.

Videos

TLC Elementary School: Life Cycles at:

http://www.unitedstreaming.com/index.cfm

This video covers types of reproduction, inherited and learned characteristics, and the role of cells. Segments include: (1) Life Cycles—explains the difference between sexual and asexual reproduction (6 minutes); (2) Heredity—discusses how genes and mutations are passed to offspring during the reproduction process (5 minutes); (3) Behavior—focuses on traits that are learned as organisms make adaptations in order to survive (6 minutes); and (4) Cell Structure—explores the biology and function of the building blocks of life (6 minutes). Recommended for Grades 3–5.

Traits T-Chart

Nature   **Nurture**

Full size form available at www.Christopher-Gordon.com/authors/KingMattox-shtml

A Traits Survey

Name_____   Date_____

Most scientists agree that the traits mentioned below are inherited (due primarily to nature). Please complete the survey for yourself. When you are finished, ask a parent, grandparent, or two other people you know to complete the survey. What did you find?

Person 2 is _____

Person 3 is _____

Trait	Me Yes	Me No	Person 2 Yes	Person 2 No	Person 3 Yes	Person 3 No
I am a male.						
I am a female.						
I have dimples on my cheeks.						
I am right handed.						
I cross my left thumb over my right.						
I have freckles.						
I have naturally curly hair.						
I have a dimple in my chin.						
I have allergies.						
I have a widow's peak.						
I have attached earlobes.						

Full size form available at www.Christopher-Gordon.com/authors/KingMattox-shtml

Definition Cards

NURTURE:	NATURE:
Nurture refers to things related to your upbringing, such as: where you live, what you like to do, the people you know, and what you've learned.	Nature means the characteristics or traits you inherit from your parents, such as curly hair. You are born with these traits.
NURTURE:	NATURE:
Nurture refers to things related to your upbringing, such as: where you live, what you like to do, the people you know, and what you've learned.	Nature means the characteristics or traits you inherit from your parents, such as curly hair. You are born with these traits.
NURTURE:	NATURE:
Nurture refers to things related to your upbringing, such as: where you live, what you like to do, the people you know, and what you've learned.	Nature means the characteristics or traits you inherit from your parents such as curly hair. You are born with these traits.
NURTURE:	NATURE:
Nurture refers to things related to your upbringing, such as: where you live, what you like to do, the people you know, and what you've learned.	Nature means the characteristics or traits you inherit from your parents, such as curly hair. You are born with these traits.

Full size form available at www.Christopher-Gordon.com/authors/KingMattox-shtml

Letter Planning Sheet

You are a geneticist writing a letter to one of your relatives. Use this planning sheet and fill in the blanks below. You may use your Traits T-chart, your Traits Survey, or your Nature and Nurture cards to help you think. Once you have recorded the information you need, write your letter on a new sheet of paper.

Dear _____,

Name two traits you share with this relative:

1.

2.

Name two traits you do not share with this relative:

1.

2.

Explain <u>why</u> you do not share these traits. Write at least two reasons:

1.

2.

Full size form available at www.Christopher-Gordon.com/authors/KingMattox-shtml

Dear _____,

_____

_____

_____

_____

_____

_____

_____

_____.

Sincerely,

_____

Full size form available at www.Christopher-Gordon.com/authors/KingMattox-shtml

Teacher's Shopping List for Nature and Nurture

- ☐ Colored sticky notes, one color per group of students

- ☐ Markers

- ☐ One sheet of paper per student

- ☐ Traits T-chart, one for each group

- ☐ Large Traits T-chart, drawn on large chart paper

- ☐ A Traits Survey Data Collection sheet, one for each student

- ☐ Nature and Nurture definition cards, one set for each group

- ☐ Chart paper

- ☐ Printed copies of computer screen image showing results of Internet search, one copy for each student

- ☐ Letter Planning sheet, one for each student

- ☐ Blank Letter form, one for each student

- ☐ Internet access in the computer lab

- ☐ Internet access in the classroom with a projector

Full size form available at www.Christopher-Gordon.com/authors/KingMattox-shtml

Chapter 5

Birdie Buffet

Introduction

Understanding behavioral and physical adaptations is key to understanding the theory of natural selection. This understanding begins when we observe similarities and differences between ourselves and our family members, which was the focus of the unit in chapter 4 of this book. We notice that we share certain similar characteristics but still remain a unique individual. Once this observation is made and understood, we are ready to begin exploring two processes in evolution: the occurrence of new traits in a population and their effect on survival. When teaching these processes, it is important to articulate that when populations change, it is the result of the survival of a few individuals, not the gradual change of all individuals in the population (American Association for the Advancement of Science [AAAS], 2001). This understanding can help us better explain why and how animals adapt to their environment.

This unit on animal adaptations comes from the Outdoor Biology Instructional Strategies work done in 1975, and we felt it was important to include it here, since it is a classic. We also realize a unit on adaptation would not be complete without addressing, at least minimally, the current controversy surrounding the topic. It is not our intention to enter into that discussion. However, the topic does provide an excellent opportunity for further inquiry and exploration, if you and your students so desire. The Talk Origins Foundation of Houston, Texas, is a non-profit corporation that sponsors a news group, which provides mainstream scientific information about biological and physical origins. Visit http://www.talkorigins.org/ for more details. In addition, the National Center for Science Education (NCSE) is an organization devoted to defending the teaching of evolution in public schools. It is a nationally recognized clearinghouse for information and advice and is the only national organization to specialize in this issue. For more information, visit http://ncseweb.org/.

Big Idea: Different plants and animals have external features that help them thrive in different kinds of places. Some plants and animals survive well, some survive less well, and some cannot survive at all (AAAS, 2001, p. 83).

Key Science Question: How are animals adapted to survive in nature?

National Science Standard: As a result of activities, all students should develop an understanding of organisms and environments.

National Language Arts Standards: Students read a wide range of print and nonprint texts to build an understanding . . . Students apply a wide range of strategies to comprehend, interpret, evaluate, and appreciate texts . . . Students conduct research on issues and interests . . . They gather, evaluate, and synthesize data from a variety of sources to communicate their discoveries in ways that suit their purpose and audience.

Thinking Tools: Concept Cartoon tool

Action	Hands-On Activities	Literacy/Thinking Activities
Phase 1: Engage		
Students will choral read with the teacher to identify ways in which birds use their beaks. Discuss what students have observed or learned about bird beaks. Record on the Knowledge Chart.		Begin Concept Cartoon thinking tool.
Phase 2: Explore		
Using tools to simulate bird beaks, students will determine which one tool is most effective for eating individual foods.	Eating simulation done in small groups	Record data and interpret it.
Phase 3: Explain		
Use open-ended questions to guide discussion of the group's findings. Debrief on the purpose of the simulation and lead students to articulate a "Big Scientific Idea."		Continue with Concept Cartoon thinking tool.
Phase 4: Elaborate		
Research other books and Web sites on adaptations in order to read about, identify, discuss, and label additional ways in which animals adapt for survival.	Create adaptation posters. Share posters with classmates.	Research animal adaptations.
Phase 5: Evaluate		
Apply new learning by classifying types of adaptations identified in the Elaborate phase.		Classifying information

Figure 5:1   A framework for science literacy.

Teacher Background

Before presenting this unit, students should know the basic needs that all living things require to live (i.e., food, water, air, light, shelter, protection). Animals have specific adaptations that help ensure their survival. Animals that cannot adapt to their surroundings eventually die. Some adaptations are physiological. For example, fish have gills to allow them to breathe underwater. When it is cold outside, cats and dogs put on an extra coat of hair to keep warm. Some animals, such as birds, migrate to a warmer spot for the winter. Woodchucks, bears, reptiles, and amphibians hibernate. Physiological adaptations also help animals get food and water or protect themselves. Animals in the desert are specially adapted to deal with the lack of water. Some desert animals acquire water through their food and then store it in their body, while others are specially adapted to tap into prickly cacti and other desert plants to get water. Other examples of these types of adaptations are: being able to move very quickly, sharp claws or teeth, keen eyesight, or the shape of the bird's beak.

Animals can also adapt to their environment by making changes in their behaviors. One significant adaptation, for some animals, has been adjusting to urban sprawl. As cities grow, people encroach on the habitat of wild animals. As a result, we often see bears in urban areas, eating food from dumpsters. Humans have even tried to direct the movement of large groups of animals by installing huge fences along the highway to keep animals from crossing. In western Canada, "crosswalks" have been built across the highway to insure animal and driver safety.

Estimated Time: 3 to 4 periods, 60 minutes each

Materials Needed: See the Teacher's Shopping List in the Teacher Resources section at the end of this unit.

Phase 1: Engage

Materials Needed:

> Chart paper, two sheets
>
> *Beaks!* by Sneed Collard, one book for each pair of students

Procedure:

1. Begin by sharing one of your observations of a bird eating, which provides the introduction to the Concept Cartoon tool. Say something like, "I saw a bright red cardinal this morning at my birdfeeder. He broke open a sunflower seed and ate it. The cardinals at my feeder just love to eat sunflower seeds. I noticed his beak was a yellow color, and it was cone

shaped. It reminded me of a great book that we are going to read to-gether. It is called *Beaks!*."

2. Distribute *Beaks!* to the class. Entice students by having them look at the colorful cover and striking paper-collage images in the book. Point out the structure of the text (i.e., large print followed by small print that serves as an example). Tell them we will take turns reading this book together. Students will read aloud the large print. You will read aloud the small print. Before reading begins, remind students that the purpose for reading is to learn more about how birds use their beaks. Begin reading *Beaks!* and stop at the end of page 7.

3. Begin creating a Knowledge Chart to record students' observations dur-ing the unit and record your cardinal observation. Ask students to tell you what they have observed or learned about bird beaks. Record their responses on the chart. When appropriate, ask them to substantiate their responses using information from *Beaks!*.

4. Also, ask students what the book, *Beaks!,* makes them wonder about. Create an "I Wonder . . ." heading, and record students' "I Wonder" state-ments. Model by giving an example such as, "I wonder if cardinals would come to my feeder if I did not have sunflower seeds in it." Record student responses. This discussion helps to eventually generate the Big Scientific Idea you are leading students to formulate on the Concept Cartoon. You will return to the chart after the Explain phase of this unit, so you will want to keep it visible throughout the unit.

5. Conclude the Engage phase by asking students if they think there is a connection between *what* a bird eats and *how* it eats its food. Encourage them to make predictions, or hypotheses, just like actual scientists do, and to base their predictions on evidence.

Phase 2: Explore

Materials Needed:

Staple puller, one per group

Tweezers, one per group

Wooden skewer, one per group

Sieve, one per group

Pipette eye dropper, one per group

Sunflower seeds, one small handful for each group

Test tubes or floral tubes (the kind used to keep single flowers fresh) with a small amount of water at the bottom, one per group

Small bucket or tub filled with water and styrofoam peanuts, one per group

Small bucket or tub filled with water and rubber fish or frogs (gummy fish or large marshmallows may be substituted as long as they don't sink), one per group

Green Easter basket grass with plastic bugs spread through it, one per group

Small piece (6 x 6 inch) of foam rubber, one per group

Student Data sheet, one per group *or* science notebooks

Bird photo cards, at least five per group

Food item labels, one set for each group

Paper plates, one for each group

Advanced Preparation:

1. Students will work in small groups. Have one set of utensils (e.g., pliers, staple puller, pipettes, sieve, wooden skewer, and tweezers) and the different "foods" (e.g., seeds, water, styrofoam, bugs, rubber fish/frogs, foam rubber) at each table. Do *not* place the appropriate utensil next to its food source.

2. Make copies of the Student Data sheet (one for each student) and place on each table.

3. Place at least five bird photo cards on each table. These can be created using photos from magazines, books, or online images, such as those on Google Images. Be sure the beaks are prevalent in the photos.

4. Label "food" items as follows so that students will know what the items represent in the simulation.

    Label the seeds: Break open the seeds

    Label the sugar water: Suck up nectar

    Label the bucket with the floating styrofoam: Scoop up food from pond

    Label grass with bugs: Catch the bugs

    Label the bucket with the rubber fish or frogs: Spear this food

    Label the foam rubber: Tear off pieces of meat

Tips for management of groups:

- Groups of 3 or 4 children work best.
- Have all group members be responsible for testing at least one tool beak.
- Have each member of the group record information on his or her own record sheet.

- Have all group members agree on the most effective tool and discuss their justification.
- Each group member should present part of his or her observations in some way.
- Explain "safe use" of materials with class before beginning.

Procedure:

1. Tell students that they are going to simulate how birds eat by using the tools at their table as beaks. Ask students if they know what *simulate* means. Explain that simulations are one way scientists reproduce something real, so they can study it under test conditions. Simulations can help scientists formulate new hypotheses, or help explain their observations. Explain that there are limitations to using simulations, since they must be tested or validated by comparing the observations to what occurs in nature. For our simulation, explain a few ground rules:

   - Students must hold one hand behind their backs while using the other to manipulate the tool.
   - Students must do what the label on the food says to do (i.e., break open the seed, tear off pieces of meat, suck up nectar), and then put the foraged food onto the paper plate.
   - Group members must agree and decide which one tool will be most effective at helping to eat each individual food.
   - While working in groups, members should verbally connect what they are doing with what they heard about in *Beaks!*.

2. If you choose to use science notebooks instead of the Student Data sheet, have students record the data table in their notebooks to be completed during the simulation.

3. Students work as a group to decide which tool beak works best with which food and then individually record their data on the Student Data sheet. Once observations have been recorded, students will answer the question in the second column of their record sheet, "Why does this type of beak work best with this type of food?" (Birds use their particular shaped beaks in order to eat a particular type of food. The shape of the beak helps them survive.)

Phase 3: Explain

Materials Needed:

> *Beaks!* by Sneed Collard, one book per pair of students
>
> Knowledge Chart begun earlier in unit
>
> Marker
>
> Birdie Buffet Concept Cartoon, one for each student

Procedure:

1. After students have finished filling in their record sheets, have the groups present and justify their findings to the class. Add new observations to the Knowledge Chart, including any conclusions students may have reached regarding an "I Wonder . . ." statement.

2. Use questions such as the following to guide a discussion of the groups' findings. Remind students to explain and justify their observations, just as scientists do. Also, remind them that scientists produce evidence when needed, so they will also need to show their evidence when explaining their observations.

    *   Which type of bird would have a beak that is best for tearing meat? Why would this type of beak work best? (Birds of prey, such as hawks and owls, have sharp, curved bills for tearing meat.)

    *   Which bird(s) would have a beak for cracking seeds? Explain why this type of beak would work best. (Cardinals and sparrows have short, thin, cone-shaped beaks for cracking seeds.)

Note. At this point, students may not have enough knowledge to answer these questions. If this is the case, return to *Beaks!* and reread up to page 7 for the purpose of gathering more information on the correlation between specific birds and what they eat. Be sure to explicitly tell students your purpose for reading, so they can make a mental note of the appropriate information.

Continue questioning:

*   Which bird(s) would have a beak like tweezers? Describe how they would use it. (Insect eaters, such as warblers, have thin, pointed beaks to reach and grab for insects in small, tight places.)

*   Which bird(s) would have a beak like a straw? What would they use it for? (Hummingbirds have long, slender beaks to probe flowers for nectar.)

*   What is physically different about these different bird beaks? (Answers may be shape or size, sharp ends, or straight or flat bills. Lead students to

come up with the generalization that these all have to do with a physiological characteristic, which is shape.)

- What other physical characteristics help a bird survive? (Examples may be talons, wings, feathers, eyesight, etc.)

3. If you have not already done so, finish reading *Beaks!* for the purpose of gathering more information. Remind students of their "I Wonder" statements and encourage them to look for explanations, or create new "I Wonder" statements, based on information in the book.

4. Revisit the Knowledge Chart and discuss "I Wonder" statements.

5. Refocus students' attention on the simulation just completed. Tell students the purpose of the simulation was to show them one way birds are adapted to survive in nature. Lead students to develop a "Big Scientific Idea," which is the next phase of the Concept Cartoon thinking tool. Discuss items such as the following:

    - What was the best tool for cracking open the seeds? (The pliers.)

    - I wonder what would happen if the cardinal that came to my feeder did not have a cone-shaped beak for cracking open sunflower seeds? (The bird would not be able to open its favorite food.)

    - How did you figure that out?

    - So, what might happen to cardinals with cone shaped beaks if a blight came along and all of the sunflowers died?

    - What might happen to birds with curved-shaped beaks (such as owls) if rats and mice died out?

    - What might happen to puffins if an oil spill killed the fish they eat?

    Record the answers to these questions on the Knowledge Chart and label them "Big Scientific Ideas." It's okay to record more than one big idea. The important point is to help students realize the shape of a bird's beak is a physiological adaptation that enables the bird to get its food, and this is necessary for survival. Record this big scientific idea on the Knowledge Chart, using a different color marker, and label it "The Big Idea."

6. Distribute the Birdie Buffet Concept Cartoon. Have students select one Big Scientific Idea and add it to the top-left call-out balloon. Working in pairs, have students ponder the "What Do You Think?" challenge question on the bottom of the Concept Cartoon. Ask them to brainstorm the BUT call-outs. The goal here is to help them explore the theories in their heads and to express diverse, complex scientific viewpoints. Now that they have begun to make some links between beaks and food as an example of adaptation, you can help them think further about environmental

changes and the links between physiology and survival. At this point, it is key is to encourage students to elaborate their BUT call-outs to expose their thinking.

Phase 4: Elaborate

Materials Needed:

> *How Do Animals Adapt?* By Bobbie Kalman, one or more copies
>
> Assorted trade books listed in the Teacher Resources section at the end of this unit
>
> Internet access with bookmarked Web sites
>
> Computer printer
>
> Long strip of paper to write on and place on a blank wall
>
> Tape and glue
>
> Poster paper, at least 8 x 11 inch or larger, one sheet per pair of students
>
> Markers, one per pair of students
>
> Sticky notes, two for each student

Procedure:

1. Begin by reminding students that they now know a lot about bird adaptations, but you are wondering about how other animals adapt to their environment. Write the statement "I wonder how animals adapt to their habitat …" on a strip of paper and tape it to a blank wall. Ask students to share what they know about other animal adaptations.

2. Then, tell them you are going to read a few pages of a new book, and their job is to listen for examples of ways in which animals adapt. Or, you may choose to have students read the book independently for the same purpose stated above. Read a few pages from *How Do Animals Adapt?* by Bobbie Kalman, and review the concept of behavioral adaptation, using examples from the book, such as migration or storing food for the winter. You might ask:

   - Did anyone notice any interesting words? Why was this word interesting to you?

   - Did anyone notice any interesting photos or pictures? Why was this interesting to you?

3. Form pairs. Ask students to use trade books and Web sites to research animal adaptations. Remind them to look for interesting words, phrases, and pictures, because their task is to create a poster that visually shows at

least two examples of animal adaptations. (See the list of appropriate book titles and Web sites in the Teacher Resources section at the end of this unit.) You may want to take your class to the computer lab or media center for this segment.

4. When posters are complete, have pairs form quads and share their posters. Encourage students to discuss whether the adaptations are behavioral or physical. Repeat with new partners until students have shared their posters with at least two other pairs. Ask students about the process just used:

    • Tell me how your group discussion went. What went well?

    • What kinds of questions were raised?

5. Give each pair two sticky notes. Students will create a label for their adaptations. Examples may include: camouflage, storing food, hibernate, migrate, curved beaks, etc. Attach the labels to the posters.

6. Hang the posters on the wall, underneath the "I wonder how animals adapt to their habitat . . ." strip.

Phase 5: Evaluate

1. Distribute the Adaptations T-chart. Explain the directions: Students will categorize kinds of adaptations noted on the class posters as either Physical or Behavioral by writing the adaptation in the proper column. You may want to complete one together as a class as an example, such as the following:

Adaptations

Physical	Behavioral
curved beaks	migrate

2. Conclude by asking students questions such as:

    • Why would a scientist categorize animal adaptations?

    • What purpose would it serve?

    • Can you think of any other examples where scientists categorize things?

Teacher Resources

Trade Books

Allen, Judy, & Humphries, Tudor. (2001). *Are you a dragonfly?* Boston: Kingfisher, 31 pp.; ISBN: 0-7534-5805-5 (paperback); $4.95.

> This charming book, which is part of the *Backyard Books* series, introduces readers to characteristics of a dragonfly and explains why a dragonfly behaves the way it does. Written in the second person, the text and illustrations explain a dragonfly's life and compare it with a child's life.

Arnosky, Jim. (1995). *All about owls.* New York: Scholastic, 24 pp.; ISBN: 0-439-05852-X (paperback); $5.99.

> This beautifully illustrated book provides many facts about all types of owls. It answers questions such as: How many kinds of owls are there? Where do they live? Why are owls' eyes so big? And what do owls eat? It is sure to inspire young naturalists. This book received the NSTA's Outstanding Science Trade Book for Children Award in 1995.

Collard III, Sneed. B. (2002). *Beaks!.* [Robin Brickman, Illus.] Watertown, MA: Charlesbridge, 30 pp.; ISBN: 1-57091-388-9 (paperback); $6.95.

> Written by acclaimed children's science writer, Sneed B. Collard III, this book explores the amazing diversity of our planet's birds by looking at their vastly different beaks. The book is written at two levels: one suited for beginning readers, while the other, more detailed text provides insights into the birds' biology and behaviors. Illustrator Robin Brickman has created stunning three-dimensional cut-paper collages to make these birds come alive. This is an NSTA recommended book.

Fowler, Allan. (1999). *Arms and legs and other limbs.* Danbury, CT: Children's Press, 31 pp.; ISBN: 0-516-26478-8 (paperback); $4.95.

> In this *Rookie Read About Science* book, Fowler shows children how their own limbs (i.e., arms and legs) compare and contrast with the limbs of various mammals, birds, insects, and amphibians. Using simple text and photos, it explains how limbs are used for eating, walking, jumping, flying, and swimming. A section called "Words You Know" is a picture dictionary to reinforce terms used in the text. An index is also included.

Hewitt, Sally. (1998). *All kinds of animals.* Danbury, CT: Children's Press, 30 pp.; ISBN: 0-516-26338-2 (paperback); $6.95.

> Part of the *It's Science* series, this book introduces readers to the ways in which scientists group animals according to their characteristics. Topics are introduced using a 2-page spread and cover topics, such as amphibians and insets. Outstanding photographs, as well as Think About It, Look Again, and Try It Out boxes, encourage readers to make discoveries and develop new ideas for themselves.

Hickman, Pamela. (2004). *Animals and their mates: How animals attract, fight for and protect each other.* [Pat Stephens, Illus.] Tonawanda, NY: Kids Can Press, 40 pp.; ISBN: 1-5337-546-7 (paperback); $5.95.

> Striking illustrations and technical text provides detailed, accurate, and interesting examples and explanations of mating rituals of a variety of animals. For instance, did you know that male honeybees explode and die after they mate with a queen? These and other fascinating facts are included in sections on attracting a mate, finding a mate, keeping a mate, mating time, and mating spaces.

Jenkins, Martin. (1997). *Chameleons are cool.* [Sue Shields, Illus.] Cambridge, MA: Candlewick Press, 30 pp.; ISBN: 0-7636-1139-5 (paperback); $6.99.

> Using great illustrations, this book, which is part of the *Read and Wonder* series, dispels the myth that chameleons only change color to match their surroundings. Different kinds of chameleons—their physical characteristics, behavior, and their ability to change color—are explained in a straightforward, interesting way. A simple index is included.

Kalman, Bobbie. (2000). *How do animals adapt?* New York: Crabtree, 32 pp.; ISBN: 0-86505-957-8 (paperback); $6.95.

> Part of the *Science of Living Things* series, this book describes physical and behavioral adaptations animals make in order to survive. Using beautiful drawings and photographs, topics such as using camouflage, mimicry, poisons, defense, adaptation to weather, feeding, mating, and adapting to people are explained. Definitions of highlighted vocabulary are provided in context and reinforced in photos or drawings. A glossary and an index are included.

Kalman, Bobbie, Langille, Jacqueline, & Walker, Niki. (1998). *Birds that don't fly.* New York: Crabtree Publishing, 32 pp.; ISBN: 0-86505-764-8 (paperback); $5.95.

> This beautifully photographed book provides a wealth of information on how flightless birds have adapted in order to survive. Physical descriptions and characteristics of ostriches, emus, rheas, kiwis, cassowaries, and penguins

are given. Frequent "More About" pages provide additional facts and statistics on flightless birds. A very interesting read. This book could also be used as a reference tool, as it includes a glossary and index.

Knight, Tim. (2003). *Super survivors.* Chicago: Heinemann Library, 32 pp.; ISBN: 1-4034-3262-7 (paperback); $6.95.

Two types of adaptation are explored in *Super Survivors*: changes that occur over time and sudden changes that plants and animals make as a result of forest fires or floods. Survival essentials, such as food, water, light, and warmth, are discussed. Part of the *Amazing Nature* series, great photographs, a fact file, glossary, section for further reading, and index make this a valuable addition to the classroom or school library.

Lock, Deborah. (2004). *Feathers, flippers, and feet.* New York: DK Publishing, 32 pp.; ISBN: 0-7566-0264-5 (paperback); $3.99.

Using stunning photographs and a unique question and answer format, this book is perfect for explaining the different ways in which birds and animals use their feathers, flippers, and feet to move. A fact box appears every fourth page and offers additional questions and information for curious readers. A simple index is included.

Morgan, Sally. (1996). *Animals and their world.* New York: Kingfisher, 32 pp.; ISBN: 0-7534-5498-X (paperback); $7.95.

Packed with interesting information, this book describes how different kinds of animals are adapted to survive in different environments. It explains how animals use their senses to search for food, how they avoid predators, and communicate. Colorful graphics complement the text, and simple experiments are suggested. A table of contents and index are included.

Pascoe, Elaine. (2003). *How and why birds use their bills.* [Dwight Kuhn, Illus.] Huntington Beach, CA: Creative Teaching Press, 17 pp.; ISBN: 154-471-1659X (paperback); $3.30.

Outstanding photographs help explain how different kinds of birds use their bills for such things as eating, preening, building nests, and courtship. The last page of the book lists six questions and can be used as a good review of how and why various birds use their bills.

Pfeffer, Wendy. (1996). *What's it like to be a fish?* [Holly Keller, Illus.] New York: HarperCollins, 32 pp.; ISBN: 0-06-445151-8 (paperback); $4.99.

This *Let's Read and Find Out Science* book teaches children how pet goldfish feed, breathe, swim, and rest in water. Large, clear, labeled pictures drawn with pen and ink, watercolor, and pastels complement the simple, informative text and explain how scales and slime keep fish healthy, how their sleek shapes help them swim, and what it means to be cold-blooded. The final pages provide a step-by-step approach for setting up a goldfish bowl.

Robinson, Claire. (1998). *Bears.* Chicago: Heinemann Library, 24 pp.; ISBN: 1-57572-463-4 (paperback); $7.25.

Simple text and corresponding photographs provide information on habitat, food, mating practices, hibernation, and cubs of bears commonly found in North America. A simple glossary, index, and More Books to Read section are included. Part of the *In the Wild* series, this book would make a good addition to any classroom or school library.

Schwartz, David M. (1998). *Animal skin & scales.* Cypress, CA: Creative Teaching Press, 16 pp.; ISBN: 1-57471-325-6 (paperback); $3.30.

Part of the *Look Once, Look Again* series, this engaging book uses highly detailed, close-up photographs to inspire readers to guess what animal part appears in the photograph. The skin or scales of an iguana, butterfly, worm, snake, turtle, fish, and even a human boy are described. The last 2 pages of the book serve as a review of the content.

Settel, Joanne. (1999). *Exploding ants: Amazing facts about how animals adapt.* New York: Atheneum Books for Young Readers, 40 pp.; ISBN: 0-689-81739-8 (hardcover); $16.95.

The title alone is enough to create curiosity on the reader's part! From small worms in a dog's nose to blood-sucking insects, this book tells of the unusual ways animals find food, shelter, and remain safe in their natural world. Although a bit technical in some of its explanations, the gory details are sure to interest even the most reluctant readers.

Sill, Cathryn. (1997). *About mammals: A guide for children.* [John Sill, Illus.] Atlanta, GA: Peachtree Publishers, 41 pp.; ISBN: 1-56145-174-6 (paperback); $7.95.

Full-page watercolors are paired with minimal text in this introduction to mammals. Beautiful illustrations explain what mammals are, how they live, and behave. A simple yet beautiful book.

Sill, Cathryn. (1991). *All about birds: A guide for children.* [John Sill, Illus.] Atlanta, GA: Peachtree Publishers; 34 pp.; ISBN: 1-56145-147-9 (paperback); $7.95.

Full-page watercolors are paired with minimal text in this introduction to birds. Beautiful illustrations explain the world of birds from eggs to flight and from songs to nests. A simple yet beautiful book.

Web Sites

Note. The authors realize that Web site addresses are not guaranteed to work, as they change, move, or are removed from the Internet. Therefore, the authors have included the sponsoring organization of the Web site in the event the link provided here does not work. Simply type in the name of the organization in your search engine, and it will direct you to a new URL.

The Norman Bird Sanctuary, Bird Adaptation—Feathered Feeders at:

> http://www.normanbirdsanctuary.org/beak_adaptation_unit01.shtml

This site contains a unit encouraging students to think like hungry birds, who must find food at a sanctuary. Students will investigate variation in bird beaks and the interrelationships of form and function by: *classifying* birds with similar beak shapes; *inferring* about the possible bird foods based on beak shapes; and *locating* and *identifying* possible bird foods in the field.

Family Education Network, Animal Adaptation Web Adventure at:

> http://www.teachervision.fen.com/tv/curriculum/weeklywebadventures/animal_adapt/t_home.html

This site contains a variety of activities on adaptation for classroom use. These include: Mystery Feature; Web Research; Article and Questions; Classroom Projects; and Tying It All Together. Each activity includes a Teacher's Guide.

Science NetLinks, Animal Adaptations at:

> http://www.sciencenetlinks.com/units.cfm?DocID=232

This site contains a unit plan designed to expand students' knowledge of animal features and behaviors that can help or hinder their survival in a particular habitat. Students will participate in classroom discussions and visit a Web site to learn more about animals and how well (or poorly) they've adapted toward satisfying their needs in their natural habitats.

Project WILD at:

> http://www.projectwild.org/

Created by the Council for Environmental Education, Project WILD is one of the most widely used conservation and environmental education programs used in schools today. It is based on the premise that students and their teachers have a vital interest in learning about our natural world. This site contains a wealth of information regarding curriculum, educator workshops, online resources, and success stories from states using the Project WILD program.

Minnesota DNR, Fish and Wildlife Today at:

http://www.dnr.state.mn.us/fwt/back_issues/march97/whittail.html

This Web site is a good example of a real-life application of adaptation. It describes an ongoing DNR research project looking into the adaptations of deer to winter. The project verifies that these animals are indeed well suited to surviving Minnesota's cold months.

EcoKids Online, Animal Adaptations game at:

http://www.ecokids.ca/pub/eco_info/topics/climate/adaptations/index.cfm

This site offers a timed game, where students have to correctly select three adaptations for each of the following: a monarch butterfly; a polar bear; a Blanding turtle; and a beluga whale.

Videos

Animals Around Us: Animal Adaptations: What Are They?

Available at: http://www.unitedstreaming.com

Naturalist Paul Fuqua narrates as he explores fascinating examples of how animals have adapted to survive in, and make the most of, their environments. From buffalos to badgers, this video explains the role of both physical and behavioral adaptation in the survival of animals. (14 minutes) Recommended for Grades 3–5.

Concepts in Nature: Adapting to Changes in Nature

Available at: http://www.unitedstreaming.com

This video explains how animals cope with both routine and unpredictable changes in nature. Footage of deer, a great horned owl, rabbits, and bears helps viewers understand why some animals seem to adapt to change better than others. Finally, the role that humans play in creating change is questioned and analyzed from several points of view. (14:06 minutes) Recommended for Grades 3–5.

Name_____

Student Data Sheet

Food	Tool	Why does this type of beak work best with this type of food? Explain.
Seeds		
Meat		
Nectar		
Food from pond		
Insects in grass		
Frogs and Fish in lakes and ponds		

What have you learned about a bird's beak and the bird's ability to survive?

_____

_____

_____

_____

Birdie Buffet Concept Cartoon

WHAT DO YOU THINK?

Full size form available at www.Christopher-Gordon.com/authors/KingMattox-shtml

Name_____

Directions: Complete the following T-chart using the labels from our Animal Adaptations posters. Ask yourself, is this adaptation a physical adaptation OR a behavioral adaptation? Record your responses below.

Animal Adaptations T-Chart

Physical Adaptations	Behavioral Adaptations

Food Item Labels

Break open the seeds	**Suck up nectar**
Scoop up food from pond	**Catch the insects**
Spear this food	**Tear off pieces of meat**

Full size form available at www.Christopher-Gordon.com/authors/KingMattox-shtml

Teacher's Shopping List for Birdie Buffet

☐ Chart paper, one or two sheets, and marker

☐ Staple puller, one per group

☐ Fine-pointed tweezers, one per group

☐ Wooden skewers, one per group

☐ Small sieves, one per group

☐ Pipette eye droppers, one per group

☐ Pliers, one per group

☐ Foam rubber to simulate meat, 6 x 6 inch pieces, one for each group

☐ Sunflower seeds, one small handful for each group

☐ Styrofoam peanuts (or use pieces of a styrofoam cup), about eight per group

☐ Rubber fish or frogs (or large marshmallows if they will float in water), about

   five per group

☐ Green Easter basket grass, one large handful for each group

☐ Plastic insects, about five per group

☐ Test tubes or floral tubes (the kind used to keep single flowers fresh) with a

   small amount of water at the bottom to simulate nectar

☐ Small buckets or tubs filled with water, two per group (Put styrofoam pieces in

   one and rubber fish or frogs in the other.)

☐ Paper plates, one per group

☐ Student Data sheets, one for each student *or* use science notebooks

☐ Labels for "bird" food items, one set for each group

(Continued on next page)

☐ Bird photo cards, at least five per group. Get from magazines, books, or online resource, such as Google Images. Be sure the beak can be seen clearly.

☐ Birdie Buffet Concept Cartoon, one for each student

☐ Animal Adaptations T-chart, one for each student

☐ Poster paper, at least 8 x 11 inch or larger, one sheet per pair of students

☐ Tape and glue

☐ Long strip of paper to write on and place on a blank wall

☐ Computer printer

☐ Internet access with bookmarked Web sites

☐ Markers, one per pair of students

☐ Sticky notes, two for each student

☐ *Beaks!* by Sneed Collard, one copy for each pair of students

☐ *How do Animals Adapt?* by Bobbie Kalman, one or more copies

☐ Additional trade books listed in the Teacher Resources section

Full size form available at www.Christopher-Gordon.com/authors/KingMattox-shtml

Chapter 6

What Matters about
the States of Matter?

Introduction

Knowledge of the properties of matter is important because it allows us to gain a deeper understanding of the role and function of different matter in the universe. We understand why certain substances look, move, or react the way they do because we understand their properties. For example, in northern climates, rain changes to snow and ice during the winter. In the spring, when the temperature gets warmer, the snow and ice begin to melt. If the snow and ice melt gradually, the melt replenishes our groundwater, as well as flows into rivers and streams. If the melting process occurs too rapidly, however, flooding may occur.

When we know properties or characteristics of things, we know what to expect and we can predict what is likely to happen. Scientists study properties of matter so that they can understand why certain things happen (i.e., changes in weather), and so that they can predict what will happen next. As children work through this unit, they will determine the physical properties of three states of matter. This will provide a foundation for the further exploration of matter.

Big Idea: We divide matter into three categories we call *states*: solid, liquid, and gas. Each state has properties that distinguish it from the other. Understanding these properties is foundational to understanding how the physical world works around us and how we utilize the resources of our world (American Association for the Advancement of Science [AAAS], 2001, p. 58).

Key Science Question: What are the properties of a solid, a liquid, and a gas?

National Science Standard: As a result of activities, all students should develop an understanding of the properties of objects and materials.

National Language Arts Standards: Students use a variety of technological and informational resources to gather and synthesize information, and to create and communicate knowledge.

Thinking Tools: Moving Visual Imagery tool

Action	Hands-On Activities	Literacy/Thinking Activities
Phase 1: Engage		
Discuss properties of matter.		
Phase 2: Explore 1: Racing Raisins!	Observe three states of matter.	Record data.
Phase 2: Explore 2: Observing the Shape of Solids		
	Observe solids.	Record data.
Phase 2: Explore 3: Observing the Shape of Liquids		
	Observe liquids.	Record data.
Phase 2: Explore 4: Observing the Shape of Gases		
	Experiment with air.	Record data.
Phase 3: Explain 1: Defining Volume		
		Locate definition. Compare/contrast. Pair-Share
Phase 2: Explore 5: Observing Volume of Gas		
	Observe balloon demonstration.	Record data.
Phase 4: Elaborate 1: Molecule Activity		
	Use our bodies to represent molecules in three states.	Record data.
Phase 4: Elaborate 2: Visualizing Molecules		
		Moving Visual Imagery
Phase 5: Evaluate		
Three options for applying knowledge of the properties of matter		

Figure 6:1   A framework for science literacy.

Teacher Background

The purpose of this inquiry is to guide students toward independently determining the properties of matter. Remind students to use all of their senses to observe materials, but do not taste any of them. Use questioning strategies to help students notice patterns and draw conclusions. Try not to provide any of the answers.

Most of the materials used in this unit are easily classified as one of the three states. Milk, for instance, is almost always observed as a liquid. Gas is more difficult to observe because the only way we can see it is if it is encased in a solid or a liquid. For example, solids such as a balloon or a baggie hold air, which is a gas. Soda pop is a liquid that contains carbon dioxide gas bubbles. When identifying gas in this unit, we are really identifying gas within a solid or liquid.

Steam is not a gas; it is a liquid, and it is visible. Steam is the condensing of water vapor and, therefore, is a liquid, but a common misconception is to classify it as a gas. Water vapor, which is invisible, is a gas. Be careful when choosing materials to teach these concepts, since some science resources put water vapor into the incorrect category.

Estimated Time: 4 periods, approximately 60 minutes each

Materials Needed: See the Teacher Shopping List in the Teacher Resources section of this unit.

Phase 1: Engage

Begin by asking students questions such as the following:

- Why do we use air in car tires? Why not use water to fill up the tire or make it out of stone? (Water would be too heavy. If you got a leak, it would be messy. Stone would wear down or be too heavy to turn.)

Air is the best option for all the reasons mentioned above. Air has the right characteristics, or properties, to keep a tire inflated and round. When we clean old buildings made of concrete, we use something called "sand blasters," which blow air and sand at a very powerful pressure at the building. The cleaners get close to the building—about 2–3 feet away to focus the air on the cement, and then the air shoots out.

- Can you think of a reason why we don't use water or scrape it with a metal tool? (The water might break down the concrete. The tool couldn't get into the concrete cracks, and it might break off some of the concrete.)

Yes, the qualities of high-pressure air make it the best option for cleaning cement. It will get into the cracks and push dirt out, but it won't dissolve the concrete like water could. We choose air in these two circumstances because the qualities, or properties, of air make it the best choice. But air is not always the best choice.

- If you were bowling, would it be a good idea to pour 1 gallon of water at the top of the lane to knock down the pins? (No. The water would just run all over. It wouldn't knock down the pins.)

- How else could we knock down the pins? (With high-pressure air, if the air pressure was strong enough.)

- What do you think happens to the air after about 3 feet? (The air, i.e., gas, goes all over the room.)

- Why then do we use a bowling ball instead of water or air pressure in bowling lanes? (The ball can knock down the pins because its energy, or momentum, stays focused.)

The bowling ball is a solid, and it keeps its shape or stays together even when it hits the pins. The bowling ball has the best properties or qualities for knocking down the pins. In this unit, we are going to look at the properties of three states of matter: solid, liquid, and gas. We are going to see how they are alike and how they are different.

Phase 2: Explore #1: Racing Raisins!

Materials needed:

> Two tall glass containers marked #1 and #2
>
> Ginger ale or other clear soft drink
>
> Raisins
>
> *Starting with Science: Solid, Liquids, and Gases* by the Ontario Science Center

Tell students they are going to watch a demonstration so they can observe the states of matter and how matter interacts. This activity is an adapted version of an activity from the book *Starting with Science: Solid, Liquids, and Gases* by the Ontario Science Center. Complete the activity as a demonstration in front of the class.

Procedure:

1. Take two clear, tall glass containers and mark them #1 and #2 (beakers or vases may work well).

2. Carefully pour the ginger ale or other clear soft drink into the container marked #1 by tipping the container to the side while pouring the soda pop slowly down the side. This prevents releasing all the drink's carbonation. Fill the container three quarters full.

3. Pour water into beaker #2. Fill this container three quarters full.

4. Add a few raisins to each beaker.

5. Have students observe and record their observations on the Raisin Race record sheet. *Or,* if you prefer, have them record their observations in their science notebooks. Remind them to complete the following:

   - Draw an illustration to show what is happening.
   - Describe, in words, what is happening.

Once observations are recorded, ask questions such as:

- What do you notice happening in beaker #1? (The raisins are rising and falling.)
- What do you notice happening in beaker #2? (The raisins stay at the bottom of the beaker.)
- Create a hypothesis as to why you think the raisins in beaker #1 are moving. Think about why they go up *and* down. Think for a minute, and then record your hypothesis. (Soda has gas bubbles in it. When the gas bubbles adhere to the raisins, they cause the raisins to float.)
- Now do the same for the activity you see in beaker #2. Again, record your hypothesis.

Discuss students' answers. If the students do not see the connection between bubbles and the movement of the raisins, ask them to think about the bubbles and how they may have caused the raisins to move. Then, read aloud the "What's Happening?" section of *Starting with Science: Solids, Liquids, and Gasses* on page 26 to explain students' hypotheses.

Phase 2: Explore #2: Observing the Shapes of Solids

Tell students they are going to explore three states of matter: solids, liquids and gases, and they will describe their differences. Explain that one thing scientists do when they investigate something is create charts and graphs to keep track of their information. Scientists call this information *data*. It is important to keep track of data because when scientists make observations over time, data help them make discoveries, ask important questions, or notice patterns.

Draw students' attention to the Three States of Matter chart at the front of the room. Tell the class this chart will help organize information, or *data*. Point out the column headings, which are characteristics, or properties, of matter that describe the three states: shape, volume, visibility, and molecular activity. Tell students they are going to do some experimentation that will help them complete each cell of the data chart.

Materials Needed:

> Two differently shaped, empty, clear containers marked #1 and #2
>
> A small ball
>
> A block
>
> A piece of clay

Procedure:

1. Place students in small groups, and give each group the materials needed. Tell students to put the ball, block, or clay into container #1 and gently shake it. Remind them that these are all solids. Ask them to observe what happens to the solids.

2. Repeat this by placing items in container #2. Observe.

3. Ask students:

   - Did you see any changes in the three items in the first container or in the second container? (Listen to a few responses, but there should be no change. If there is a change, talk to students about what may have caused the change—perhaps the clay was pushed, but the container itself did not cause the change.)

4. Model how to complete the Three States of Matter chart hung in front of the class. Then, ask:

   - Do solids keep their shape when they are put in a different-shaped container? (Yes.)

So, in the row marked "solid" and the column marked "shape," what would we write? Changes shape or does not change shape? (Does not change shape.) Write "does not change shape" in the cell. Give students a few minutes to record observations on their own States of Matter chart or in their science notebooks. Explain that students will be using this sheet to record their observations of the next activities.

Phase 2: Explore #3: Observing the Shape of Liquid

Materials Needed:

> Two differently shaped, empty, clear containers marked #1 and #2
>
> A small container of milk

Procedure:

1. Have students remove the solids from the container.

2. Put milk in container #1, gently shake it, and observe.

3. Pour the water into container #2, gently shake it, and observe. Ask students:

- What changes to the milk did you observe when it was in container #1? (None.)

- What changes to the milk did you observe when it was in container #2? (Listen to a few responses. There was a change in shape.)

- How are milk and water alike? (Answers will vary, but direct students' attention to the fact they are both liquids.)

- So, what should we write in this cell? (Changes shape.)

Model recording the correct response on the class chart, and have students record their observations of the changes in the liquids on their own charts or in their science notebook. Ask:

- How did the milk act differently from the ball, block, and clay?

- How did it react when we shook the container gently? (The milk took the shape of the container.)

- What can we conclude about the differences between a solid and a liquid? (Solids do not change shape, and liquids do change shape.)

Phase 2: Explore #4: Observing the Shape of Gases

Materials Needed:

Self-sealing sandwich bags

Procedure:

1. Have 1 student from each group blow air into a self-sealing sandwich bag and quickly seal the bag. Remind students of the variables used in our experiment: solids, liquids, and gases. Ask students:

- Which material represents the solid, the liquid, and the gas? (The sandwich bag is the solid. Air is the gas. There is no liquid.)

2. Have students push on the bags gently. Then, ask:

- What did you notice about the shape of the gas when we pushed on the bag? (The gas changes shape in the same way that the bag's shape changes.)

Record this observation in the appropriate cell on the Three States of Matter chart or in their science notebooks. Continue discussing:

- Does the air, which is a gas, behave more like the solids (ball, block, and clay) or the liquids (milk and water)? (Gas behaves more like a liquid because its shape changes and takes the form of the container. Solids do not change shape.)

- Can gas change shape? (Yes, gas takes the shape of the container it is in.)
- What can we conclude about the differences between a solid and a gas?

Phase 3: Explain #1: Defining Volume

Materials Needed:

Dictionaries, one for each pair of students

Trade books on solids, liquids, and gases

Procedure:

At this point, students have observed that matter can be distinguished by the property of shape. Now they will examine volume. Do a partner study of the word *volume* by providing pairs of students with dictionaries and trade books (see Teacher Resources at the end of this unit for a list).

1. Tell students they will explore the word *volume* in the materials provided. Read the passage from *Science Answers: Solids, Liquids, and Gasses* by Carol Ballard to focus students' attention on definitions of volume that deal with space. The text reads, "the first person to understand what *volume* meant was Archimedes, a scientist in ancient Greece. When he got into his bath, he realized that his body made the level of the water rise. The amount of water pushed up was exactly the same as the amount of space his body took up—his volume" (p. 29).

2. Tell students they will now use a dictionary to learn more about the definition of volume. Model how to search for the appropriate definition. Say something like, "My dictionary has four definitions for volume, so I will need to read them all to find the one we're looking for—something to do with taking up space. This is not the space we think of when we are studying the solar system, but physical space." Gesture with your hands a small area including height and width, then gesture a larger area. Then, continue: "Definition 1 says a series of printed sheets bound in book form. No, that does not deal with space, so I'll look further. Definition 2 says the degree of loudness or the intensity of a sound. No, that does not deal with space. I should read on. Definition 3 says space occupied as measured in cubic units, such as inches. The synonym given is "capacity." Hmmmm. That sounds like the kind of definition I want because it deals with space [gesture with your hands], but I'm going to read the last definition just to be sure. Definition 4 says amount, bulk,

mass. Well, the definition I want is either number 3 or 4, so I will write both of them on the board and look for another source to verify which definition is best." Write the definitions on the board.

3. Allow time for pairs of students to locate the appropriate definitions of the term *volume*.

4. Have a class dialogue to develop a shared definition of the word. Begin by asking students to offer their "best" definition. Record these on the board. Have students note similarities in definitions and, if need be, re-read the example using Archimedes, or other examples students have found helpful.

5. Reach a consensus, and have students record the consensus definition of *volume* on the Three States of Matter chart or in their science notebooks.

Phase 2: Explore #5: Observing the Volume of Gas

Note. Practice this activity before doing it as a demonstration. The amount of vinegar and baking soda you use depends on the size of the bottle and balloon you have. Check your proportions before showing this to the class. Carry this out as a demonstration. Be sure to blow the balloon up a number of times before the activity to make it easy to expand.

Materials Needed:

> Water balloons
>
> A 12-ounce soda pop bottle
>
> Vinegar (about ¾ cup)
>
> Baking soda (about 2 tablespoons)
>
> Funnel

Procedure:

1. Blow up the balloon in front of students and ask:
   - Hypothesize why you think the balloon expanded.
   - Explain what is inside the balloon now. (Your breath)
   - What can we conclude about our breath? (Is it a solid, liquid, or gas? A gas.)

Begin the next activity. Be prepared for "oohs" and "ahhhs."

2. Pour vinegar into a 12-ounce soda pop bottle. Fill it almost to the half-way mark (about ½ to ¾ cup). Put 2 large spoonfuls of baking soda into the balloon, using the funnel.

3. While pinching the neck of the balloon so the baking soda will not come out, stretch the balloon opening over the mouth of the bottle. (You will probably need help with this.)

4. When ready, release the balloon neck. You may need to tap the balloon so the baking soda falls into the vinegar. Squeeze your fingers around the mouth of the bottle where the balloon attaches to ensure it will not blow off.

5. Once the baking soda is out of the balloon, keep the balloon upright as it fills with carbon dioxide gas, which results from the chemical reaction of the vinegar and baking soda.

Let the students discuss this. Encourage students to explore what blew up the balloon. If they are having trouble with the response, draw parallels to when you blew up the balloon and have them return to the trade books for a possible explanation. Share student findings and connect their observations and new information gathered with the definition of *volume* discussed previously. Explain that in this experiment, the gas took up the space inside the balloon and stretched it or filled it up. Ask the students:

- Did the *volume* of the gas change or stay the same? (It changed.)

- Did the space the gas took up stay the same or expand? (It expanded.)

- What might happen to the gas if the balloon were removed from the bottle? Would it stay in the balloon and occupy the space of the bottle, or would it expand out into the room? (It would expand out into the room.)

- So, what can we conclude? (The volume of gas changes to fill the container.)

Encourage students to think about and discuss the definition of volume they just explored, and apply the definition to what they just observed. Allow conversation and discussion, but end the discussion with the correct understanding that gas volume does change. Have students record this on their States of Matter chart or in their science notebooks.

Phase 4: Elaborate #1: Molecule Activity

Materials Needed:

A circle of rope, large enough for the entire class to stand inside

Drawings of gas, liquid, and solid molecules

Water

Clear container or beaker

Small solid object, such as a block or a ball, to put into the container

Procedure:

1. Explain to the students that scientists using powerful microscopes have discovered that matter is made up of things we cannot see, called *molecules*. Molecules are very, very small bits of matter that move. The molecules in solids and gases look different from those in liquids. Show students molecule models, such as the ones below:

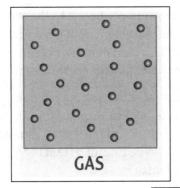

GAS

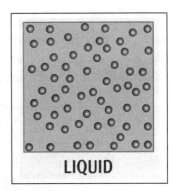

LIQUID

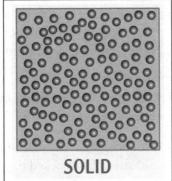

SOLID

Tell students they are going to "become" molecules, and it is their job to decide what kind of matter they are representing. You may choose to have the entire class participate, or have a smaller group participate as a demonstration for the class. Make a large circle of rope on the classroom floor, and tell students the rope represents a container like the ones we used in our earlier experiments. Ask:

- Think about a time when you have seen children "huddle" together on the playground on a cold day.

Explain that some molecules do the same thing. They slow down and move close together.

2. Have students come into the rope circle and huddle close together. Then, encourage them to move even closer to one another. Ask:

- Can you move very easily? (No.)
- Why not? (Too close together.)
- Predict what kind of matter has molecules that are huddled close together, like you are now. (Solid.)
- Look at where you're standing in relationship to the rope. Tell me where you are. (Inside the rope.)

Refer students to the model previously drawn and connect it to the rope activity. Show students they are closely packed together, just like the molecules in the drawing.. Place a cube or other solid inside a glass container or beaker. Explain to students that this solid is inside a container, just like they are inside the rope.

3. Explain that some molecules are more active and spread out away from each other. They spread out a little bit, but they stay inside their container. Have the students bounce slightly and push apart, but stay inside the rope circle. Encourage students to be careful so that bigger students do not hurt smaller ones. Ask students:

- What kind of matter has molecules that move around but still stay inside their containers? (Encourage students to think about their earlier observations as well as the molecule model.)
- Predict what state of matter takes the shape of its container. (Liquid.)
- Look at where you're standing in relationship to the rope. Tell me where you are. (Inside the rope.)

Refer students to the model previously drawn and connect it to the rope activity. Show students they are less tightly packed together, just like the molecules in the drawing. Pour water inside a glass container or beaker. Explain to students that this liquid is inside the container, just like they are inside the rope.

4. Explain that some molecules are very active and spread out away from other molecules, just as children like to spread out on the playground when it is hot outside. Have students act out being warm molecules. Direct them to spread out and "bounce" carefully. They can move outside the rope circle. Ask students:

- Predict what kind of matter has molecules that spread out and bounce around: a solid, a liquid, or a gas? (A gas.)

Refer students to the model previously drawn and connect to rope activity. Show students they are far apart, bouncing all around, just like the molecules in the drawing. Have them look at the bottle and balloon from Explore #5: Observing Volume. Ask students:

- What did you observe about the gas in the bottle container? Did the gas stay in the bottle container or did it move to fill up the balloon? (It moved to fill up the balloon.)

Explain to students that gas behaves differently than solids and liquids. Gas expands to fill space, or it changes its volume, just like students did when they moved beyond the rope when they were pretending to be gas.

5. Have the students get back into the rope circle, and huddle close together.

    - What kind of molecules are we again? (Solid.)

    - What is a property or characteristic of a solid? (Solids keep their own shape.)

    - Do solid molecules expand beyond their container? (No.)

    - So, what can we conclude about solid molecules and volume? (Solid molecules do not change volume.)

6. Again, have students carefully bounce slightly and push apart, staying in the rope circle.

    - What kind of molecules are we now? (Liquid.)

    - What is a property or characteristic of a liquid? (They change shape, depending on their container.)

    - Do liquids expand beyond their container? (No.)

    - So, what can we conclude about liquid molecules and volume? (Liquid molecules do not change volume.)

7. Have students return to the States of Matter chart or science notebook. Be sure they record, in the Volume column, "does not change volume" for solids and liquids, and record "does change volume" for gas.

8. Refer to the Molecule Activity column, and ask students: Which molecules were far apart and very active? (Gas.) Record that in the gas row. Repeat for other states of matter.

9. Consider the visibility of the three states of matter. Ask students:

    - Think of the three states of matter that we used. Which ones were visible? Invisible? (Solids and liquid were visible, gas was invisible.)

    - How do you think the chart should be filled out for visible or invisible? (If students say water is invisible, ask them if they can see when a glass is half full. If they say yes, then explain that you can see the water by where it ends. If you had a cup half full of gas, you would not know because gas is not visible. Water is visible and *clear*.)

Complete the States of Matter chart.

Phase 4: Elaborate #2: Using Visual Imagery

Use a moving visual imagery tool to help students solidify and synthesize their new knowledge of matter and molecules. Invite them to really use their imaginations. Encourage them to see, hear, smell, and taste the images created in their mind. The more senses this imagery tool uses, the more impact it will have in the students' minds and memories. Use expressions such as the following:

"Now, sit quietly and imagine what it would be like to be a molecule. Close your eyes. Picture yourself as a molecule floating in space. Imagine you are a water molecule, and you are liquid. You are moving with the rest of the molecules, and you feel them around you. What does it feel like? Smell like? Sound like?

"Now it's getting hotter. You are moving more quickly, and look, the other molecules are moving farther and farther away from you. You hardly see or feel them, and you are moving so quickly now, darting here and there. What does it feel like? You feel different now. You are a gas called water vapor, and you are moving very fast! What can you see? What do you hear? What does it smell like?

"Wait, now it is getting colder. Much colder. You feel yourself slowing down. Other molecules are gathering around you. You feel the familiar feeling of being water again, but wait, things are even colder and you feel the other molecules getting closer, and closer, and closer. You feel yourself moving slower and slower. The other molecules pack up against you tightly. You feel packed in and you can barely move. You have become solid ice! What does it feel like to be ice? What does it sound like? What can you see?"

Finally, have students choose one state of matter: solid, liquid, or gas. Their task is to draw the image they imagined on a piece of paper or in their science notebooks.

Phase 5: Evaluate

Remind students how the unit began—with a discussion of the question: "Why do we use air in car tires?" Have students record the question in their science notebooks and answer the question again, using evidence they have collected. Encourage students to use data from the States of Matter chart as well as their notes. (Students should correctly use the data and descriptions on their chart to explain why gas is better in a tire than a solid or liquid. Air changes shape and volume, so it expands to fill the tire. Solids and liquids don't expand to fill the tire space. Solids won't even take the shape of the tire.)

Or, use this optional scenario. When people clean old buildings made of concrete, they use "sand blasters," which blow air and sand at a very powerful pressure at the building. The cleaners get close to the building—about 2–3 feet away to focus the air on the cement—and then the air shoots out. Why do they use air, which is a gas, and not a solid, such as a metal tool? (Again, students should use the chart information to answer this question. A solid holds its shape and would not move into the crevices.) Why do they have to be so close to the building? (The air is a gas and it expands to fill the space, so if the cleaners are far away, the air will expand before it gets to the building.)

Or, use this optional evaluation. Ask students to locate three items from home, or three pictures from a magazine or newspaper, representing all three states of matter. Students will list or paste the items on index cards. On the back of the card, they must identify what state of matter is represented, then write a description of its properties. Encourage students to include details about shape, volume, visibility, and molecular activity.

Teacher Resources

Trade Books

Appleby, Leanne & Russell, Peter. (2001). *Wally and Deanna's groundwater adventure.* Waterloo, Ontario, Canada: Waterloo Hydrogeologic Inc., 24 pp.; ISBN: 0-9697833-0-2 (paperback); $5.00.

> Wally, a worm, follows Deanna, a water droplet, as she percolates through the ground and moves through the water cycle. This book is an excellent, accurate, and engaging tool describing how water changes states. The final drawing is simple, but is a perfect summary of the water cycle.

Ballard, Carol. (2004). *Solids, liquids, and gases: From ice cubes to bubbles.* Chicago: Heinemann Library, 32 pp.; ISBN: 140343552-9 (paperback); $7.50.

> Part of the *Science Answers* series, this experiment book explores the role physical science plays in our world. Readers will learn how life on Earth depends on the simple physical changes that happen with water, as well as understand the importance of investigating the physical world around us. A section entitled "People Who Found the Answers" puts a human face onto important scientific finds. A glossary and index are also included.

Glover, David. (1993). *Solids and liquids.* New York: Kingfisher, 32 pp.; ISBN: 0-7534-5513-7 (paperback); $7.95.

> Readers will learn how the everyday objects around them, both natural and artificial, can change and be changed. The composition and strength of materials, both solid and liquid, and chemical reactions, including how metal rusts, liquid evaporates, and plastic can melts, are explored. The Do-It-Yourself pages feature simple experiments to clarify concepts. An index is included.

Graves, Kimberlee. (1997). *Where did it go?* [Catherine Leary, Illus.] Cypress, CA: Creative Teaching Press, 16 pp.; ISBN: 1-57471-314-0 (paperback); $3.30.

> This book explains several science concepts in a very simple story format. These concepts include: the appearance, taste, and state of matter; water can be changed by heating and cooling; some substances can be dissolved in water to form solutions, which affect the properties of the solution. This book is appropriate independent reading for struggling and English as a second language (ESL) students.

Lanczak Williams, Rozanne. (1994). *What happened?* [Gwen Connelly, Illus.] Cypress, CA: Creative Teaching Press, 16 pp.; ISBN: 0-916119-47-5 (paperback); $3.30.

> Similar in format to *Where Did It Go?*, this book also explains several science concepts in a simple format. These concepts include: matter exists in three states; water can be found in three states; the state of water is affected by heat; some solids can be dissolved in liquids. This book is appropriate for independent reading for struggling and ESL students.

Riley, Peter. (1998). *Materials and processes.* New York: Franklin Watts, 32 pp.; ISBN: 0-531-15369-X (paperback); $6.95.

> Part of the *Straightforward Science* series, this book does just that: It demonstrates that materials are solids, liquids, or gases, and while they have special distinguishing features called properties, they can be changed in ways known as processes. Everyday examples are found on each 2-page spread, which focuses on a single concept. The Investigate! boxes encourage readers to explore the concept independently.

Royston, Angela. (2002). *Solids, liquids, and gases.* Chicago: Heinemann, 32 pp.; ISBN: 1-4034-4-0044-X (paperback); $6.95.

> Part of the *My World of Science* series, this book provides a basic introduction to the properties and characteristics of solids, such as hardness, softness, and changing shape; characteristics of liquids, including melting and freezing; and gases and the air. The simple explanations and accompanying photos highlight key vocabulary that is also defined in the glossary. An index is included, too.

The Ontario Science Center. (1998). *Starting with science: Solids, liquids, and gases.* [Ray Boudreau, Photog.] Tonawanda, NY: Kids Can Press, 32 pp.; ISBN: 1-55074-401-1 (paperback); $5.95.

> This is a great book, offering safe, simple experiments to explore the three states of matter and their characteristics. Experiments involve household items and show all types of children as scientists. The What's Happening box provides straightforward explanations as to why a phenomenon was observed. In some instances, additional information is provided in additional boxes for further explanation. A special page for parents and teachers provides additional activities and information to help answer children's challenging questions. An excellent book!

Whitehouse, Patricia. (2004). *Changing shape.* Chicago: Heinemann, 24 pp.; ISBN: 140345105-2 (paperback); $5.75.

> Part of the *Read and Learn* series, this book extends children's play into simple experiments about the physics of changing shape. Each section asks the reader a question, and manipulating materials, such as clay, paper, and balloons, helps children to discover answers about their basic properties. A simple picture glossary and index are provided. Colorful photos of a variety of children are included.

Web Sites

Note. The authors realize that Web site addresses are not guaranteed to work, as they change, move, or are removed from the Internet. Therefore, we have included the sponsoring organization of the Web site in the event the link provided here does not work. Simply type in the name of the organization in your search engine, and it will direct you to a new URL.

Harcourt School Publishers at:

> http://www.harcourtschool.com/activity/states_of_matter/

This site provides a moving graphic and sound to illustrate the arrangement of particles in a solid, liquid, and gas.

Andrew Rader's Chem4Kids at:

> http://www.chem4kids.com/

This site was created by Andrew Rader, whose background is in physiology, cell biology, and computers. The Chem4Kids site contains tutorials and activities to encourage learners to explore their personal interests related to all aspects of chemistry, including states of matter.

Racing Raisins Record Sheet

Name _____

1. Write what you notice happening in the beaker with the soda pop.
    Draw it if you like.

2. Write what you notice happening in the beaker with water.   Draw it
    if you like.

3. Hypothesize why the raisins are doing what they are doing in beaker
    #1

4. Hypothesize why the raisins are doing what they are doing in beaker
    #2.

Full size form available at www.Christopher-Gordon.com/authors/KingMattox-shtml

States of Matter Chart

State	Shape Options to write "changes shape" or "does not change shape"	Volume Options to write "changes volume" or "does not change volume"	Visibility Options to write "visible" or "invisible"	Molecule activity Options "far apart and very active" or "apart and active" "close together or still"
Solid				
Liquid				
Gas				

Full size form available at www.Christopher-Gordon.com/authors/KingMattox-shtml

Observations of States of Matter Activities

1. Compare what happens to the solids when they are put in container #1, then container #2. Do the solids change at all?

2. Compare what happens to the milk in containers #1 and #2. Does its shape change?

3. How do the solids act differently than the milk in the containers?

4. What happens to the shape of the gas when you push on the bag?

Full size form available at www.Christopher-Gordon.com/authors/KingMattox-shtml

Teacher's Shopping list for What Matters about the States of Matter?

Materials Needed:

- *Starting with Science: Solids, Liquids, and Gases* by the Ontario Science Center (See Teacher Resources above for bibliographic information.)
- Solids: small ball, clay, and block
- Liquids: water, milk, ginger ale, or other clear soda pop
- Large beakers (2) or large, clear glass bowls for each group of students. Each group needs to have two beakers of a different shape with a mouth wide enough to put the solids through.
- Raisins
- Two clear containers, tall and big enough for students to see the raisin activity. A tall vase would work well.
- Two empty soda pop bottles (12-ounce)
- Balloons that will fit over the top of the soda pop bottle
- Vinegar (about ¾ cup) and baking soda (about 2 tablespoons)
- Funnel
- Large piece of string, big enough to make a circle on the floor for all students to stand in without being crowded
- Self-sealing sandwich bags
- Dictionaries
- Art paper
- Science notebooks
- Assorted trade books
- Student Response sheets

Full size form available at www.Christopher-Gordon.com/authors/KingMattox-shtml

Chapter 7

Roll It!

Introduction

Forces are an important part of our everyday life. Some forces, called contact forces, work when two objects touch. We use contact forces when we pull our sneakers' shoelaces to tie them, or when we push a child in a swing. Other forces are invisible. Gravity, which is the force that pulls objects to the ground on Earth, is one example. Magnetism is another.

Objects need forces to make them move or to help them stop moving. Friction is a force that helps moving objects stop. It is present when the rubber backing on a carpet keeps it in place when we walk on it. Friction allows the brakes to stop a moving car. It also helps control direction and speed. For instance, friction is present when the tires of a car rub against the road and when sneakers on a basketball court help us make sudden stops and quick turns. Sometimes it is beneficial and necessary to reduce friction. For instance, we want our roller-blade wheels to rotate smoothly, ice-skate edges to be sharp and smooth, and our skis to be waxed. In these examples, we want to control where and when we stop by reducing friction.

In this unit, students will explore movement, friction, and its impact. They will also develop their own experiments to explore how to reduce the force of friction.

Big Idea: The same basic rules govern the motion of all bodies, from planets to billiard balls. Students need to be familiar with many different kinds of motion before they can make sense of these laws. Changes in speed or direction of motion are caused by forces. The greater the force is, the greater the change in motion will be (American Association for the Advancement of Science [AAAS], 2001, p. 62).

Key Science Question: How does force affect the motion of objects?

National Science Standard: The position and motion of objects can be changed by pushing or pulling. The size of the change is related to the strength of the push or pull.

National Language Arts Standard: Students read a wide range of print and nonprint texts to . . . acquire new information . . . and for personal fulfillment. Students apply a wide range of strategies to comprehend, interpret, evaluate, and appreciate texts. Students conduct research . . . and gather, evaluate, and synthesize data from a variety of sources.

Thinking Tool: Concept Frame

Action	Hands-On Activities	Literacy/Thinking Activities
Phase 1: Engage		
	Rub soles on surfaces. Compare/ contrast results.	
Phase 2: Explore 1: Teacher Modeling		
Set up inclined plane and car experiment. Measure distance car travels. Calculate average distance.		
Phase 2: Explore 2: Guided Experiments with Friction		
	Repeat car experiment, vary track surface. Calculate average distance.	Record data.
Phase 3: Explain		
Class meeting/discussion. Teacher read aloud.	Thumbs Up/Down	Create chart. Interpret data. Use text to explain experiment.
Phase 4: Elaborate 1: Independent Experiments with Friction		
Jigsaw groups	Repeat car experiment but add friction reducers.	Form hypothesis. Record data. Discuss data.
Phase 4: Elaborate 2: Concept Frames		
Use trade books and/or Web sites. Class meeting.		Locate information to complete Concept Frame. Carousel Posters.
Phase 5: Evaluate		
Use information and structure of Concept Frame.		Write report on force and motion.

Figure 7:1   A framework for science literacy.

Teacher Background

Isaac Newton developed the three laws of motion that explain how all things move. Law 1 states: Objects in motion stay in motion; objects at rest remain at rest (i.e., inertia) unless a force acts on them. Law 2 states: An object's acceleration depends on its mass and on the size and the direction of the force acting on it. Law 3 states: For every force there is an equal, opposite force.

A force is a push or pull that is needed to make an object move. A force can start a motion, stop a motion, or change the direction of a motion. For example, pulling a drawer will open it; pushing shuts it. A person can pull a wagon to make it move. He pushes against it to stop it. The pitcher in a baseball game pushes the ball toward the hitter, and the hitter changes the direction of the ball by pushing the bat against the ball when he or she hits it. Force can also change the shape of something. For instance, when a baker kneads bread dough, he or she is stretching and squashing the dough, which changes its shape. Force also causes the elastic in a pair of socks to expand when we put them on and contract as it compresses around our calves and ankles.

Friction is the force that resists the movement of one object against another. Friction causes an object to slow down and eventually stop. Without friction, an object would continue moving. There is friction when a towel rubs against your wet skin and when water rubs against a swimming fish. The amount of friction between two objects depends on the roughness or smoothness of the material. Materials that are rougher create more friction. Materials that are smoother create less friction. When there is more friction, the motion of objects will slow down faster.

Gravity is a force that pulls things toward Earth. Gravity pulls on everything inside the Earth's atmosphere. For example, gravity causes skiers to ski downhill and a ball to drop when it is thrown. The more mass an object has, the more gravity pulls on it. When lifting a heavy box off the ground, a person will feel the pull of gravity because the box has a large mass. A lighter box will be easier to lift because gravity pulls less on objects that have less mass.

Estimated Time: 4 periods, approximately 60 minutes each

Materials Needed: See the Teacher Shopping List in the Teacher Resources section of this unit.

Phase 1: Engage

Materials Needed:

> Different types of surfaces (e.g., carpet, tile, wood floor, plastic garbage bag, grass, or asphalt) for students to share

Procedure:

> As a group, have the students compare and contrast the soles of their shoes. Discuss as a class the similarities and differences of soles. With shoes on, have students rub the soles of their shoes in a skating-like motion on three different types of surfaces (e.g., carpet, tile, wood floor, plastic garbage bag, grass, or asphalt). Have them observe the motion of their shoes, then describe it. If students can't verbalize observations, you might ask:

- What did you observe about the motion of your shoes while sliding across the different surfaces? (The smoother the surface, the easier it was to move. The rougher surfaces gripped more or made it harder to "skate" with your shoes on.)

Results will vary, but most rubber soles will yield the same response whether or not they are bumpy or smooth. Leather soles will be more slippery.

Phase 2: Explore #1: Teacher Modeling

Materials Needed:

> Student Data Collection sheet, one for each student, *or* have students recreate this chart in their science notebooks
>
> A plank to be used as an inclined plane
>
> Two or three textbooks for height (approximately 10 cm)
>
> Toy car to roll on the plank
>
> Wax paper over 120 cm long
>
> Measuring tape
>
> Duplicate Student Data Collection sheet in chart form on board or overhead

Procedure:

> Students may want to focus on speed during this experiment; however, keep the focus on measuring distance, not speed. Model this experiment for students.

1. Make an inclined track by leaning a plank on two or three textbooks.
2. Place the length of wax paper (120 cm long) at the end of the plank to make a track.

3. Release the car (don't push it!) from a point near the top of the plank. Encourage students to observe how far the car moves, not its speed.

4. Measure the distance traveled from the bottom of the plank to the stopping point on the track, using a measuring tape. Measure in centimeters, not inches. In the row marked Wax Paper, record the distance in the Trial Distance #1 column of the Student Data Collection sheet.

5. Repeat this process twice. Remember to release the car from the same place each time, and measure and record the distance each time. Explain to students that when scientists conduct experiments, they carefully control the *variables*. In this experiment, the angle of the plank, the person releasing the car, the car itself, and the material it will travel on are important *variables*.

6. Model how to calculate the average distance the car rolled by adding the total of all three trials and dividing the sum by three to get the average. Record the average on the data collection chart.

Phase 2: Explore #2: Guided Experiments with Friction

Materials Needed:

Note. You will need the following materials for each center. The number of centers needed depends on the number of students in your classroom. Plan for 3 or 4 students at each center.

Planks of equal length with starting lines in equal placement

Books to raise the planks to make an inclined plane

Toy cars (such as a Match Box™ car) of equal mass

Four to six smooth and rough surfaces in equal numbers, such as wax paper, newspaper, paper towel, sandpaper, crinkled foil, Velcro, or burlap

Measuring tapes

Student Data Collection sheets or science notebooks

Overhead transparency of Student Data Collection sheet, one for each group

Transparency pens, one for each group

Motion by Ben Morgan

Assorted trade books on forces and motion

Advanced Preparation:

Students will be conducting their own experiments to explore force and motion. Set up centers for students to move through in groups of three or four.

Teams of no more than four students are best. You may need to duplicate centers to keep teams small.

The set-up must be the same for each center to minimize differences in results based on different set-ups or variables. This is why toy cars at each center must have the same mass. In addition, if planks are placed at a higher incline in one center than in another, the distance the car travels will be different, in part, due to the difference in angle of incline and partly due to the surface upon which the car travels. If the angle of incline, car, and starting point are the same for each center, the difference in results will be due to the surface the car rolls on or to the force of friction the car encounters. By carefully setting up each center, you are modeling how scientists carefully control variables during an experiment. Be sure to explain this to your students before they begin with their experiments.

Each center should have a plank resting at a uniform height to create an inclined track. Using the same number of textbooks at each center will insure consistency of height throughout. A starting point should be indicated on each plank. This should be the same point on all tracks. Place a surface for the car to roll on at the end of each plank. Two centers should have a smooth surface (i.e., wax paper, newspaper, or paper towel) and two should have a rough surface (i.e., sandpaper, crinkled foil, or burlap). Be sure the surface is long enough to extend beyond the length the car rolls. Test the centers before the students do their experiments to be certain the track is adequate.

Procedure:

1. Put students in teams and have them select a reporter and recorder.
2. Give students the following directions. Remind them that the car, books, and person releasing the car need to stay constant throughout the experiment. These are the *variables* we want to control in this experiment. (The track surface is the uncontrolled variable in this experiment.) Tell them to start their car at the point marked on the track, and be very careful not to move the track or books. After they release the car, they will need to measure and record the distance the car rolled. Then, they will compute the average distance rolled for each type of surface tested, just as you modeled for them.
3. Allow groups time to experiment with multiple surfaces in all four centers.
4. When groups are finished, invite the recorder to record the group's findings on an overhead transparency.

Phase 3: Explain

Have a class meeting where you discuss the process used in the experiments. You might ask questions such as:

- What are you doing as a scientist today?
- What are some important things to remember when conducting an experiment?
- Did you experience any problems today?
- What would a scientist do if he or she ran into these same problems while doing this experiment? What else could we do to solve this problem?

Next, encourage reporters to explain their results to the rest of the class using the overhead to show their chart. Ask questions such as the following to help groups explain and interpret their data:

- What information on this chart is most interesting? (The distances traveled, surface.)
- What do scientists call this kind of information? (Data.)
- What do these data tell us? (The car traveled farther on smooth surfaces as compared with rough surfaces.)
- What is your evidence? (The measurements taken.)
- Why did we take several measurements and record our results? (Three trials will give more accurate, consistent results.)

Create a class chart using each group's average distances column. Continue the discussion.

- What are some of the variables in this experiment? (Variables are anything that can change, i.e., be "varied" or is "vary—able." Controlled variables are variables that remained consistent. For example, one controlled variable is the placement of the car, and a second controlled variable is the car itself. The car was consistently placed in the same spot, and each car has the same mass, so this variable is controlled. Uncontrolled variables are those that change. In this experiment, the track surface differed in each center, so it is an uncontrolled variable.)
- How can we compare group results? What would we need to examine? (Look for similarities and differences across the groups and discuss possible reasons for differences. Students should notice that slippery surfaces produce greater distances.)

Next, read aloud *only* pages *5, 7, 15,* and *17* from the book, *Motion* by Ben Morgan. Tell students this book is about force, energy, and motion. Tell them their purpose for listening is to identify any information that would be helpful in explaining the experiments just completed. Encourage active listening by playing Thumbs Up. When students hear information they think is helpful, they stick their thumbs up in the air. If a student raises a thumb, continue reading to the end of a paragraph, stop, and ask the student about the connection made. Create a list of students' connections on the board. When you have finished reading page 17, briefly discuss the list.

Conclude by asking:

- What force caused the car to move? (Gravity.)
- What force caused the car to stop in our experiments? (Friction.)
- What surface caused the most friction? (Those with shorter distances.)
- What surface caused the least friction? (Those with longer distances.)
- What is your evidence? (The measurements.)
- What might happen if you pushed the car a little bit as you released it? (It would have gone farther because it was pushed.)
- Why? (The way to change the movement of an object is to push it.)
- Is there anything else you are wondering about? [Allow for student discussion that may lead to further exploration.]

Phase 4: Elaborate #1: Independent Experiments with Friction

Materials Needed:

A plank marked with a starting point

Books to raise the plank to an inclined plane

Measuring tapes

Various surfaces for track (aluminum foil, bath towel, newspaper, sandpaper, etc.)

Small amounts of oil, grease, or wax

Experiment Design sheets, one for each student

Procedure:

1. Remind students they have done experiments to show the effects of friction on a traveling car. In the book just read, it says that friction slows things down. Ask:

- What are some ways to reduce friction? (Solicit suggestions based on the surfaces used in the centers.)

- What else could we use to reduce friction? (If they have trouble thinking of things, ask what skiers or snow boarders use to make their skis and boards go faster, or when a door creaks from friction in the hinges, what do we put on them? Students will likely list oil, wax, or grease.)

2. Tell the students that scientists do not rely on what they think might work or what people believe. Scientists do experiments to show physically how things work. Tell them they are going to create their own experiment to determine what reduces friction on the track surfaces in the centers previously used. Explain that each team will get a plank marked with a starting point, books to raise the plank to an incline plane, a car, a measuring tape, a surface for the track, and their choice of oil, grease, or wax. Call these materials "friction reducers." Their task is to create an experiment to see what effect the friction reducers have on the car's distance.

3. Have students return to their groups. Each group will answer questions 1–4 on the Experiment Design sheet. Model how to create a hypothesis and give an example such as the following: "My hypothesis is: With oil on the wheels, the car will travel farther than it did without the oil."

4. When students have completed questions 1–4, discuss the responses. Be sure to revise hypotheses so they accurately state the experiment's focus. Be sure students understand how to carry out the experiment. Ask them:

    - As scientists, how should we conduct this experiment?

    Record the steps on the board. They include:

    - Form a hypothesis.
    - Set up the inclined plane.
    - Run three trials to determine distance without the friction-reducing substance and record. (This serves as a control.)
    - Compute the average.
    - Apply the friction-reducing substance (either on the track surface or on the car wheels).
    - Run three trials and record distance with the friction-reducing substance.
    - Compute the average.

    Allow students time to conduct their own experiments. Circulate around the room to be sure students are following directions. As they continue to work, create a chart or overhead such as the following to chart each group's results.

Group #	Track Surface	Average Distance Traveled	Friction Reducer Used	Friction Reducer Placement	Average Distance Traveled

6. Have reporters place their group's results on the chart or overhead. Ask:

   - Why would scientists record information on a data chart like this one?

   - Explain how a scientist might use this chart.

7. Then, using the data on the chart or overhead, have groups complete items 7–13 on their Experiment Design sheet.

8. After a few minutes, create jigsaw groups by selecting one person from each group. One way to do this is to give each student within a group a color, such as blue, red, green, or yellow. When creating a jigsaw group, put all of the blues together, all of the reds together, etc. Then, you will have members in the jigsaw groups from each of the original teams. This is a quick and easy way to share across groups. Give jigsaw groups a few moments to reach a consensus on items 7–13.

9. Then review items 7–13 with the entire class. End with a brief conversation about questions that still remain.

Phase 4: Elaborate #2: Concept Frames

Materials Needed:

Trade books and/or prebookmarked Web sites

Roll It Concept Frame sheet, one for each student

Four sheets of poster paper

Procedure:

1. Keep students in the same jigsaw groups (four groups is ideal). Remind students of the questions they had after the last set of experiments. Tell them they will now have the opportunity to find more information about

motion and forces, and hopefully, the answers to their questions. Distribute the Roll It Concept Frame and explain how this sheet will help them organize the information they are gathering. Decide ahead of time how many items you want students to include in each square.

2. Distribute trade books or take students to the computer lab.

3. Model for students how you would locate information in a trade book. (If you are at the computer lab, refer to chapter 4, Nature and Nurture, for details on searching Web sites.) Show them the index indicating where specific information is located. Show them the table of contents as well as section or chapter headings. Point out boldface words and captions on pictures. Tell students that all of this information may be used to complete each square on the Concept Frame. Remind them that scientists often work together in their search for knowledge, and they acknowledge the contributions made by fellow scientists. Indicate to students that it is a good idea to share books and information with others in their group. The goal is to work collaboratively to find appropriate information that relates to the experiments just completed.

4. Allow students time to work together and complete the Concept Frame.

5. Create four posters to represent each square of the Concept Frame. Hang the posters around the room with enough space in between for groups to stand in front of them. Give each group a different-colored marker and assign a reporter.

6. Station each group at a poster and tell them to begin writing on the poster significant information they have recorded on their Concept Frame. Ask students to stop after an appropriate amount of time.

7. Groups will rotate to the next poster, read the information on it, and compare with their own Concept Frame. Groups may add information to the poster, but only if it is a new idea and is not duplicated information.

8. Rotate twice more until each group has visited each poster.

9. Have a class meeting and discuss the most significant information. Encourage students to share their original question and what they learned about it. Debrief and ask questions such as:

   • What have you learned most recently as a reader and a scientist?

   • What do you want to remember from this experience?

Phase 5: Evaluate

Students will use Concept Frame posters to reflect and write a report on the key question: *How does force affect the motion of objects?* Help students begin writing by telling them to use the unshaded square on the Concept Frame. This information will provide a definition of *force* and is a good starting point. The shaded areas can be used to write the body of their report. Students should use scientific vocabulary (e.g., friction, force, gravity, least, most) and specific examples from their experiments and their reading. The information might be written as a simple sentence or as full paragraphs to indicate deeper knowledge.

Teacher Resources

Trade Books

Bryant-Mole, Karen. (1997). *Forces.* Chicago: Rigby Education, 24 pp.; ISBN: 1-4034-0050-4 (paperback); $6.95.

> Part of the *Science All Around Me* series, this colorful, simple text explains the basic principles of force and movement through direct observation and looking at everyday experiences. Each 2-page spread has a "See for Yourself" page that encourages and shows children conducting hands-on exploration of concepts explained on the adjacent page. A table of contents, glossary, and index are included.

Graham, John. (2001). *Hands-on science: Forces and motion.* [David Le Jars, Illus.] New York: Kingfisher, 40 pp.; ISBN: 0-7534-5349-5 (paperback); $6.95.

> In this experiment book, scientific principles and fascinating facts are brought to life using everyday materials. Over 40 experiments on a variety of topics, including friction, speed, acceleration, and pressure, are explained with colorful illustrations and photos. A table of contents, glossary, and index are included.

Hewitt, Sally. (1998). *Forces around us.* Danbury, CT: Children's Press, 30 pp.; ISBN: 0-516-26390-0 (paperback); $6.95.

> Part of the *It's Science* series, this book entices young readers with introductory information, simple experiments, and a "Think About It!" feature. Force is explained as something that pushes or pulls and includes a discussion of forces, such as gravity, wind, magnetism, weight, and water. A table of contents, glossary, and index are included.

Morgan, Ben. (2003). *Gravity.* Farmington Hills, MI: Thompson Gale, 24 pp.; ISBN: 1-41030-199-0 (paperback); $9.95.

Part of the *Elementary Physics* series, this book is a simple and concise text that explains gravity, weight, orbit, and balance. It uses colorful photos and diagrams to make examples real for young readers. Scientific terms are highlighted and introduced in context. A table of contents, glossary, and index are included.

Morgan, Ben. (2003). *Motion.* Farmington Hills, MI: Thompson Gale, 24 pp.; ISBN: 1-41030-200-8 (paperback); $9.95.

Part of the *Elementary Physics* series, this book is a simple and concise text that explains force, inertia, friction, and acceleration. It uses colorful photos and diagrams to make examples real for young readers. Scientific terms are highlighted and introduced in context. A table of contents, glossary, and index are included.

Murphy, Patricia. (2002). *Push and pull.* New York: Children's Press, 32 pp.; ISBN: 0-516-26864-3 (paperback); $4.95.

This *Rookie Read About Science* book introduces children to pushing and pulling. Colorful photos and simple text encourage independent reading as well as learning how force affects the movement of different objects. Each 2-page spread has a large photo with accompanying text to explain it. A short picture glossary is included.

Trumbauer, Lisa. (2004). *What is friction?* New York: Scholastic, 31 pp.; ISBN: 0-516-25843-5 (paperback); $4.95.

Part of the *Rookie Read About Science* series, this simple text defines friction and gives multiple examples of how friction causes moving objects to stop. Each 2-page spread has a large photo with accompanying text to explain it. A short picture glossary is included.

Trumbauer, Lisa. (2004). *What is gravity?* New York: Scholastic, 31 pp.; ISBN: 0-516-25844-3 (paperback); $4.95.

Part of the *Rookie Read About Science* series, this provides a simple introduction to gravity. Several read-world examples are used to illustrate how gravity works, including the influence of mass. Large, colorful photos accompany the text, and a short picture glossary is included.

Whitehouse, Patricia. (2003). *Sliding.* Chicago: Heinemann Library, 24 pp.; ISBN: 1-4034-34719 (paperback); $5.95.

Part of the *Read and Learn* series, this very simple book provides hands-on experiments to demonstrate the properties that make sliding easier or more difficult. Scientific vocabulary is highlighted and defined in context, and reappears in the picture glossary. A table of contents and simple index are also included.

Web Sites

Note. The authors realize that Web site addresses are not guaranteed to work, as they change, move, or are removed from the Internet. Therefore, the authors have included the sponsoring organization of the Web site in the event the link provided here does not work. Simply type in the name of the organization in your search engine, and it will direct you to a new URL.

Passport to Knowledge at:

> http://passporttoknowledge.com/scic/

Sponsored by NASA, the NSF, and the NOAA, this site includes a series of interactive learning adventures connecting key life, Earth, space, and physical science concepts with exciting real-world phenomena. The site uses a suite of video programs shown on PBS in 2002–2003, hands-on activities, and online resources linking users with scientists. One module deals with force and motion.

Educational Resources in Science at:

> http://www.cln.org/themes/force_motion.html

Sponsored by the Community Learning Network of British Columbia, this site is an educational portal linking hundreds of Web sites on the Internet. Each site has been reviewed and selected by K–12 educators involved in promoting distance learning. The link above contains several links for resources involving the topic of force and motion.

Thinking Fountain: Friction at:

> http://www.sci.mus.mn.us/sln/tf/f/friction/friction.html

This site, maintained by the Science Museum of Minnesota, offers insightful hands-on experiments with everyday materials that model several aspects of friction, including the use of ball bearings to reduce friction.

The Exploratorium's Science Snack at:

> http://www.exploratorium.edu/snacks/gas_model.html

This site features several great demonstrations about forces, including friction, magnetism, and gravity.

TryScience at:

> http://www.tryscience.org/

Do you think you understand inertia well enough to save an egg in a toy truck? This Web site features fun online experiments that look at several aspects of mass, motion, and friction.

Videos

TEAMS: Forces & Motion: Measuring Forces

> Available at: http://www.unitedstreaming.com

This video is an excellent, engaging investigation of forces and motion with numerous student activities and teacher demonstrations. It includes ways to measure frictional forces and a description of the forces related to roller coasters. (30 minutes) Recommended for Grades 3–5.

The Magic School Bus Plays Ball

> Available at: http://www.unitedstreaming.com

This popular program explores forces and motion by playing "frictionless" baseball. (24 minutes) Recommended for Grades 3–5.

Physical Science: Forces and Gravity

> Available at: http://www.unitedstreaming.com

This video features five segments on force and motion. It includes an excellent description of key aspects of gravity. (20 minutes) Recommended for Grades 3–5.

Student Data Collection Sheet

Name:_____

NAME OF SURFACE	TRIAL 1 DISTANCE (cm)	TRIAL 2 DISTANCE (cm)	TRIAL 3 DISTANCE (cm)	AVERAGE DISTANCE (cm)
Wax Paper				
Surface #2:				
Surface #3:				
Surface #4:				
Surface #5:				

Full size form available at www.Christopher-Gordon.com/authors/KingMattox-shtml

Experiment Design Sheet

Names of Group Members:

Directions: As a group, write answers to the following items.

1. What are we trying to learn about friction and the substance we chose (oil, grease, or wax)?

2. If friction is reduced, we predict _____will happen. To answer this, think about the results of the previous experiment and the surface material your track is made of.

3. What is our hypothesis about the effect of the oil, grease, or wax on the distance the car travels?

4. What will we need to do to test our hypothesis? What steps will we carry out and why?

Full size form available at www.Christopher-Gordon.com/authors/KingMattox-shtml

5. What are the lengths of our first three trial runs <u>without</u> the friction-reducing substance?

      Trial #1 _____

      Trial #2 _____

      Trial #3_____

Total Distance_____ ÷ 3 = _____ Average Distance

6. What are the lengths of our second three trial runs <u>with</u> the friction-reducing substance?

      Trial #1 _____

      Trial #2 _____

      Trial #3_____

Total Distance_____ ÷ 3 = _____ Average Distance
                                                  (with friction
                                                reducers)

After the experiment is over and you have added your data to the class chart, use it and discuss these questions with your group.

7. What do the distances show?

8. Do these results make sense?

Full size form available at www.Christopher-Gordon.com/authors/KingMattox-shtml

9. Based on the results, what can we infer or assume about friction?

10. Do the results support our hypothesis?

11. If the results do not support our hypothesis, what might have affected them?

12. What did this experiment teach us?

13. What do we still want to know? What questions do we have?

Full size form available at www.Christopher-Gordon.com/authors/KingMattox-shtml

Roll It Concept Frame

Directions: Find information from trade books and Web sites to complete each sentence below.

A force is . . .	A force can . . . A force can be . . .
Examples of forces are . . .	A force has . . . Forces have . . .

Full size form available at www.Christopher-Gordon.com/authors/KingMattox-shtml

Teacher's Shopping List for Roll It!

- ❏ Different surfaces for students to rub soles on, such as: carpet, tile, wood floor, plastic garbage bag, grass, asphalt

- ❏ A long, flat surface such as a smooth floor or long counter or tabletop (about 2 m). Make sure there is plenty of room at the end of the track for the car to roll.

- ❏ Several planks to use as an inclined plane

- ❏ Several textbooks (10 cm thick) to help form an inclined plane

- ❏ Metric measuring tapes

- ❏ Several Match Box™ cars of equal mass

- ❏ Several sheets of wax paper (120 cm long)

- ❏ Variety of surfaces for students to choose from while working in centers. For example: several sheets of sandpaper taped together (about 60 cm long), a bath towel, several sheets of aluminum foil (about 120 cm long), foam rubber, plastic, newspaper, Velcro strips

- ❏ Copies of Student Data Collection sheet, one for each student (if students are not recording information in science notebooks)

- ❏ Transparencies of Student Data Collection sheet, one for each group

- ❏ Overhead transparency pens, at least one for each group

- ❏ Experiment Design Sheet, one for each student

- ❏ Oil, grease, or wax

- ❏ Science notebooks

Full size form available at www.Christopher-Gordon.com/authors/KingMattox-shtml

Chapter 8

Light Blockers

Introduction

Light is a basic component of the universe and is essential to our survival. It enables us to see, gives us color, and helps our crops to grow. It is responsible for the way we define our seasons and our days. Humans need light and darkness to maintain health. For instance, light enables us to break down vitamins in our food, and night provides an opportunity to rest our brains and our bodies. Light influences the way we live our lives. People and animals living in polar regions behave very differently from those living in other latitudes.

The goal of studying light is to understand the complexities of this basic component of survival. In this introductory unit, students will explore how light travels, how it is absorbed and reflected, and how it causes shadows.

Big Idea: Light travels and tends to maintain its direction of motion until it interacts with an object or material. Light can be absorbed, redirected, reflected, or allowed to pass through (American Association for the Advancement of Science [AAAS], 2001, p. 65).

Key Science Questions: How is a shadow created? What does this tell us about light?

National Science Standard: Light travels in a straight line until it strikes an object. Light can be reflected by a mirror, refracted by a lens, or absorbed by an object.

National Language Arts Standard: Students read a wide range of print and nonprint texts to build an understanding of text . . . and to acquire new information.

Thinking Tool: Visual Imagery

Action	Hands-On Activities	Literacy/Thinking Activities
Phase 1: Engage		
	Play Shadow Tag.	Summarize-Pair-Share
Phase 2: Explore 1: How Is a Shadow Formed?	Use different shapes to create shadows.	Record data.
Phase 2: Explore 2: Moving Shadows		
	Internet simulation	Record observations.
Phase 3: Explain		
		Visual Imagery. Find shadow examples in books.
Phase 2: Explore 3: Light Travels in a Straight Line		
Demonstrate light traveling using styrofoam and toothpicks.	Observe	Explore books to explain observations.
Phase 4: Elaborate: Light Is Absorbed, Reflected, and Refracted		
Demonstrate light absorption, reflection, and refraction.	Predict, draw, and observe	Visual Imagery. Summarize-Pair-Share. Record data.
Phase 5: Evaluate		
Two options for applying knowledge of shadows and how light travels to draw conclusions		

Figure 8:1   A framework for science literacy.

Teacher Background

Shadows can be anywhere. Cats have shadows and so do chairs. What makes a shadow? A light source, an object that blocks light, and a surface are the three things that are needed to make a shadow. Shadows are made on surfaces when objects are placed in the path of light. For example, if sunlight shines on a dense, thick cloud, a shadow is made on the ground beneath the cloud because the cloud blocks out the sunlight in that area. The area beneath the cloud is in shadow.

Shadows come in different shapes and sizes. These different shapes and sizes are due to the distances and angle between a light source, such as the sun, and the object blocking the light. Sometimes a small object, such as a cup, can have a big shadow if the light source is far away from the cup or at a low angle. When the light is moved closer to or above the cup, the shadow gets smaller. When you are outdoors, your body may make a long skinny shadow, and at other times, it makes a very short shadow. Your body doesn't change size. The change in the shadow size or shape is caused by the sun's change of location in the sky.

As the Earth rotates on its axis, the sun appears to move across the sky from east to west. However, the sun is not moving; the Earth is moving. As the Earth keeps rotating, the sun seems to move higher and higher, making shadows shorter and shorter during the middle of the day. After noon, the sun seems to be moving downward and westward, which makes shadows grow longer. The biggest shadow on Earth is called night. This occurs when the sun shines on one side of the Earth, creating daylight while also blocking the sun's light to the other side of Earth, creating night. The side of Earth that is experiencing night is actually cast in shadow.

Estimated Time: 4 days, approximately 60 minutes each

Materials Needed: See the Teacher Shopping List in the Teacher Resources section of this unit.

Phase 1: Engage

On a sunny day, take the students outside to play a game of Shadow Tag. One student is "it," and he or she has to tag or stand on the shadow of other students to make them be "it" instead. The object of the game is to keep your own shadow from getting tagged. Halfway through the game, stop the students and discuss the following questions:

- What do you think is making your shadow? (The light from the sun is being blocked by your body.)
- Why do trees, houses, and other objects have shadows? What do they have in common? (The sun is shining on them, and they are solid objects, so the sun's light is being blocked.)
- How would you describe your shadow? (Students will give various responses, such as shadows are dark, shadows change sizes, shadows stay by me, they disappear when I'm in the shade, etc.)

Have students Summarize-Pair-Share an observation they had in common regarding shadows. Help students to construct a generalization about shadows, based on their experience.

- When you were "it," how did you know where the shadow was going to be to tag the next person? (The shadow will be on the opposite side of the sun from the person, since the person needs to block the light from the sun to create their shadow.)

If time permits, play Shadow Tag again and ask students to make additional observations about shadows.

Phase 2: Explore #1: How Is a Shadow Formed?

Materials Needed:

> Flashlights, one for each pair of students
>
> Shapes cut from construction paper, three shapes for each pair of students
>
> Shapes cut from transparencies, three shapes for each pair of students
>
> Blank wall or floor
>
> Science notebooks or How Is a Shadow Formed? Observation sheet

Procedure:

1. Working with a partner, students will use a blank spot on the wall or floor, a flashlight (as a light source), and the shapes to attempt to create shadows. Allow students to explore where the object, light source, and surface need to be in relationship to each other in order to create a shadow. Encourage students to think about their game of Shadow Tag and make connections.

2. Ask students to record their observations in their science notebooks. You might have them respond to items such as the ones below:

   - Show how you created a shadow by drawing a picture and labeling each part.

   - Using the drawing, explain how you formed shadows. List the materials you used to create shadows. (Opaque materials, such as construction paper, block out the light and create a shadow.)

   - Also, explain why some materials did not create a shadow. (Transparent materials, such as the transparency, allow the light to shine through and will not create a shadow.)

   Or, if you prefer, have students answer the questions on the "How Is a Shadow Formed?" sheet in the Teacher Resources section of this unit.

3. When pairs have completed their work, have a class discussion to explore insights.

Possible questions to ask include:

   - In what order did the light source, object, and surface have to be to create the shadow? Show your drawings. (The object has to be between the light source and the surface to be able to block the light and cast a shadow.)

   - Explain how you formed shadows. (Blocking all or part of the light forms a shadow.)

- What happens to the shadow when you twist the shapes? (The shadow changes shape.)
- What happens to the shadow when you move the flashlight further from the shape and closer to the shape? (The shadow gets larger, then smaller.)

Phase 2: Explore #2: Moving Shadows

Materials Needed:

Science notebooks or Moving Shadows Observation sheet

Computer with projection screen

Internet access

If each student has access to a computer, and you choose to have them do this activity independently, walk them through these instructions. If not, project your computer screen via your AV system. If that is not available, you may cycle groups of students through this Web exercise while they are doing their trade book investigations (during the Explain phase). You may use the Moving Shadows Observation form for students to carry out this activity without your direction. Encourage them to work together to answer questions.

Procedure:

1. Go to this Web site from Learning Media at:
   http://www.learningmedia.co.nz/staticactivities/online_activities/
   theshadow/

2. Observe the shadow of the umbrella changing throughout the day.

   If each student has access to a computer, tell them to click on the DO button in the lower right-hand corner. They will use the cursor to move the towel for a person to sit on in the shade. Place the towel in the place where the shadow will be. Have students practice the simulation before asking questions. You may ask questions such as:

   - What do you notice about the direction the shadow is moving? (West to east.)
   - In what direction does the sun move as the Earth rotates? (East to west.)
   - What does this tell us about shadows? (There is a correlation between the sun and where a shadow falls.)
   - What do you think is making the shadow longer? (The lit surface of Earth is rotating away from the sun.)

- What do you think is making the shadow the shortest? (The sun is directly above the umbrella.) At what time does this happen? (Noon.)
- If you were sitting on the towel, at what time of day would you be in the shadow of the umbrella? (The afternoon.) Why?
- At what time of day is half of the Earth blanketed by a shadow? (Night) Why? What causes this? (Half of the Earth is blocking the sun's light, so the second half is cast in shadow.)

Phase 3: Explain

Materials Needed:

Trade books

Procedure:

1. Use a visual imagery tool to help review students' observations of shadows. Say something like: "Let's close our eyes and imagine. We are going to create mental pictures in our head of light hitting an object and stopping. Now picture the shadow on the wall behind the object. Try to see it clearly in your mind's eye. Notice how the shape of the object is also the shape of the shadow. Notice how clear the edges of the shadow are."

2. Have groups of students find photographs of shadows in various trade books. Tell students to discuss with group members how the shadow in the photo is created.

3. Have a class meeting to show and discuss the photos. Also, discuss how shadows form, and urge students to think about the mental images they made previously.

4. As a class, create a written explanation that summarizes and generalizes the groups' findings. An example might be: "The shadow in this picture is caused when the arm of the sundial blocks the sun's light."

Phase 2: Explore #3: Light Travels in a Straight Line

Materials Needed:

Styrofoam shapes

Flashlight

Student helper

Trade books

Chart paper

Procedure:

1. Have the student hold the flashlight so it is shining directly on the styrofoam. Position the styrofoam so that a shadow forms on the wall or floor.

2. Use toothpicks as examples of the light shining directly on the styrofoam by positioning the toothpicks as though they were the beams of light coming from the flashlight. Stick the toothpicks into the styrofoam as if they were light hitting the styrofoam and being blocked. Be certain that the toothpicks do not go through the styrofoam. The goal is to demonstrate how an object blocks light.

3. Demonstrate the light that goes past the styrofoam by placing toothpicks alongside the styrofoam. Help students see that the light going passed the styrofoam is shining on the wall. Ask students to think about these questions.

   • What do you think happens to the light that is not shining on the wall?

   • How can you explain where the light goes?

   • Do you have any "I Wonder" questions about light? What are they?

4. Place students in groups of three and give them a variety of trade books. Then, explore the books for:

   • Information on how light travels, including diagrams. Ask them to compare this information to the pictures they created in their head.

   • Answers to their "I Wonder" questions about light

   • Learn new information about light

   • Raise new questions about light

   Circulate around the room as groups are working and ask them to show you what they are finding. Encourage students to notice information about light that is absorbed, reflected, and refracted.

5. After some time exploring multiple books, place two triads together and let students share new information, questions, and interests. Encourage students to help each other by answering each other's questions and by sharing information. Have one person record interesting things learned as well as unanswered questions.

6. Hold a class meeting where a reporter from each group of six shares what was discussed. Record this new information and unanswered questions on the chart paper so the class can refer back to it as they continue with their study of light. Record students' unanswered questions on an "I Wonder" chart and invite students to seek answers either independently

or in teams. When answers are obtained, or when additional questions arise, take time to share them for additional learning.

Phase 4: Elaborate

Materials Needed:

One sheet of blank paper for each student

Chart paper

Blank transparencies

A piece of white poster board

A piece of black poster board

Mirror

Glass of water

Flashlight

Chart paper

Procedure:

Introduce the next activity for students. Remind them that in their reading they discovered that when light hits an object, it can be absorbed, reflected, or just pass through. However, a scientist doesn't rely on what books say or what people believe to be true. A scientist relies on observations and experiences in the real world. So, the next phase of our lesson will show us how light acts when it "hits" certain objects.

1. Have students get into teams of four, and give each student a piece of paper. Tell them to fold it in half two times to create four sections. Say to them, "Close your eyes again and visualize the light coming up to an object. [Pause] Now visualize the light beams going directly through the object in straight lines. [Pause] Now visualize the beams coming up to the wall. [Pause] Imagine the light beams are now bouncing off the wall. [Pause] Now open your eyes, and in the upper-left section of your paper, and draw what you saw in your head." Allow them just a few minutes to draw. Have students write "pass through" as a caption in that picture section.

2. Have the students close their eyes again. Say, "Again, visualize the light beams coming up to the object, but now visualize them getting absorbed into the object. [Pause] Notice the darkness behind the object making a shadow on the wall. [Pause] Visualize it in your head. Now open your eyes, and in the upper-right section of your paper, draw what you saw in

your head." Allow them just a few minutes to draw. Have students write "absorbed" as a caption in that picture section.

3. "Now close your eyes and visualize the light coming up to the object as you have done before. [Pause and give them time to see it in their heads.] Now visualize the light bouncing off the object. [Pause] Let your mind's eye look behind the object. The light did not go through but bounced off the object. Is there a shadow on the wall? What does it look like in your mind's eye? [Pause] Now open your eyes and draw in the lower-left corner section of your sheet what you saw in your head." Allow them just a few minutes to draw. Have students write "reflected" as a caption in that picture section.

4. Use Summarize-Pair-Share to have students quickly share their pictures and notice similarities and differences. This should take only 2–3 minutes.

5. Then, draw this chart on chart paper. You might want to duplicate it so that each student has his or her own copy. Or, ask students to draw the chart in their science notebooks and complete it as the lesson progresses. You will be placing checkmarks in the cells, so they do not have to be extremely large.

Material	Reflects	Absorbs	Passes through	Refracts
Transparency				
White poster board				
Black poster board				
Mirror				
Water				

6. Select volunteers to hold the materials, including the flashlight. Have one person hold the flashlight for each material. The others will hold each one of the materials about 1 foot (12 inches) away from the flashlight. As materials are "tested," put a checkmark on the chart indicating what happens to light when it hits that material. For instance, light passes through a transparency, so place a checkmark in the "passes through" column.

7. Make the room as dark as possible. Have the student with the transparency place it about 12 inches in front of the flashlight and shine the light toward the wall. Ask students:

   • What do you see on the wall? (Light.)

- How would you explain this observation? (The light beams are passing through the transparency.)
- Does this agree with the picture you had in your head, the one that you drew in the upper-right corner of your paper?

Describe verbally what is happening to the light. The beams come from the flashlight and move straight through the sheet. They aren't stopped or bent. Turn the lights on and check "passes through" for transparency.

8. Next, have the student with the piece of black poster board come forward. Again, hold the poster board about 12 inches in front of the flashlight. Ask students:
    - What do you see on the wall? (Not much of anything.)
    - How might you explain this? (The light is being blocked.)
    - What do you see on the black poster board? (The light is bouncing off the poster board and we can see it.)

Tell them that you want to compare what happens to the black poster board with the white poster board and the mirror.

9. Repeat the process with the white poster board and flashlight. Ask students:
    - In which instance do we see more light? (From the white poster board.)

10. Have the student with the mirror come up and shine the flashlight onto the mirror. Ask students:
    - What does the light do when it strikes the mirror? (It bounces back.)
    - Compare the light we see when the light shines on the mirror as compared with the black and white poster boards.
    - Explain what you think is happening here. Did anyone read about this earlier when we were exploring our books? (If not, then provide the following explanation. The beams are hitting the mirror and the white surface and they are bouncing back to our eye, so that we see what's in the mirror and see the light shine off the paper. The black surface does not have as much light bounce off or reflect from it.)

Turn the lights back on. Have them look at the picture labeled "reflected" in the lower-left corner of their drawings. Ask:
    - How does the picture match what the light did in the mirror?

Draw Figure 8:2 on the board. Write "Reflection" above it. Explain that the light is reflected by the mirror, and so we see our reflection. Point out the illustrated light beams for emphasis. On the chart, in the mirror row, put a checkmark in the Reflection column.

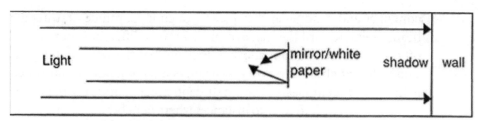

Figure 8:2   Light being reflected.

11. Explain that the white surface also reflects light, but not as efficiently as the mirror. Most of the light beams—but not all—bounce back. If more explanation is needed, refer students to Figure 8:2. Ask students:

   • What conclusion do we have about the white poster board and light? (It reflects.)

   • Why? Explain it to me. (On a white surface, most of the light beams bounce back, or reflect.) Check the appropriate column on the chart.

12. Explain that very few light beams bounce back from a black surface. Ask:

   • What do you think happens to the light beams that hit the black paper? (They are absorbed.)

   Draw Figure 8:3 on the board. Write "Absorb" above it. Explain that the light beams are penetrating the black surface, and they are stopping. It's like they are being sucked in or absorbed by the dark surface. Point out the illustrated light beams for emphasis. On the chart, in the black poster board row, put a checkmark in the Absorbs column.

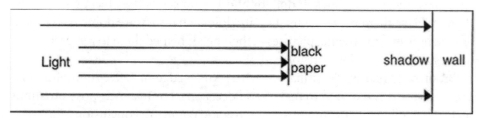

Figure 8:3   Light being absorbed.

13. Tell the students there is one action of light they have not discussed: refraction. Light is refracted, or bent, when it comes to a substance that makes the light slow down. When it slows down, the light beams bend. Have the student with the glass of water shine the flashlight on the water. Turn the lights off. Let the students see the "shadow." The shadow will be very diffuse and clearly outlined as in the others. Have the students use descriptive words to describe what the light looks like, such as fuzzy or blotchy. Turn the lights on, and draw Figure 8:4 on the board. Begin by drawing the container. Then, draw the light beams approaching the

container and bending as they pass through it. Continue drawing the beams going toward the wall and hitting it in a different spot than the others. Write "Refraction" above it. Explain that the water in the glass causes the light beams to slow down and bend. Point out the illustrated light beams for emphasis. Remind students that scientists use the words *refraction* or *refract* to refer to instances where light beams bend. On the chart, in the glass of water row, put a checkmark in the Refracts column.

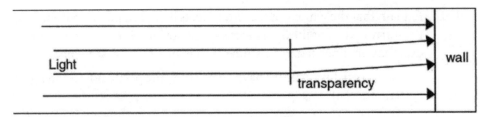

Figure 8:4   Light being refracted.

Conclude by telling students that when we observed what light actually does in the real world, we were collecting scientific data that light is absorbed, reflected, or passes through when it hits an object.

Phase 5: Evaluate

Have groups of 3 or 4 students simulate being the sun. Have them demonstrate the shadows the sun would make at 9:00 a.m., 12:00 p.m., 3:00 p.m., and 12:00 a.m. Have them use a bucket, doll, or another object as the object creating the shadow. Have them explain why they are doing what they are doing. Have them discuss how making mental pictures in their heads helped them to remember and understand how shadows are formed.

Or, provide real-world situations where knowledge of reflection, refraction, and absorption is required to make good decisions. For instance, pose situations such as the following for students to discuss and come to a conclusion:

- If you were living in a very, very hot climate, would you want windows that absorbed heat, reflected it, or passed through? Justify why.

- If you were outside on a very sunny, hot day, what color shirt would be more comfortable to wear—white or black? Justify why.

- If you were at the beach on a sunny day and were collecting rocks under the surface of the water, explain why the shadow created by the sun is diffused, fuzzy, or blotchy.

- Explain why a landscaper would need to know about shadows.

- Explain why a solar eclipse is an example of a shadow.

Teacher Resources

Trade Books

Berger, Samantha. (1999). *Light.* New York: Scholastic, 14 pp.; ISBN: 0-439-08120-3 (paperback); $2.50.

> If you think there is just one kind of light, this picture book will give you some bright ideas. Full-page photographs illustrate all types of light, ranging from starlight to firefly light to incandescent light.

Branley, Franklyn. (1998). *Day light, night light.* New York: HarperCollins, 32 pp.; ISBN: 0-06-445171-2 (paperback); $4.95.

> Part of the *Let's Read and Find Out* series, this book discusses the properties of light, including heat and its source, in child-friendly terms. For instance, did you know that light travels so fast, it can go from the moon to the Earth and back in 3 seconds? Read this book to discover more fascinating light facts.

Bredeson, Carmen. (2003). *The moon.* New York: Scholastic, 31 pp.; ISBN: 0-516-27770-7 (paperback); $4.95

> Part of the *Rookie Read About* series, this book is a simple introduction to the physical features, orbit, and efforts to explore the Earth's moon. Half of the book discusses how the moon reflects light from the sun and seems to change its shape throughout the month.

Bulla, Clyde Robert. (1994). *What makes a shadow?* [June Otani, Illus.] New York: HarperCollins, 32 pp.; ISBN: 0-060-229-160 (paperback); $4.95.

> When you run, your shadow runs. But you can never catch it! What makes a shadow? Where does it come from? When the sun is shining, everything has its own shadow—trees, houses, cars, even clouds and planes way up in the sky. You have a shadow, too. As the sun sets, all shadows become part of a much larger one—the night! With simple words and charming illustrations, Clyde Robert Bulla and June Otani explain how shadows are produced. Young readers will discover what makes the shadows they see and will be introduced to the fun of making shadows of their own. This book received the 1996 NSTA Outstanding Science Trade Books for Children Award.

Burnie, David. (1992). *Light.* New York: Dorling Kindersley, 44 pp.; ISBN: 1-879431-79-3 (hardcover); $15.99.

> This *Eyewitness* book is complete with fascinating facts about light, including explanations about the way light works, how light is used, the history of

scientific research into light, and what light has meant to our culture. The difference between refraction and reflection is explained, as well as topics such as light particles, holograms, shadows, lenses, and light in outer space. An index is included.

Challoner, Jack. (2001). *Hands-on science: Sound and light.* [David Le Jars, Illus.] New York: Kingfisher, 40 pp.; ISBN: 0-7534-5347-9 (paperback); $6.95.

A myriad of activities will help explain what sound and light are, how they work, and how important they are in our everyday lives. The majority of experiments use materials that can be found around the home. Experiments are illustrated and a few photos are included to explain concepts.

Cooper, Christopher. (2004). *Light: From sun to bulbs.* Chicago: Heinemann Library, 32 pp.; ISBN: 140343550-2 (paperback); $7.85.

This book is part of the *Science Answers* series. It includes experiments and explanations to answer questions such as: What is light? How is light made? How do you see things? How does light move? What are shadows? Why do things have color? How do lenses help you see? and, Is there light you cannot see? A section entitled "People Who Found the Answers" puts a human face onto important scientific finds. A glossary and index are also included.

Glover, David. (1993). *Sound and light: Science facts and experiments.* New York: Kingfisher, 32 pp.; ISBN: 0-7534-5512-9 (paperback); $7.95

Using a combination of explanation and simple experiments, this book helps children discover basic properties of sound and light. The experiments use materials that can be found around the home and are clearly explained.

Nankivell-Aston, Sally. (1999). *Science experiments with light.* Danbury, CT: FranklinWatts/Scholastic, 32 pp.; ISBN: 0-531-15429-7 (paperback); $6.95.

This experiment book answers many questions about properties of light, including traveling light, bouncing light, bending light, and seeing light. A glossary, index, list of materials needed, and safety concerns are included. "Keep Thinking" and "Don't Stop There" sections provide opportunities for further exploration.

Otto, Carolyn B. (2001). *Shadows.* New York: Scholastic, 32 pp.; ISBN: 0-439-29583-1 (paperback); $3.99.

Have you ever seen your shadow on a bright and sunny day? Do you know what a shadow is or how it changes shape? This *Scholastic Science Reader* is full of facts and photographs about what makes shadows and how they change shape.

Riley, Peter. (1998). *Light and color.* New York: Franklin Watts, 32 pp.; ISBN: 0-531-15371-1 (paperback); $6.95.

> Beautiful photographs and text help to introduce the scientific principles of light and color, including explanations of where light comes from, reflected light, colors in nature, and how the eye works.

Royston, Angela. (2002). *Light and dark.* Chicago: Heinemann, 32 pp.; ISBN: 1-4034-0041-5 (paperback); $7.25.

> What is light? Where does it come from? What is a shadow? This book explains the science to answer each of these questions using real-world examples and photographs.

Swinburne, Stephen R. (1999). *Guess whose shadow?* Boyds Mills, PA: Boyds Mills Press, 32 pp.; ISBN: 1-5907-80175 (paperback); $8.95.

> Depending on the angle of light, everything in the world has a shadow. Shadows can be beautiful or mysterious. Shadows also can be entertaining. Children are intrigued by shadows at an early age. Shadows appeal to children's innate curiosity. They enjoy figuring out what shadows are and how they work. They are especially delighted when they discover their own shadows. In this fascinating book, Steve Swinburne invites young children to investigate this phenomenon of nature. With a simple text and stunning full-color photographs, he introduces children to the basics of shadows. Then, he leads them on a shadow hunt, playing a game called Guess Whose Shadow? After looking at this book, children will see that there is more to shadows than first meets the eye.

Zubrowski, Bernie. (1995). *Shadow play: Making pictures with light and lenses.* New York: HarperCollins, 112 pp.; ISBN: 0-688-13210-3 (hardcover); $7.95.

> Starting with the basics, this book helps readers understand shadows using experiments in natural and artificial light. Additional investigations explain special properties of light, including how a camera works and using a shadow box. Lists of the simple materials needed to conduct experiments and explanations are provided.

Web Sites

Note. The authors realize that Web site addresses are not guaranteed to work, as they change, move, or are removed from the Internet. Therefore, the authors have included the sponsoring organization of the Web site in the event the link provided here does not work. Simply type in the name of the organization in your search engine, and it will direct you to a new URL.

The Exploratorium: The Museum of Science, Art and Human Perception at:

http://www.exploratorium.edu/snacks/iconlight.html

This link contains approximately 45 brief, fun experiments that teach viewers about many aspects of light, such as colored shadows, polarized light, diffraction, invisible light, and many more. For additional activities and information about light and other aspects of science, visit the main Web site at: http://www.exploratorium.edu/

American Association for the Advancement of Science, ScienceNetLinks at:

http://sciencenetlinks.com/resource_index.htm

This site contains a wealth of helpful information for K–12 classroom teachers. To search the site, click on Resources, then select the appropriate grade-level range and benchmark. The benchmarks are categorized according to the AAAS organization, which are different from the National Science Standards' organization.

How is a shadow formed ?

Name _____

1. What materials created a shadow?

2. How was a shadow formed?

3. In what order did the light source, object, and surface have to be to create the shadow? Draw where each was placed.

4. What happens to the shadow when you twist the shapes?

5. What happens to the shadow when you move the flashlight further from the shape? Closer to the shape?

Full size form available at www.Christopher-Gordon.com/authors/KingMattox-shtml

Shapes for Shadows

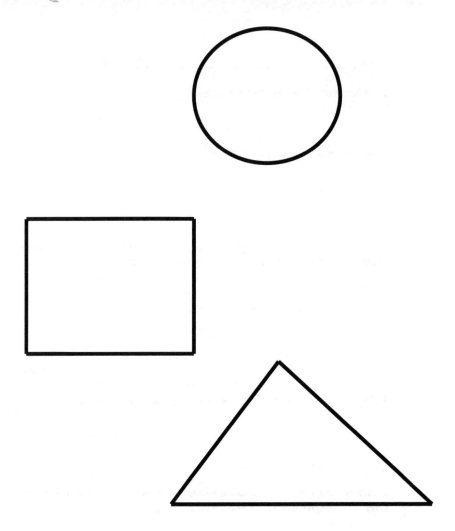

Full size form available at www.Christopher-Gordon.com/authors/KingMattox-shtml

Moving Shadows

Name _____

Observe the shadow of the umbrella changing throughout the day.

1. What direction is the shadow moving?

2. What direction does the sun appear to be moving as the Earth rotates?

3. What is making the shadow longer?

4. What is making the shadow the shortest? At what time does this happen?

5. At what time (give a range) will a person sitting on the towel be in the shadow of the umbrella?

6. What happens at night?

7. What would happen to night if light bent?

Full size form available at www.Christopher-Gordon.com/authors/KingMattox-shtml

Draw the position of the sun in relationship to the person and the umbrella at the following times.

9:00 a.m.

12:00 noon

3:00 p.m.

What does the placement of the shadows tell you about the movement of the Earth? (The umbrella needs to block the sun's light, and the Earth needs to rotate in order to create different-sized shadows.)

Full size form available at www.Christopher-Gordon.com/authors/KingMattox-shtml

Teacher's Shopping List for Light Blockers

- ☐ Sun (outdoors)

- ☐ Flashlights (one for each group of students)

- ☐ Computer with Internet access

- ☐ Overhead transparency paper

- ☐ Construction paper shapes

- ☐ Styrofoam shapes (triangle, circle, square, rectangle)

- ☐ Toothpicks

- ☐ Scissors

- ☐ Blank surface in your classroom, such as a screen, clean white board, or a light-colored wall or floor for a surface to create shadows on

- ☐ Science notebooks or Moving Shadows observation sheet, one for each student

Full size form available at www.Christopher-Gordon.com/authors/KingMattox-shtml

Chapter 9

The Earth Beneath Our Feet

Introduction

Most children display an interest about the rocks and minerals around them. It might be a pebble on the driveway or a gemstone in a ring. It might be memories of skipping stones across a pond. This natural curiosity is fortunate for us because we can use it to encourage students to describe a rock and correctly name the specimen. With additional study, we can lead students to develop deeper insight into the origins of geologic materials and the gradual construction of how the Earth has changed over time.

This unit will focus on developing students' descriptive skills of three sets of materials: igneous, sedimentary, and metamorphic rocks. A complementary lesson on minerals is provided in Appendix C, if needed. These lessons describe the most useful and common rocks. The sets are not comprehensive, but after their exploration, students will thoroughly understand some common rocks. In addition, they will be able to expand their own rock collections to include new materials they have not seen before (just like geologists do). For information on rocks most common in your state, visit the Web site of the Association of American State Geologists at: http://www.stategeologists.org/

Big Idea: Earth is made of a limited number of common materials. By learning the basics of identification, we can classify most of the Earth materials encountered (American Association for the Advancement of Science [AAAS], 2001, p. 50).

Key Science Questions: What types of materials make up the Earth? What are the origins of the different types of materials? How are Earth materials classified?

National Science Standard: Earth materials are minerals, rocks, sediment, and soils. The varied materials have different physical and chemical properties, which make them useful in different ways, for example, as building materials, as sources of fuel, or for growing plants we use as food. Earth materials are critical to our well-being.

National Language Arts Standards: Students read a wide range of print and nonprint texts . . . apply a range of strategies to comprehend, interpret, evaluate, and appreciate texts. Students participate as knowledgeable, reflective, creative, and critical members of a literacy community.

Thinking Tool: Brainstorming tool

Action	Hands-On Activities	Literacy/Thinking Activities
Phase 1: Engage		
Begin role-play.	Sort samples by characteristics	Step One: Brainstorming tool
Phase 2: Explore #1: Physical Properties of Igneous Rocks		
	Sort by color, weight, appearance	
Phase 2: Explore #2: Physical Properties of Sedimentary Rocks		
	Sort by color, hardness, reaction to acid	
Phase 2: Explore #3: Physical Properties of Metamorphic Rocks		
	Sort by layers, appearance, reaction to acid	
Phase 3: Explain		
Introduce formal vocabulary.		Read *Rocks: Hard, Soft, Smooth, and Round.* Discuss characteristics of rocks. Use *Rocks* to verify. Record descriptions.
Phase 4: Elaborate		
Use formal descriptions of rocks.		Steps Two, Three, and Four: Brainstorming tool
Phase 5: Evaluate		
		Research using additional books. Summary writing. Create a field guide to Earth materials.

Figure 9:1 A framework for science literacy.

Teacher Background

Igneous rocks all started as molten material, called magma, in the Earth's mantle or crust. The magma rises toward the surface because it is less dense than the adjacent rock. Some of the magma stops rising and cools slowly, allowing crystals to grow. These rocks are called intrusive igneous rocks, and they are later exposed by the erosion of the overlying rocks. Granite is a common intrusive rock. Other batches of the magma rise to the surface and erupt at volcanoes. The molten material, called lava, cools quickly, and there is no time for crystals to grow. These rocks are called extrusive igneous rocks, and they are found on the ocean floor and at volcanoes. Basalt, pumice, and obsidian are common extrusive rocks.

Sedimentary rocks all form at the Earth's surface. Sandstone forms when sand grains, commonly made of the mineral quartz, accumulate in beaches, along river beds, or in dunes. Shale forms adjacent to rivers when they flood or offshore in shallow oceans. These rocks are called clastic sedimentary rocks because they are made of preexisting pieces of rock. Limestone can form by direct chemical precipitation from water. These rocks are called chemical sedimentary rocks, and they are found on the ocean floor and at volcanoes.

Limestone can also form from shells. Some organisms make their shells by pulling elements (e.g., calcium, carbon, and oxygen) out of the water. When these organisms die, their shells accumulate to make fossiliferous limestone. Limestone commonly forms in shallow oceans but also forms in some freshwater lakes. Coal is formed by the accumulation and change of land plants. Swamps are a common environment for the plants to accumulate. Later, they get compressed to make coal.

Metamorphic rocks form at greater depths, tens of kilometers, within the Earth's crust. Metamorphism means a change in a solid state. Conditions needed for metamorphic rocks to form include temperatures of 600–700°C and intense pressure caused by the collision of plates. Because these rocks are not commonly found at the surface, coupled with the way they are formed, they are perhaps the most difficult for students to conceptualize.

When plates collide, deformation (i.e., squeezing) occurs. Because most metamorphic rocks form under pressure, new minerals grow perpendicular to the squeezing of the plates. This alignment of minerals forms layers, called foliation. Foliation is seen in slate and gneiss. Some metamorphic rocks, such as marble or quartzite, lack foliation and form by a change in temperature. If temperatures get too hot, perhaps more than 600–700°C, the rocks start to melt, begin to make magma, and start the process of igneous rock formation. Metamorphism is a slow process, estimated to take millions of years.

Estimated Time: 4 periods, approximately 60 minutes each

Materials Needed: See the Teacher Shopping List in the Teacher Resources section of this unit.

Phase 1: Engage

Materials Needed:

> Numerous, different rock specimens, one set for each pair of students

> Carpet samples, one for each pair of students

> Science notebooks, *or* Rock Hounds booklet found in Teacher Resources, one for each student

Advanced Preparation:

> Number the rock specimens. This can easily be done by applying a small amount of white-out correction fluid to a small area of the specimen. After the correction fluid dries, numbers can be drawn with a fine-tipped maker. Do not number all specimens of a given type consecutively. For example, choose an igneous sample to be #1, a metamorphic #2, a sedimentary #3, then start again with a metamorphic rock as #4. As new specimens are added to the collection, their numbers are added consecutively. It is a good idea to keep a running spreadsheet of your collection. Inexpensive preidentified rocks can be obtained from various sources. See the Teacher Resources section at the end of this unit for suggestions. Sediment samples can be collected from beaches, other natural areas, or even purchased at garden centers. Carpet samples can be obtained from carpet stores at a nominal price.

Procedure:

1. Begin by telling students they are scientists from another planet. They have been sent on an interplanetary mission to explore and collect rock samples from Earth. Provide pairs of students with a variety of rocks. Have each pair observe their samples and list general characteristics in their science notebooks such as: color, density (accept "heavy or light"), soft or hard, sandy, or note the presence of fossils.

2. Create a class list by writing student descriptions on the board. Label this list "Words about Rocks." Discuss the types of materials they discovered. Ask questions such as:

   • As an interplanetary scientist, how would you describe to your control center on your home planet the Earth samples you collected?

   • If you were to classify every rocky sample on Earth into two groups, what would those two groups be? (light or dark color, "heavy" or "light" weight, smooth or rough, shiny or dull, etc.).

3. Now have pairs physically sort their samples into those two groups.

4. Have students create a label for each group. Encourage them to use words to describe the characteristics of each group. Technical terms are not necessary at this point, but do encourage students to include words that evoke how the rocks look (i.e., visual image) and how they feel. This is the first step of the Brainstorming tool.

Phase 2: Explore

In this series of explorations, students will discover the physical properties of rocks. Geologists have named and described several hundred, if not thousands, of different rock specimens. Fortunately, every rock falls within one of three types, based on its origin. To facilitate learning, we will focus our students' attention on the most common, and distinctive, rocks. These rocks serve as an excellent foundation for students' emerging view of Earth materials and processes. Our line of questioning has been designed specifically to lead students to the correct identification. You may choose to ask other types of more open-ended questions and still lead to the same understandings.

Phase 2: Explore #1: Physical Properties of Igneous Rocks

Materials Needed:

> Numerous, different rock specimens, one set for each pair of students
>
> Carpet samples, one for each pair of students
>
> Science notebooks
>
> Small tubs of water, one for each pair of students

Procedure:

1. Distribute carpet and rock samples to each pair of students. Inform them that as interplanetary geologists, it is important to explore the composition and texture of the three main types of rocks found on Earth. Composition refers to the minerals in the rock. Texture refers to the size of the crystals or grains and how they are arranged. Tell students our home planet does have some information about Earth materials. For instance, we know that some of the rocks were once molten; some formed at the Earth's surface; and some were changed inside the Earth when they were heated and squeezed.

2. Have pairs of students remove the specimens of granite, basalt, pumice, and obsidian by referring to the sample numbers. Names are not important at this stage.

3. Next, ask pairs of students to write a short description of each rock sample in their science notebooks. Informal words, such as shiny or sparkle, are fine. Or, have pairs of students complete the section on Set #1 of the "Investigating Earth's Materials" page.

4. Discuss the samples with students by asking questions such as:

    *   How might you tell your four rocks apart? (They all look different. Mine is glassy. Mine is black and smooth.)

    *   Do you see any minerals, any crystals in it? (No, it is just black and smooth.)

    *   What else describes your rocks? (Color. One is black; another is black with some red streaks in it. Weight. One rock is gray and really light-weight.)

    *   Can you see any bubbles in the grey, lightweight rock? (Yes.)

    *   Let's see it if floats in water. [Students set sample in water. It floats.]

    *   Only one rock is left; what can you tell me about the last one? (It's kind of speckled. The pieces are all different colors.)

Explain that this rock has crystals in it, and that you can see each one with your eyes.

    *   Can you hypothesize what the crystals are? Have you seen them before? (They are minerals.)

Good observations! Those are the minerals that make up the rock. There are three or four different minerals in your rock.

Phase 2: Explore #2: Physical Properties of Sedimentary Rocks

Materials Needed:

Numerous, different rock specimens, one set for each pair of students

Carpet samples, one for each pair of students

Science notebooks

Weak acid, such as vinegar

Eye dropper

Paper towels, one sheet for each pair

Optional:

Hand-held magnifying lens, one for each pair, *or*

Brock Magiscope, one for each pair

Procedure:

1. Have pairs remove the specimens of sandstone, shale, limestone, fossiliferous limestone, and coal by referring to the sample numbers. Names are not important at this stage.

2. Next, ask students to write a short description of each rock sample in their science notebooks. Informal words, such as sandy or black, are fine. Or, have pairs complete the section on Set #2 of the "Investigating Earth's Materials" page.

3. Encourage students to examine and observe the samples. Guide their exploration by asking questions such as the following:

   - How might you tell your five rocks apart? Which one is easy to describe? (The black one. [coal])

   - Would all of you agree with that? [Some students might identify the sand or fossils more readily. We'll get to those samples shortly. Continue with coal.]

   - Does it have other characteristics? (Yes. It is lightweight and kind of soft. I can rub some off on the edges, and it gets my hands dirty.)

   - Yes, it is soft and has a low density compared to the other rocks. How would you describe the other rocks? (This one is sandy. I can see and rub some of the sand grains off. [sandstone])

   - You could use a magnifying glass or a microscope for a closer look. Where do you usually see sand when you are outside? (At the beach, in a dune, or along a river.)

   - Of the last three rocks, which one is most distinctive? Most unique? (This one has fossils that look like shells.)

4. Next, conduct a short experiment. Tell pairs to place all of their samples on the table. Circulate and place one drop of acid on each specimen. Tell students not to touch the acid, but to observe any reactions. Discuss what students are seeing. Ask:

   - Do all of your specimens react to the acid? (No.)

   - Which ones reacted to the acid? (The one with fossils and the other gray one.)

   - What might you conclude? (Some rocks react to acid and others do not react to acid.)

After the test, use the paper towel to dry of the drop of acid. Pairs should have one remaining sample that has not been explored.

- Can you describe it? (It's boring. It's gray, and I can't see anything in it.)
- What do you think it is made of? Really small pieces of rock or mineral? (Maybe.)
- Is it soft? Try to scratch it. (Yes, we can scratch it.)
- Does it have any layers? (Our sample doesn't, but the sample on that table does.)
- Of the rocks you have looked at so far, which one is most interesting and why?

Ask students to remember these facts about Earth materials because they will use this information later.

Phase 2: Explore #3: Physical Properties of Metamorphic Rock

Materials Needed:

Numerous, different rock specimens, one set for each pair of students

Carpet samples, one for each pair of students

Science notebooks

Weak acid, such as vinegar

Eye dropper

Paper towels, one sheet for each pair

Optional:

Hand-held magnifying lens, one for each pair *or*

Brock Magiscope, one for each pair

Procedure:

1. Have pairs remove the specimens of marble, slate, and gneiss by referring to the sample numbers. Names are not important at this stage.

2. Next, ask pairs to write a short description of each rock sample in their science notebooks. Informal words, such as flat or shiny, are fine. Or, have pairs complete the section on Set #3 on the "Investigating Earth's Materials" page.

3. Encourage students to examine and observe the samples. Guide their exploration by asking questions such as the following:

   • How can you tell your three rocks apart? (They all look different.)

   • Which one is easiest to describe? (This one. The flat one. [slate])

   • Does it have other characteristics? (Yes. It has sharp edges and sounds like a dinner plate when I tap on it. I think I see some layers in mine.)

   • Good, some of these rocks will have some layers. Do any of the other rocks have layers? (Yes.)

   • Describe them. (Almost like a cookie, gray and white. Layers of different stuff.)

   • What do you think makes the layers? (Maybe minerals.)

4. Repeat the acid experiment. Place one drop of acid on each sample. Remind students not to touch the acid, but to observe any reactions. Discuss what students are seeing. Ask:

   • Do all of your specimens react to the acid? (No.)

   • Which one reacted with acid? (The one with lots of shiny crystals.)

   • Again, what can we conclude, based on this experiment and the last one? (Some rocks react with acid and others do not.)

5. After the test, use the paper towel to dry off the drop of acid. Explain to students the reaction indicates the presence of the mineral calcite. Calcite is common in limestone, which is a sedimentary rock. So, this sample started out as limestone before it changed into a metamorphic rock.

Phase 3: Explain

Materials Needed:

Rocks: Hard, Soft, Smooth, and Round by Natalie M. Rosinsky, one copy for each group of 4 students

Rock Hounds booklet in the Teacher Resources section, one for each student *or* science notebooks, one for each student

Numerous, different rock specimens, one set for each pair of students

Carpet samples, one for each pair of students

Procedure:

1. Remind students they are role-playing scientists from another planet who observed samples of Earth rocks. This kind of scientist is called a geologist. Refer to the first list created, "Words about Rocks."

Ask students:

- Was the list scientific? (No.)
- Did we use scientific terms? (No.)

Tell students that on Earth, people use books to help them locate information and learn new things. Today, we will be reading a special book that will give us scientific vocabulary and explanations to help explain the Earth samples we explored. This is important because we don't know what the Earthlings call these samples. Since we need to report our findings to scientists at home, we will need to gather information about what geologists call these rocks on Earth.

2. Have students think for a moment. Ask them:

    - When a scientist reads something, what do you think is important to her? (Learning new information, asking new questions, etc.)
    - What do you think is important for us to notice when we read this book? (Names of samples, characteristics, origin.)
    - Why are these important for us to know? (As scientists, we need a way to categorize and organize our Earth samples.)
    - Do you think scientists just read about something and that's it? (No, they discuss it, make more observations, and even form hypotheses.)

    Tell students that's what they will be doing today: They will read this book in groups and think really hard like a scientist does.

3. Form groups of 4 students by combining two pairs. Encourage groups to pick up samples as they are discussed in the book, and stop reading and discuss the text when they think the book tells them something a geologist would think is important. Remind them they are reading this book as a scientist would, so encourage them to notice the vocabulary used, as well as information about the composition and origin of the samples.

4. Next, direct students to the "Classifying Earth Materials: Set #1" page in their Rock Hounds booklet. Have students list their samples by number in the left column, and notice their task for the right column where they are going to list descriptions of each sample. Encourage students to use more specific terminology than the words they initially thought of, which are on the board. Since they are role-playing interplanetary scientists, they will want to use fairly specific terms when they report their findings to mission control at home; so instead of saying a sample is "light" in color, encourage students to say it is "speckled gray, white, and pink." Likewise, when describing the rock's texture, encourage students to record geologic descriptions, such as "layered," "sandy," or "glassy," not just "smooth" or "rough." Encourage students to return to *Rocks: Hard, Soft,*

Smooth, and Round as needed. Allow a few minutes for students to record in the right-hand column words to describe each sample. Tell them this is the first step geologists take when they are making observations about rocks. If students struggle, you might ask again the questions asked during Explore #1.

- Where are two general places or environments igneous rocks form? (Inside the Earth and at the surface.)

- How does this environment affect the rock's appearance? (Rocks that form at the surface do not have visible crystals; they are fine grained. Rocks that form inside the Earth must be the other group, the ones with visible crystals).

Offer an explanation to students to help explain this information. Tell them that geologists say volcanic rocks are fine grained because you can't see any crystals in them. All the rocks they just described erupted from volcanoes and cooled quickly. Because they cooled so quickly, the minerals/crystals didn't have time to grow very big or at least big enough for us to see. Geologists would say this is a coarse-grained rock, since we can see all the crystals.

5. Draw students' attention to the piece of granite, and ask students to recall what the book said about this rock. (The book identifies the sample as "granite" and says that it cooled underground.) Continue explaining. Since it cooled slowly, the crystals had time to grow larger. It can take thousands of years for a batch of magma to cool and solidify. Then, weather and erosion have to break down and transport away all the rocks above it.

6. Repeat the process. Have students return to their Rock Hounds booklet and look at the "Classifying Earth Materials: Set #2" page. They will record the numbers of their samples in the left column and provide descriptions in the right column. Encourage students to record words to describe the sample's color, texture, and composition. Return to *Rocks: Hard, Soft, Smooth, and Round* as needed. If a sample has evidence of minerals being present, be sure students record that as well. If students struggle, you might ask again the questions asked during Explore #2.

   - What characteristics of these rocks give clues about places or environments where they are formed? (Sand-sized material is common on beaches, rivers, and dunes. Fossils are the remains of organisms that lived on the surface.)

   - Think about ways that humans use rocks. (Coal is burned for energy. Limestone is a common building stone. Fossils provide evidence for evolution.)

  • So what can we conclude? (Rocks have value.)

7. Offer an explanation for students to help explain this information. Tell students that sedimentary rocks form at the Earth's surface and often contain fossils. One common type of sedimentary rock is limestone [hold up a sample] and another common one is coal [hold up a sample]. Explain that coal is mined and burned in power plants on Earth to make electricity. Other sedimentary rocks include sandstone [hold up a sample]. Sandstone may be yellow, brown, or red and may have layers. [Hold up a sample of sandstone] Explain that geologists would say it is fine- to medium grained because it is made of sand-sized particles.

8. Repeat this process. Have students return to their Rock Hounds booklet and look at the "Classifying Earth Materials: Set #3" page. Again, they will record the numbers of their samples in the left column and provide descriptions in the right column. Encourage students to record words to describe the sample's color, texture, and composition. Return to *Rocks: Hard, Soft, Smooth, and Round* as needed. If a sample has evidence of minerals being present, be sure students record that as well. If students struggle, you might ask again the questions asked during Explore #3.

9. Offer an explanation for students to help clarify this information. Have students hold up the rock sample that fizzed when acid was on it (i.e., marble). Explain that the rock used to be a limestone before it was changed. Have students observe the rock's shiny crystals. Explain that when rocks grow new crystals, sometimes they increase in size. Repeat the official name of this rock—marble.

Phase 4: Elaborate

Materials Needed:

Science notebooks *or*

Rock Hounds booklet, one for each student

Procedure:

1. Encourage students to use some of the geologic vocabulary associated with Earth materials. Using information recorded in their Rock Hounds booklet and the class list written on the board, have pairs find two words in their collection that go together in some way. Examples may include: coarse and fine; light and dark; flat and round. Have students justify why the two words go together. Their explanation provides a label for the words. For instance, coarse and fine are words to describe the "texture" of the specimen. The term *texture* is the label.

Record both the label and the pair of words on the board. Ask students to nominate other words to describe texture. Ask students to justify why those words belong there. Continue the process until the majority of terms are categorized and labeled. This is Step Two of the Brainstorming tool.

2. Now create an opportunity for students to remember some characteristics and traits of their samples. Tell them they need to communicate their discoveries with their home planet, but there is a problem with the video feed. Therefore, they cannot show the command module what the samples look like. Instead, they need to create a simile to verbally describe them. Remind students that similes use the words "like" or "as" and compare two things. Give them an example. Hold up a piece of obsidian and ask them to complete the sentence, "Obsidian is like _____." (Dark, black glass) Other examples may include: "Pumice is like . . . frozen foam." Record the similes in science notebooks or in the Rock Hounds booklet. Encourage your interplanetary scientists to verbally share their similes with the class. This activity is Step Three of the Brainstorming tool.

3. Complete Step Four of the Brainstorming tool by asking scientists to elaborate on some of the words they recorded to describe these Earth samples. Encourage them to think of any feelings or emotions they may have had when exploring the Earth rocks. For example, describe what a metamorphic rock feels like when it is deep in the extremely hot Earth, where the Earth is squeezing it so hard that minerals are literally smashed into each other? Or, describe what a sedimentary rock feels like when small aquatic creatures decide to stick to it and live there for a while? Discuss these associated feelings and emotions, since these will help our interplanetary scientists remember more vivid details about the Earth samples they have explored.

Phase 5: Evaluate

Materials Needed:

> *Looking at Rocks* by Jennifer Dussling, four or five copies
>
> Numerous, different rock specimens, one set for each pair of students
>
> Carpet samples, one for each pair of students
>
> Variety of assorted trade books listed in the Teacher Resources section of this unit
>
> Geologist Note-Taking Guides, three copies for each student
>
> Cover page for Field Guide of Earth Materials
>
> Multiple copies of blank Rocks page to be included in Field Guide

Procedure:

1. Students will create a field guide to describe common rocks found on Earth. Tell them the purpose of a field guide is to record information about common rocks and materials we see in our daily lives. Show them Jennifer Dussling's *Looking at Rocks* book, which is a field guide for children. Point out distinguishing features of this field guide:

   - Name of a rock
   - Photographs
   - Description of its color and texture
   - Description of its shape and size
   - Where it is found

2. Tell your scientists they are going to create a field guide, which will serve as a valuable record of their observations of Earth materials. Each scientist will select one igneous, sedimentary, and metamorphic rock from their sample set. Using the books listed in the Teacher Resources section of this unit, as well as information recorded in their Rock Hounds or science notebooks, they will each research three rocks. To facilitate their research, show them the "Geologist Note-Taking Guide" in the Rock Hounds booklet and review the goal and components.

3. Provide assorted trade books and allow each scientist time to research their three samples.

4. After the research is completed, meet as a whole class to review what specific rocks were selected. Have the class analyze their research by asking themselves if a scientist would find the information they collected valuable. Remind students of the things they noticed when they read *Rocks: Hard, Soft, Smooth, and Rough*. Encourage students to add to their notes, if needed.

5. Next, decide on the content of the final field guide. Eliminate duplicate information and check for accuracy before writing the final class field guide. When the necessary information is assembled, have students record their final drafts on their blank Rocks page.

6. Collect the pages and ask the scientists how they might organize their information (alphabetical, by type of rock, etc.), and bind the pages, including the cover page. Ideally, all scientists will have their own copy to take back to their home planet and share with fellow scientists.

Teacher Resources

Suppliers

Great Lakes Geoscience
Steven Tchozeski
7705 N. Canfield Road
Belding, MI 48809
(616) 794-3339
tchozes@pathwaynet.com

Earth Science Educators Supply
Box 503
Lee's Summit, MO 64063
(816) 524-5635

Trade Books

Cefrey, Holly. (2003). *Metamorphic rocks.* New York: PowerKids Press, 24 pp.; ISBN: 0-8239-6466-3 (hardcover); $17.99.

> Great photographs and diagrams help define metamorphic rocks, how they make other rocks, the minerals found in them, and uses for them. A table of contents, glossary, bibliography, and index are included.

Chasek, Ruth. (2000). *Rocks and minerals.* New York: Children's Press, 48 pp.; ISBN: 0-516-23533-8 (paperback); $6.95.

> Photographs help to explain what rocks and minerals are and where to find them. Text tells how to become a rock hound and create your own collection. It includes a table of contents, safety tips, glossary, bibliography, and index.

Ditchfield, Christin. (2002). *Coal: A true book.* New York: Children's Press, 48 pp.; ISBN: 0-516-29366-4 (paperback); $6.95.

> Excellent photographs! This short chapter book defines coal, where it is found, how it is processed, what it is used for, as well as the future of coal. The text also includes a table of contents, glossary, index, and Meet the Author section.

Ditchfield, Christin. (2002). *Oil: A true book.* New York: Children's Press, 48 pp.; ISBN: 0-516-29367-2 (paperback); $6.95.

> Excellent photographs! Like other books in this series, it defines oil, explains where it is found, how it is processed, what oil is used for, as well as the future of oil. This book also includes an experiment on how to clean up oil spills. A table of contents, bibliography, glossary, index, and Meet the Author section are also included.

Ditchfield, Christin. (2002). *Soil: A true book.* New York: Children's Press, 48 pp.; ISBN: 0-516-29368-0 (paperback); $6.95.

> Great photographs. An excellent description of what soil is and how it is beneficial to both humans and animals. The text and photographs carefully explain how soil forms, types of soil, and what mankind can do to protect it. A soil experiment, a simple glossary, and index are included.

Dussling, Jennifer. (2001). *Looking at rocks.* [Deborah & Allen Drew-Brook-Cormack & Tim Haggerty, Illus.] New York: Grosset & Dunlap, 60 pp.; ISBN: 0-448- 42516-5 (paperback); $5.95.

> This easy-to-read book is a field guide for collecting rocks. It tells what you need to be a rock hound and how to keep a record of what you find. The text describes quartz, sandstone, mica, granite, sulfur, limestone, marble, graphite, slate, pumice, salt, coal, diamond, conglomerate, and fool's gold. It gives lots of tips, as well as notebook pages to record what you find.

Gallant, Roy A. (2001). *Minerals.* New York: Benchmark Books, 48 pp.; ISBN: 0-7614-1039-2 (hardcover); $22.95.

> This text uses large, easy-to-read print with clear, concise explanations of what minerals are, where they come from, how they are formed, and their physical properties. Outstanding full-page, full-color photographs appear throughout and concludes with directions for growing crystals. A table of contents, glossary, bibliography, index, and author's biography are included.

Gallant, Roy A. (2001). *Rocks.* New York: Benchmark Books, 48 pp.; ISBN: 0-7614-1042-2 (hardcover); $25.95.

> This text offers clear explanations about the ways fossils are formed and information on how to read the record they leave behind. It also includes brief descriptions of a paleontologist's work and how museum exhibits are created. Igneous, sedimentary, and metamorphic rocks are introduced. A Did You Know? section provides some additional facts. This book also contains well-selected, beautifully reproduced photographs.

Gans, Roma. (1984). *Let's go rock collecting.* New York: HarperCollins, 32 pp.; ISBN: 0-06-445170-4 (paperback); $4.99.

> Excellent diagrams, full-color photographs of specimens, and minor textual changes clarify the concepts (e.g., Mohs' scale of hardness) of basic rock formation; the characteristics of igneous, metamorphic, and sedimentary rocks; the uses of rocks in the past (Roman roads, Egyptian pyramids) and the present (cement); and rock collecting. The pair of youngsters featured in collecting, organizing, and storing rocks, convey the joy of being a rock hound.

Nayer, Judith. (2001). *Rocks and minerals.* [Francois Escalmel, Illus.] Cleveland, OH: Learning Horizons, 10 pp.; ISBN: 1-56293-547-X (paperback); $6.95.

> This board book contains brilliant colored pictures of rocks and minerals. It describes the differences between rocks and minerals, where they are found, and how they are made. The text explains how igneous, sedimentary, and metamorphic rocks, as well as metals and gemstones, are used in daily life.

Oxlade, Chris. (2002). *Soil.* Chicago: Heinemann, 32 pp.; ISBN: 1-4034-0088-1 (paperback); $7.25.

> A fine book that answers these questions: What is soil? Where does it come from? and How do we use soil? This book includes a Fun Fact File, a Can You Believe It? page, a glossary, an index, and illustrative photographs.

Rosinsky, Natalie M. (2003). *Rocks: Hard, soft, smooth, and rough.* [Matthew John, Illus.] Minneapolis, MN: Picture Window Books, 24 pp.; ISBN: 1-4048-0015-8 (hardcover); $14.95.

> A nice bridge from the simplest rock books toward a true understanding. This book covers the three rock types, how they form, and common examples and also contains two activities. A table of contents and glossary, as well as At the Library and On the Web sections, are included.

Squire, Ann. (2002). *Rocks and minerals.* New York: Children's Press, 48 pp.; ISBN: 0-516-26985-2 (paperback); $6.95.

> This book provides a good description of minerals in our everyday life, layers of the Earth, definition of a mineral and properties, rock types and how they form, uses, and materials. Only error: nickel, iron, and sulfur (p. 12) are elements, not minerals.

Web Sites

Note. The authors realize that Web site addresses are not guaranteed to work, as they change, move, or are removed from the Internet. Therefore, the authors have included the sponsoring organization of the Web site in the event the link provided here does not work. Simply type in the name of the organization in your search engine, and it will direct you to a new URL.

Mineral Information Institute at:

> http://www.mii.org

This site contains many free resources for teachers. It is especially helpful in investigating how we use minerals and rocks each day. It is a great resource for integrating geography and math with the science investigations.

K. Brannon's Rocks and Minerals Detectives at:

http://cte.jhu.edu/techacademy/fellows/brannon/webquest/kmbindex.html

On this site, students become rock and mineral detectives. They collect clues about rocks and minerals from the Internet and other resources and share their findings in a multimedia presentation. They have to find out what minerals are, their characteristics, where they are found, and how they are used. They have to identify the three types of rocks and how they were formed.

Coal Education. Your House Comes from a Mine at:

http://www.coaleducation.org/lessons/MII/doc5.htm

This Web site lists things that are found in your house and where they come from. For example, doorknobs, locks, and hinges are brass or steel (i.e., copper, zinc, iron ore, and alloys), and toilets, sinks, and bathtubs are made of porcelain (i.e., clay) over iron, or plastic (i.e., petroleum).

Videos

Geologist's Notebook: Three Rocks

Available at: http://www.unitedstreaming.com

This video examines three stones: a piece of igneous, a piece of sedimentary, and a piece of metamorphic rock, and investigates how they formed, and how they are related to the rock cycle. Formal terms complement the objectives of this lesson. (11 minutes) Recommended for Grades 3–5.

Rock Hounds

Scientist_____

Date_____

Full size form available at www.Christopher-Gordon.com/authors/KingMattox-shtml

Investigating Earth's Materials

Scientist's Name:_____

Date:_____

You have been given materials found on Earth. Your job is to describe and classify them. Record your observations by listing the sample numbers and a description of each sample.

Set #1:

Sample numbers:	Description:

Set #2:

Sample numbers:	Description:

Set #3:

Sample numbers:	Description:

Full size form available at www.Christopher-Gordon.com/authors/KingMattox-shtml

Classifying Earth Materials: Set #1

Igneous Rock	Composition	Texture	Origin

Notes:

Classifying Earth Materials: Set #2

Sedimentary Rock	Composition	Texture	Origin

Notes:

Full size form available at www.Christopher-Gordon.com/authors/KingMattox-shtml

Classifying Earth Materials: Set #3

Metamorphic Rock	Composition	Texture	Origin

Notes:

Full size form available at www.Christopher-Gordon.com/authors/KingMattox-shtml

Key to "Classifying Earth Materials"

Set #1

Igneous Rock	Composition	Texture	Origin
Granite	quartz, feldspar, mica, hornblende	coarse grained, crystals large enough to be seen	forms inside the Earth
Pumice	similar to granite, but individual crystals cannot be seen	glassy with many small holes, frothy, vesicular	forms on the surface and cools very quickly
Basalt	olivine, augite, plagioclase feldspar	very fine grained, crystals often too small to be seen	forms on the surface and cools quickly
Obsidian	similar to granite, but individual crystals cannot be seen	glassy	forms on the surface and cools very quickly
Diorite*	mostly hornblende and feldspar	coarse grained, crystals large enough to be seen	forms inside the Earth
Gabbro*	olivine, augite, plagioclase feldspar	coarse grained, crystals large enough to be seen	forms inside the Earth

Set #2

Sedimentary Rock	Composition	Texture	Origin
Sandstone	sand particles	medium 2- to 1/16 mm	old sand dunes or deposited by water
Shale	clay	very fine < 1/256 mm	lake or marine deposits in quiet water
(Fossiliferous) Limestone	calcite	may be fine grained, crystalline, or contain fossils	marine deposits precipitation of calcite
Coal	organic material	fine grained	swamp deposits
Conglomerate*	pebbles, sand, could contain clay	coarse > 2-mm particles are rounded	glacial or river deposits

Full size form available at www.Christopher-Gordon.com/authors/KingMattox-shtml

Set #3

Metamorphic Rock	Composition	Texture	Origin
Slate	individual crystals cannot be seen; contains clay minerals, mica	very fine	changed from shale by low temperature and pressure
Marble	calcite	crystalline	changed from limestone by heat
Gneiss	variable, may contain mica, quartz, hornblende, feldspar	coarse, and rock shows layering or foliation with color bands.	Very intense heat and pressure may change other rocks into gneiss.
Schist*	variable, may contain mica, quartz, hornblende; garnets are common.	coarse, and rock shows fine layering or foliation	Intense heat and pressure may change other rocks into schist.
Quartzite*	quartz	looks like coarse sugar	changed from sandstone by heat
Metaconglomerate*	rock fragments	coarse	changed from sedimentary conglomerate by heat

* Denotes challenge specimens.

Full size form available at www.Christopher-Gordon.com/authors/KingMattox-shtml

Rock Note-Taking Guide

Scientist name: _____

1) Name of rock: _____

2) What does this rock look like?
   What is its texture? _____

_____

_____

3) How did this rock form? _____

_____

_____

_____

4) How is this rock used on Earth? _____

_____

_____

5) I found a picture or photo of this rock here (list source):

_____

_____

Now write a sentence or two that combines the information from items 1–4 above. Write your summary below:

Full size form available at www.Christopher-Gordon.com/authors/KingMattox-shtml

SAMPLE
Rock Geologist Note-Taking Guide

Geologist name: Elliot

1) Name of rock: pumice

2) What does this rock look like? a hard sponge
   What is its texture? it's like foam with lots of bubbles

3) How did this rock form? it forms from cooled lava

4) How is this rock used on Earth? my mom rubs pumice on her

feet to keep them smooth

5) I found a picture or photo of this rock here (list source):

Images at Google.com

Now write a sentence or two that combines the information from items 1–4 above. Write your summary below:

Pumice is a rock that looks like a hard sponge and is formed by lava. My mom rubs pumice on her feet to keep them smooth.

Full size form available at www.Christopher-Gordon.com/authors/KingMattox-shtml

Field Guide of Earth Materials

by

The scientists in _____'s class
(Teacher's name)

Published on _____
(Date)

Full size form available at www.Christopher-Gordon.com/authors/KingMattox-shtml

Rocks

Name of rock:

Description and uses:

Photo or drawing:

SAMPLE
Rocks

Name of rock: pumice

Description and uses: Pumice is a rock that looks like a hard sponge with holes in it. It is formed from lava, and some people use it to keep their skin smooth.

Photo or drawing:

Teacher's Shopping List for Earth Beneath Our Feet

This list of rocks is only a recommendation and is by no means all-inclusive. The materials chosen may vary according to your geographic location. The varieties listed below represent economically important and common rocks. Selecting as few as two or three specimens of each type of material serves as a good foundation.

- ☐ Igneous rocks such as granite, pumice, basalt, and obsidian
- ☐ Sedimentary rocks such as sandstone, shale, limestone, fossil-rich limestone, and coal
- ☐ Metamorphic rocks such as marble, slate, and gneiss
- ☐ Small carpet samples (These provide a soft surface to protect table tops and reduce noise.)
- ☐ Acid bottles with weak acid (Vinegar works fine.)
- ☐ Copies of *Rocks: Hard, Soft, Smooth, and Rough* by Natalie M. Rosinsky, one copy for each group of 4 students
- ☐ White-out correction fluid
- ☐ Fine-tipped marker
- ☐ Eye dropper
- ☐ Small tubs of water, one for each pair of students
- ☐ Paper towels
- ☐ *Looking at Rocks* by Jennifer Dussling, four or five copies
- ☐ Variety of assorted trade books listed in the Teacher Resources section of this unit
- ☐ Geologist Note-Taking Guides, three copies for each student
- ☐ Cover page for Field Guide of Earth Materials
- ☐ Multiple copies of blank Rocks page to be included in Field Guide

Optional:

- ☐ Hand lenses (Magnification is helpful when students are observing specimens.)
- ☐ Brock Magiscopes (http://www.magiscope.com/) are ideal for these investigations.

Full size form available at www.Christopher-Gordon.com/authors/KingMattox-shtml

Chapter 10

Away We Go!

Introduction

Weathering and erosion are perhaps the most common geologic processes. We can easily observe blowing sand or a muddy river, while large landslides are commonly reported on the daily news. Many states are blanketed in layers of glacial deposits or have rugged mountains that were sculpted by ice. Understanding these basic geologic processes is critical to interpreting the Earth's past, as well as planning for risks today.

The lessons in this unit will allow students to compare and contrast the factors that influence the movement and deposition of geologic materials by wind, water, and ice. The activities serve as simple models of actual natural processes and are stepping stones for observing features we see in our communities.

Big Idea: Waves, wind, water, and ice shape and reshape the Earth's land surface by eroding rock and soil in some areas and depositing them in other areas (American Association for the Advancement of Science [AAAS], 2001, p. 51).

Key Science Question: How do water, wind, and ice cause changes on Earth?

National Science Standard: The surface of the Earth changes. Some changes are due to slow processes, such as weathering and erosion, and some changes occur rapidly, such as with volcanic eruptions and earthquakes.

National Language Arts Standards: Students read a wide range of print and nonprint texts to build an understanding . . . Students apply a wide range of strategies to comprehend, interpret, evaluate, and appreciate texts . . . They gather, evaluate, and synthesize data from a variety of sources to communicate their discoveries in ways that suit their purpose and audience.

Thinking Tools: Multi-Flow tool; Short- and Long-term Consequences tool

Action	Hands-On Activities	Literacy/Thinking Activities
Phase 1: Engage		
Take a walk around the neighborhood and look for signs of erosion. Use a digital camera to record evidence.	Observe the neighborhood.	
Phase 2: Explore #1: Wind Erosion		
	Simulate wind erosion.	Observe. Record data. Write up findings.
Phase 2: Explore #2: Water Erosion		
	Simulate water erosion.	Observe. Record data. Write up findings.
Phase 2: Explore #3 Erosion by Ice		
	Simulate erosion by ice.	Observe. Record data. Write up findings.
Phase 3: Explain		
Participate in guided discussion to verbalize findings. Students use their findings as support.		Begin Multi-Flow tool.
Phase 4: Elaborate		
Search for more examples of how wind and water continually change the Earth's landscape, using teacher read aloud, nonfiction books, and videos. Use open-ended questions to encourage critical thinking.	Become Information Detectives.	Add to Multi-Flow tool. Begin Short- and Long-Term Consequences thinking tool. Make text connections.
Phase 5: Evaluate		
Two options for applying knowledge to realistic situation		Writing, based on information on Multi-Flow tool, observation

Figure 10:1 A framework for science literacy.

Teacher Background

Weathering is the process of breaking down earth materials by physical and chemical means. Soil, which is a product of weathering and biologic action, is a mixture of earth materials (i.e., sand, silt, and clay), living plants, animals, and organic debris. The top layer of soil is rich with nutrients and supports plant life on Earth.

Erosion is the process of carrying away the broken-down material. Erosion is caused by wind, water, ice, and gravity. Erosion by running water is the greatest cause of soil loss. Gravity makes water flow downhill. When land is barren of plant life, water runs across bare soil and takes soil with it. Gullies or miniature river valleys are formed and grow larger with each new rainfall. The steeper the hill, the faster the water flows, increasing the rate of erosion.

Wind can also cause erosion. Very fine particles of soil can be picked up by the wind and transported over great distances. Shifting sand dunes move due to wind erosion. The Dust Bowl of the 1930s was also caused by wind erosion. The size of the particles picked up by the wind, the climate, the make-up of the surface of the Earth, and lack of plants can play a role in wind erosion.

Glaciers move Earth materials from one place to another. Again, gravity causes glaciers to move. Glaciers also cause erosion by abrasion and plucking. Abrasion occurs when rocks at the bottom of the glacier grind and scrape the Earth as the glacier moves. Plucking occurs when a glacier moves, melts, and refreezes, taking some of the Earth materials with it as it moves. As the glacier melts, it deposits materials that were once frozen in the ice. Additional materials are washed out of the glacier by streams.

Estimated Time: 4 periods, approximately 60 minutes each

Materials Needed: See the Teacher Shopping List in the Teacher's Resources section of this unit.

Phase 1: Engage

Materials Needed:

Digital camera for the teacher

Procedure:

Take a walk around the neighborhood with your class and look for signs of erosion. Take photos of the evidence of erosion. If erosion is not active near your school, visit a construction site, or share photos with your students of a construction site that they might be aware of. Prompt student thinking by asking:

- What do you see?

- What seems to be moving?

- Why do you think this area is disturbed?

- What could we do to protect the soil and rocks to keep them in place? Do you see any evidence of this happening?

- Predict what would happen if the soil and rocks were transported away.

Phase 2: Explore #1: Wind Erosion

Materials Needed:

Student Observation sheets, one per student *or* science notebooks

Newspaper to cover desks

Safety glasses, one per student

Drinking straws, one per student

4 x 6 inch index cards, two per group

Plastic teaspoons, one per group

Cup of dry topsoil, one per group

Cup of dry sand, one per group

Plastic cups, two per group

Advanced Preparation:

Cover desks with newspapers and distribute materials. Have dry sand and topsoil available in a tub or bucket for easy access.

Procedure:

1. Give each child a Student Observation sheet, *or* have students recreate it in their science notebooks. Students will identify *wind* for this part of the investigation. Give each child safety glasses and a straw.

2. Divide the class into groups of 3 or 4 students. Give each group two 4 x 6 inch index cards, a plastic teaspoon, and a plastic cup of sand and soil. Instruct students to put a spoonful of dry sand on one index card and a spoonful of dry soil on the other.

3. Direct students' attention to the Student Observation sheet. Ask students to divide both boxes in half and label one half "Sand" and the other half "Soil." Tell them to observe carefully the two piles on their index cards and draw a picture to represent what each pile looks like.

4. Tell students that in this investigation, they are going to use the straw to represent the wind blowing. Model using the straw to blow on a spoonful of soil or sand. Blow softly at first, then blow harder.

5. Instruct students to blow across the sand and soil and observe. Students may pile up the sand and soil and repeat as necessary.

6. After students finish, bring the class together for a whole-group discussion. Ask questions such as:

- Compare what happened when you blew on the sand and the soil. (A lot of the soil moved. Some of the sand moved.)

- Explain the relationship of the wind speed (how hard you blew) and how much material is transported. (With stronger wind, more of the sand and soil moved. With less wind, less of the sand and soil moved.)

- Explain the relationship of a constant wind speed and how soil and sand is transported. (With less wind, only soil is moved. With stronger wind, more sand moved.)

- Speculate why farmers might find your observations interesting. (Small amounts of wind can remove valuable soil.)

7. Have students return to their Student Observation sheet or science notebooks and draw a picture of what their piles now look like. Have them use their pictures to help them write a response to the question on the second page. Remind students that when scientists write about findings of their investigations, they make reference to the *data* they collected during the experiment. In this investigation, student drawings are the "data" so they should refer to the drawings in their written explanation.

Phase 2: Explore #2: Water Erosion

Materials Needed:

Student Observation sheet, one per student *or* science notebooks

Paint trays, one for each group

Plastic cups, two per group

Styrofoam cups, three per group

Dry topsoil

Dry sand

Bucket of water

1/2 cup measure, two are needed

1/3 cup measure, one is needed

Advanced Preparation:

Have dry sand and dry topsoil in individual tubs or buckets for easy access. If desired, label the paint trays near the top of the slope to indicate where students should put the sand and soil. Each group of students will receive three styrofoam cups; one of them needs to be prepunctured. Use a paper clip to put a hole on the side at the bottom of the cup.

Procedure:

1. Give each child a Student Observation sheet *or* refer them to their science notebooks. Have students identify *water* for this part of the investigation.

2. Give each group a paint tray; three styrofoam cups (one which has been prepunctured); and two plastic cups. Have students scoop 1/2 cup of sand and 1/2 cup of soil to put in their plastic cups. Instruct students to pour the sand on one side of the high end of their paint trays and pour the soil on the other side of the high end of their paint trays.

3. Direct students' attention to the Student Observation sheet. Ask students to divide both boxes in half and label one half "Sand" and the other half "Soil." Tell them to observe the two piles carefully and draw a picture to represent what each pile looks like.

4. Take the bucket of water around and have 1 student measure out 1/2 cup of water and put in the cup without a hole.

5. Tell students to pour this water into the cup with the hole while holding it over the sand in the tray. Tell students that in this investigation, the water represents rain. Ask students to observe carefully what is happening as the water comes in contact with the sand. Tell students to talk to their group about what they see happening to the sand.

6. Now have students pour the water over the soil and observe.

7. Discuss the results of water traveling across the sand and the soil. Ask students questions such as the following:

   - Compare what happened when you dripped water on the sand and on the soil. (As water dripped on the sand, the water traveled through the sand, then down the pan, leaving much of the sand behind. As water dripped on the soil, the water picked up more soil and then traveled down the pan, taking more of the soil with it. Less of the sand traveled down with the water as compared to the soil.)

   - Explain the relationship of the water to the movement of the sand and the soil. (The water will move easily through the sand. Some of the water seeps into the sand. At the end of the tray, students should see more water with little sand in it. The water will also drain from the sand, leaving most of the sand dry. When the water moves across the soil, it will take some of the soil with it and students should see more soil and less water at the end of the tray.)

   - Speculate why you observed this.

8. Explain why students saw these differences. Tell them two factors affect the outcome, porosity (i.e., the open space between grains), and the size

of the particles. The sand has larger particles and a higher porosity. So, more water drains away, and because the particles are bigger, they are harder to move and are more resistant to *erosion*. Erosion is the transport of geologic materials. A small amount of sand is transported to the bottom of the tray. On the other hand, the soil is made of smaller particles and has lower porosity. Because the particles are smaller, rather than seeping through the soil, the water runs off and creates erosion. That is why more soil traveled with the water to the end of the tray.

9. Have students return to their Student Observation sheet or science notebooks and draw a picture of what their sand and soil now look like. Have them use their pictures to help them write a response to the question on the second page. Remind students that when scientists write about findings of their investigations, they make reference to the *data* they collected during the experiment. In this investigation, student drawings are the "data" so they should refer to the drawings in their written explanation.

Phase 2: Explore #3: Erosion by Ice

Materials Needed:

Student Observation sheets, one per student *or* science notebooks

Rocks frozen in ice, one per group

Paint trays with sand and soil in it, one per group

Advanced Preparation:

Fill large paper cups of water with varying sizes of rock (three quarters full of rock) and freeze. Different sizes of beads may be used if rock is not available. On the day of the demonstration, thaw just enough to remove the ice or tear a paper cup off of ice. Set up a paint tray with a combination of sand and soil. Place the ice cube (glacier) at the top of the slope of the paint tray just at the top of the incline (see Figure 10:2).

Figure 10:2 As "glacial" ice melts, coarse material is deposited on the land surface, and streams erode and transport material.

Procedure:

1. Give each student a Student Observation sheet *or* a science notebook. Students will identify *ice* for this part of the investigation.

2. Have students draw the set-up of the investigation.

3. Tell students that in this investigation, the ice cube represents a glacier. Ask students to predict what will happen as the ice cube melts. This will take some time.

4. Periodically, check the ice cube and note any change in its position. Have students draw these changes and record the time they were observed.

5. Repeat the process until the ice cube is fully melted.

6. Discuss the results with students. Ask questions such as the following:

   • Explain the relationship between the melting ice and the movement of geologic materials. (As the ice melted, the water flowed away, making a "river" and transporting some soil. The rocks in the ice were gradually lowered onto the soil and piled up, making a little ridge.)

   • Describe any changes caused by the ice to the adjacent soil. (The melting ice pushed the rocks and soil as it melted.)

Phase 3: Explain

Materials Needed:

Multi-Flow tool, one per student

Student Observation sheet, one per student

Procedure:

1. Discuss with students the findings of their investigations. Tell them scientists use a technical word to tell about what we have done. It is called *erosion*. Erosion is the transport of geologic materials. Our experiments were examples of erosion. During questioning, have students support their explanations by showing their recorded observations from the Student Observation sheet *or* their science notebooks. Ask the following:

   • How did we demonstrate erosion in our first experiment? (We blew wind on the sand and soil, and now the original pile of sand or soil is smaller.)

2. Introduce the Multi-Flow tool. Direct students to record in the Causes column, "blowing wind on the sand and soil." Continue with the discussion.

- Why did the original pile become smaller? What happened to all of the sand or soil? (Some of the sand or soil was moved to another place.)

Have students record this in the Effects column of the Multi-Flow tool.

- In our second experiment, how did we show erosion? (The water caused the some of the sand or soil to move downhill.)

- What are some other examples of ways in which water causes erosion? (Sometimes, I see farmer's fields with gullies in them. I saw a steep river bank; I think it was eroded by a river. I was at the beach and saw sand getting pushed around.)

Add to the Causes and Effects columns on the Multi-Flow tool.

- In our third experiment, how did we demonstrate erosion? (The melting ice washed some of the sand and soil down the slope.)

- How did we demonstrate deposition? (As the rocks melted out of the ice, they piled up to make a little ridge.)

Explain that geologists call this a *moraine*.

- Can you think of any more examples of ice causing erosion? (Sometimes, the rocks frozen in the bottom of the glacier might scratch or scrape the rocks under it.)

Add to the Causes and Effects columns on the Multi-Flow tool.

Phase 4: Elaborate

Materials Needed:

The Sun, the Wind, and the Rain by Lisa Westberg Peters, one copy

Multi-Flow tool (same copy used in Explain)

Internet access with projector

Sticky notes, one packet for each pair of students

Variety of trade books listed in the Teacher Resources section of this unit

Procedure:

1. Introduce the book, *The Sun, the Wind, and the Rain* by Lisa Westberg Peters. In this book, a girl builds a sand mountain on the beach and then watches as wind, rain, and waves wear it down. The analogies to real Earth processes are excellent and are illustrated with accurate art on the facing page.

2. Tell students you will be reading the book aloud and their job is to listen carefully. Tell them their purpose for listening is to learn how wind and water affect Elizabeth's mountain, as well as the whole Earth's landscape.

3. As you are reading aloud, be sure to make some "text to self" connections, where you verbalize similarities between the investigations students just completed with the content of *The Sun, the Wind, and the Rain*. For example, after reading page 12, which states: "An afternoon shower blew in suddenly and Elizabeth watched as the water began to destroy the mountain she had worked so hard to build," and say something like: "This reminds me of our experiment when we poured water on sand. But our sand was not destroyed like Elizabeth's mountain was. Hmmmm. Maybe if we had poured more water on it, it would have reacted like the sand mountain in this book." Continue modeling how to connect the knowledge gained from doing the experiments with information found in this text.

4. Next, go to http://www.unitedstreamingvideo.com and access the video *TLC Elementary School: Protecting our Planet*. Tell your students that their purpose for viewing it is to find examples of erosion that remind them of the experiments they conducted. View the 8-minute section of the film called "Erosion," which visually shows students examples of how water and ice cause various types of erosion. Discuss briefly, encouraging students to make "text to text" connections by relating new information in the video (i.e., text) with the book *The Sun, the Wind, and the Rain*, or their investigations.

    You might also consider viewing the video *Weathering and Erosion* also available at http://www.unitedstreamingvideo.com This 20-minute video gives more detailed explanations of landforms, weathering, erosion, and agents of change, including mankind. Tell your students their purpose for viewing is to find examples of erosion that remind them of the experiments they conducted. Discuss briefly, encouraging students to make "text to text" connections by relating information in the video (i.e., text) with either the book *The Sun, the Wind, and the Rain*, or their investigations.

5. Encourage students to add information to their Multi-Flow tool, based on what they observed in the video and book.

6. Next, pair students and give each pair a packet of sticky notes and a variety of trade books. Tell students they are going to become Information Detectives. Each set of detectives is going to look for an example of weathering or erosion and its affects on the Earth. Write on the board the key question of the unit: *How do water, wind, and ice cause changes on*

Earth? This is the mystery they will be trying to solve. When detectives find an example, they will use a sticky note to mark the page. Encourage students to also use photos as evidence, just as the police do when solving a crime.

7. Follow up with a discussion that helps your students make "text to world" connections by using the Short- and Long-Term Consequences thinking tool. This thinking tool can be an extension of the Multi-Flow tool and helps students broaden their perspective by analyzing physical, psychological, and ethical consequences or outcomes. Select one Cause and Effect example a student pair has identified, and ask the class to consider what might be a short-term consequence. For example, if a photo of blowing sand is selected, a short-term consequence might be: Sand gets in your eyes if you are on the beach. Accept all reasonable answers from students, and encourage detectives to share their "evidence," marked with their sticky notes.

8. Using the same initial example, ask students to consider what might be a long-term consequence. For example, if large amounts of sand are blown away, dunes along the shoreline might be eroded. This would affect vegetation, animals, and the people living along the shoreline. You might ask:

   • How would you feel if your house fell into the water because the dune it was built on had eroded?

   • How would you feel if your house and yard were being buried by a migrating dune?

   • If you were an animal living in the dune, how might you adapt to its changes?

   These answers require a psychological response.

9. Continue with the same example and tell students when people own a home, they buy insurance that pays the homeowner money if the home is damaged. Ask:

   • Is it fair for insurance companies to pay for rebuilding homes in areas where erosion (or flooding) is likely to continue?

   This answer requires an ethical response. Encourage detectives to think about current events, such as the effects and aftermath of hurricanes or tornadoes.

10. Select a different example, and repeat the process.

   • What might be a short-term consequence? What is your evidence?

   • What might be a long-term consequence? What is your evidence?

   Be sure to elicit physical, psychological, and ethical responses.

Phase 5: Evaluate

Materials Needed:

> Away We Go! Student Evaluation sheet, one for each student
>
> Completed Multi-Flow tools

Procedure:

> Give students the Away We Go! Student Evaluation sheet, which contains the scenario below. You may also choose a similar scenario, based on your neighborhood.
>
>> In the spring, road construction began on the highway near Jose's house. Jose observed a cone-shaped pile of soil approximately 6 feet tall left by the construction crew. A heavy rain occurred, lasting 2 days. After the rain, Jose noticed the pile had changed.
>
> Students will draw a picture and write an explanation of what happened using information located on their Multi-Flow tools. Encourage students to also comment on the short- and long-term consequences of erosion.
>
> Or, take another walk around the neighborhood or visit nearby construction areas and look for signs of erosion. Take the digital camera and let students take pictures of the evidence of erosion. When you return to the classroom, have students print the photos and write a description to explain what happened. Encourage them to include information from their Multi-Flow tool, and comment on the short- and long-term consequences of erosion.

Teacher Resources

Trade Books

Banks, Kate. (2001). *A gift from the sea.* [Georg Hallensleben, Illus.] New York: Francis Foster Books, 32 pp.; ISBN: 0-374-32566-9 (hardcover); $15.99.

> A beautifully illustrated picture book about a boy who finds a rock on a beach. The book traces the long history of the rock and describes how a volcano, glacier, erosion, and a river have influenced it. This book is excellent for introducing the rock cycle.

de Paola, Tommie. (1977). *The quicksand book.* New York: Holiday House, 27 pp.; ISBN: 0-8234-0532-X (paperback); $5.95.

> This classic story explains everything a child might want to know about quicksand: where and how it forms; why people sink into quicksand; what happens

to animals in quicksand; how people can watch out for quicksand; and what people should do if they fall into quicksand. This book includes simplistic, yet effective, visual aids.

Fowler, Allan. (2001). *North America.* New York: Children's Press, 32 pp.; ISBN: 0-516-27299-3 (paperback); $5.95

Part of the *Rookie Read About Geography* series, this book is a simple introduction to the geographic features, people, and animals of the continent of North America. It includes a glossary, index, and spectacular color photographs.

Gallant, Roy A. (1999). *Glaciers.* New York: Franklin Watts, 64 pp.; ISBN: 0-531-15956-6 (paperback); $6.95.

Using stunning photographs and thorough explanations, this clearly written and informative book explains the nature of glaciers, their formation, and movement. It also explores how glaciers have changed the surface of the Earth and how scientists learn about the past from cores of glaciers. A section on where glaciers can be found today neglects to mention the glaciers of western Canada.

Gibbons, Gail. (1996). *Deserts.* New York: Holiday House, 30 pp.; ISBN: 0-8234-1519-8 (paperback); $6.95.

The text and illustrations briefly describe the formation and characteristics of deserts around the world. Full-color illustrations depict the flora and fauna that thrive in this harsh environment, but no distinction is made between the plants and animals found in the American West and those of the other desert areas. The lifestyle of desert people is touched upon, but there is no indication as to where these nomads might roam.

Hiscock, Bruce. (1988). *The big rock.* New York: Aladdin, 26 pp.; ISBN: 0-689-82958-2 (paperback); $5.99.

Outstanding! Excellent! A big rock in New England is used as the center point of the rock cycle. Numerous geologic processes are described accurately and well. The art is excellent and accurate. A female geologist is also shown.

Hooper, Meredith. (1996). *The pebble in my pocket: A history of our Earth.* [Chris Coady, Illus.] New York: Viking, 31 pp.; ISBN: 0-670-86259-2 (hardcover); $17.99.

Few books for children are done this well. This book fuses geologic time with life, evolution, changes in the landscape, and changes in geologic materials, such as sand, mud, and rock. The geologic timeline provides a colorful visual overview of the Earth's history.

Llewellyn, Claire. (1998). *Glaciers.* Chicago: Heinemann, 32 pp.; ISBN: 1-58810-973-9 (paperback); $6.50.

> This book has excellent text, photos, and selection of content that describes how glaciers are formed, different kinds of glaciers, what their surface is like, how they change the landscape, how they move rocks, and how they provide fresh water. The three maps of glaciers are excellent. This book also includes a table of contents, glossary, bibliography, and index.

Locker, Thomas. (2001). *Mountain dance.* San Diego: Silver Whistle, 30 pp.; ISBN: 0-15-202622-3 (hardcover); $16.00.

> This book engages the reader with excellent, brief descriptions of the common types of mountains. Accurate paintings are a perfect match. Locker is a writer and artist—not an expert in geology—and in the About Mountains section, he implies magma is involved in making fault-block mountains. This is not true; they result from heating and stretching of the lithosphere. However, the overall high quality of the book overrides this minor flaw.

Owen, Andy, & Ashwell, Miranda. (1998). *Mountains.* Des Plaines, IL: Heinemann Interactive, 32 pp.; ISBN: 1-5881-0976-3 (paperback); $7.25.

> Amazing photographs and well-designed diagrams! This book explains how mountains are formed, their parts, sources of water, and hazards and also provides several maps and the diagrams to explain them. This book includes a table of contents, glossary, bibliography, and index.

Peters, Lisa Westberg. (1988). *The sun, the wind, and the rain.* [Ted Rand, Illus.] New York: Henry Holt, 28 pp.; ISBN: 0-8050-1481-0 (paperback); $6.95.

> Outstanding! A girl builds a sand mountain on the beach and then watches as wind, rain, and waves wear it down. The analogies to real Earth processes are excellent and illustrated with accurate art on the facing page.

Simon, Seymour. (1994). *Mountains.* New York: Mulberry Paperback, 28 pp.; ISBN: 0-688-15477-8 (paperback); $6.99.

> Spectacular full-color photographs and well-designed diagrams! Information is provided about the major ranges and the different types of mountain formations. This book also covers the forces of erosion, their effect on weather and climate, and their impact on vegetation and animals, including humans.

Spickert, Diane Nelson. (2000). *Earthsteps: A rock's journey through time.* [Marianne Wallace, Illus.] Golden, CO: Fulcrum Kids, 32 pp.; ISBN: 1-55591-986-3 (hardcover); $17.95.

> Wow! The introduction alone is outstanding. Rarely in a children's book is the geologic time scale so well explained. Process, material, and time are intertwined in a good story of the rock cycle. This book could be used to springboard your class anywhere in geology!

Trueit, Trudi Strain. (2003). *Rocks, gems, and minerals.* New York: Franklin Watts, 63 pp.; ISBN: 0-531-16241-9 (paperback); $8.95.

> Rocks, gems, and minerals are the basic things that make up the Earth. This book explores how heat, pressure, water, wind, and time combine to make rocks, gems, and minerals. Trueit explains how these materials are common, yet precious and essential, substances. Good glossary and index. Illustrative photographs, too. This makes for a good reference book.

Web Sites

Note. The authors realize that Web site addresses are not guaranteed to work, as they change, move, or are removed from the Internet. Therefore, the authors have included the sponsoring organization of the Web site in the event the link provided here does not work. Simply type in the name of the organization in your search engine, and it will direct you to a new URL.

U.S. Geological Survey Landslide Hazards Program at:

> http://landslides.usgs.gov/learningeducation/images.php

This Web site is rich in content and images. It summarizes some of the most recent and most significant landslides from around the world.

How Glaciers Erode and Transport Sediment (has pictures) at:

> www.geography-site.co.uk/pages/physical.html#Glaciers

This Web site works much like a glossary. It provides thorough lists of glacial topics and features. By following a link, you can learn details and see excellent images related to the topic.

The Dirt on Soil by Discovery School at:

> http://school.discovery.com/schooladventures/soil/recipe_soil.html

This well-thought-out Web site explores the major factors that influence soil: parent rock, weathering, time, and biology and includes an interactive Soil Safari.

Videos

Earth: A First Look

> Available at: http://www.unitedstreaming.com

Oceans, mountains, rivers, and volcanoes are major features of the Earth. This video describes these features and explains how water, air, and land provide valuable resources. The structure of the Earth, including the crust, mantle, and core, is also explained. Students will see that the Earth's crust changes because of earthquakes, volcanoes, weathering, and erosion. (20 minutes) Recommended for Grades 1–3.

Junior Geologist: Our Planet Earth.

> Available at: http://www.unitedstreaming.com

From views of the Earth from a space shuttle, students begin their exploration of the science of geology. Spectacular footage of the many different land formations across our planet's surface help to excite students about the geology of our planet. Segments addressed include: What is geology? What is inside the Earth? How has the Earth changed over time? and Why does the Earth's surface differ from place to place? (11 minutes) Recommended for Grades 2–4.

Physical Geography

> Available at: http://www.unitedstreaming.com

Physical Geography examines the Earth's oceans and freshwater sources, the major continents and basic landforms, and the changes that are constantly occurring to the Earth's surface. The video also examines the world's climates and the factors that shape those climate zones, as well as the world's natural resources and the many ways people use them. In addition, this video considers how these aspects affect not only where people live, but also how they live as well. Through live-action video footage, graphics, and animation, this comprehensive program helps students to better understand the physical forms and forces that create the world around us and encourages them to apply this knowledge to gain an understanding of human, or cultural, geography. In this context, students will also be introduced to basic map and globe skills. (29 minutes) Recommended for Grades 3–5.

The Living Earth

> Available at: http://www.unitedstreaming.com

Explore what life was like on Earth hundreds of millions of years ago. Learn about the super-continent Pangaea and how the planet's shifting plates of crust formed the world we know today. Then, follow scientists as they uncover dinosaur fossils. Produced by Discovery Channel School. (27 minutes) Recommended for Grades 3–5.

AWAY WE GO!
Student Observation Sheet

Name _____ Date _____

Wind, Water, Ice (Circle one)

Draw a picture before erosion.

```



```

Draw a picture after erosion.

```



```

Full size form available at www.Christopher-Gordon.com/authors/KingMattox-shtml

AWAY WE GO!
Student Observation Sheet, Page 2

Name _____   Date _____

Wind, Water, Ice (Circle one)

Describe what happened to the soil in the investigation before and after erosion. Use the drawing of the investigation to help you.

_____

_____

_____

_____

_____

_____

_____

_____

_____

_____

Full size form available at www.Christopher-Gordon.com/authors/KingMattox-shtml

AWAY WE GO!
Student Evaluation

Name _____   Date _____

In the spring, road construction began on the highway near Jose's house. Jose observed a cone-shaped pile of soil approximately 6 feet tall left by the construction crew. A heavy rain occurred lasting 2 days. After the rain, Jose noticed the pile had changed.

Task: Draw and write an explanation to show what happened to the soil after the storm.

Full size form available at www.Christopher-Gordon.com/authors/KingMattox-shtml

Multi-Flow Learning Tool about Erosion

List what you know about the causes and effects of erosion by wind, water, and ice.

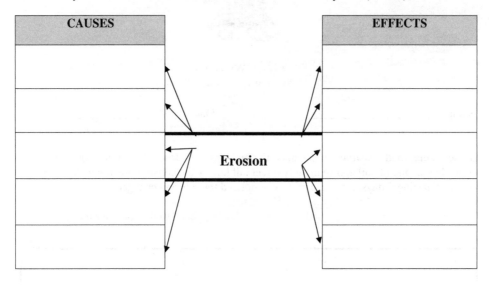

Full size form available at www.Christopher-Gordon.com/authors/KingMattox-shtml

Teacher's Shopping List for Away We Go!

Note: Provide enough materials for students to work in groups of three or four.

☐ Safety glasses, one pair for each child

☐ Dry sand

☐ Dry topsoil (Do not use potting soil.)

☐ 1/3 measuring cup

☐ Index cards

☐ Paint tray (one per group)

☐ One straw per child

☐ Styrofoam cups

☐ Plastic cups

☐ Water

☐ Bucket for water

☐ Two tubs for sand and soil

☐ Copies of the Student Observation sheet (three per student) *or* science notebooks

☐ Newspaper to cover work area

☐ Sticky notes (one packet for each pair of students)

☐ One digital camera for the teacher

☐ *The Sun, the Wind, and the Rain* by Lisa Westberg Peters

☐ Internet access with projector

☐ Trade books listed in the Teacher Resources section of this unit

Full size form available at www.Christopher-Gordon.com/authors/KingMattox-shtml

Chapter 11

The Earth in the Solar System

Introduction

We've observed that students are naturally curious about the world around them, as well as the objects they see in the sky. Since it is difficult to provide students with inquiry-based activities and investigations about the actual solar system, this series of lessons uses models and simulations to encourage students to conduct creative, thoughtful investigations. The activities are designed to deepen their understanding and directly address common misconceptions about our solar system.

The lessons in this unit will focus on the physical descriptions of the sun, planets, and natural satellites or moons, and activities will be based on student observations. The activities are designed to provide teachers with the "tools" to help students develop a conceptual understanding of the nature of the solar system. Activities focus on the following: comparing the sun, moon, and Earth; and exploring the general characteristics of the planets.

Big Idea: Two objects, the sun and the moon, dominate the sky. Comparing and contrasting their characteristics with those of Earth provide a basic understanding of the solar system.

Key Science Questions: How do the sun, moon, and Earth compare in respect to their physical characteristics? What are the important characteristics of each planet?

National Science Standard: The sun, moon, and stars all have properties that can be observed and described in relationship to Earth. Other members of the solar system also have unique characteristics and properties.

National Language Arts Standards: Students read a wide range of print and nonprint texts to build understanding. Students apply a range of strategies to comprehend, interpret, evaluate, and appreciate texts. Students adjust their use of spoken, written, and visual language to communicate effectively. Students conduct research by generating questions. Students participate as knowledgeable, reflective, creative, and critical members of a literacy community.

Thinking Tools: Meaning Grid tool

Action	Hands-On Activities	Literacy/Thinking Activities
Phase 1: Engage		
Assess students' prior knowledge of the Earth, moon, and sun.		Create a three-column chart
Phase 2: Explore #1: Exploring the Moon through Literature		
Students will collect facts about characteristics of the moon.		Research moon facts. Introduce the Meaning Grid tool.
Phase 2: Explore #2: Comparing and Contrasting the Earth, Moon, and Sun		
	Create a human graphic organizer.	Research Earth, moon, and sun facts. Practice and explain metacognitive thinking. Use the Meaning Grid tool. Justify location within the human graphic organizer.
Phase 2: Explore #3: Scale Model of the Sun, Earth, and Moon		
The teacher constructs a scale model of the inner solar system.	Walk around the solar system.	
Phase 3: Explain		
		Discuss key characteristics. Use information on the Meaning Grid tool.
Phase 2: Explore #4: Super Solar System		
Students collect facts about all planets in the Milky Way galaxy.		Begin paper graphic organizer.
Phase 2: Explore #5: Using *Postcards from Pluto*		
Collect new planet facts.		Read, self-monitor comprehension, summarize text. Add to graphic organizer.
Phase 4: Elaborate		
	Students physically recreate the solar system.	
Phase 5: Evaluate		
Demonstrate factual knowledge of planets.		Students create and write postcards about planets and send them home.

Figure 11:1 A framework for science literacy.

Teacher Background

Comparing and contrasting the Earth, sun, and moon is an efficient way to teach the characteristics of stars, planets, and moons and is an important way to convey content knowledge about the solar system. The sun is a middle-aged (4.6 billion years old), average star made mostly of the gases hydrogen and helium, which release light and other radiation as the gases undergo nuclear reactions. The sun is about 800 times larger than the Earth, and because of its great mass, the gravity of the sun holds the planets in their orbits. The Earth is the third planet from the sun. It is unique in its dense, oxygen-rich atmosphere, abundant water and life, moderate surface temperature, and active tectonics. It is also unique because the moon orbits the Earth. The moon's early history, similar to Earth, was dominated by cratering and volcanism. Unlike the Earth, the moon has no atmosphere and undergoes extreme temperature changes over a monthly period. There is no life on the moon, but frozen water has been discovered at its poles.

A planet is a large, spherical object that orbits a star. Pluto, which was once thought to be a planet, is now considered to be a "dwarf" planet. Recent discoveries of multiple objects in a Pluto-like orbit has prompted the International Astronomical Union (IAU) to revise the definition of "planet." Thus, in late 2006, our sun is orbited by eight planets. Outward from the sun, the planets are: Mercury, Venus, Earth, Mars, Jupiter, Saturn, Uranus, and Neptune. The mnemonic devices we once learned to help us remember the order of the planets no longer make sense. Such is the nature of science, which is continually changing based on observation and new discoveries.

The first four planets (Mercury, Venus, Earth, and Mars) are relatively small and rocky. Because of their rocky characteristics, they are called terrestrial planets. In addition, craters are observed on each terrestrial planet. Whereas volcanism occurred during specific periods on Venus and Mars, we continue to observe volcanic activity on Earth today. At one time in the past, water was present on Mars, and water is certainly vital to Earth's past and present.

The next four planets (Jupiter, Saturn, Uranus, and Neptune) are made of gas and are much larger than the terrestrial planets. These planets are called gas giants. Pluto, a "dwarf" planet, is about one fifth the diameter of the Earth and is rocky. Its atmosphere is frozen on the surface. NASA is exploring the solar system with many new space missions, and new discoveries are announced every week. To learn the latest, visit NASA's Web site at http://www.nasa.gov

Estimated Time: 4 periods, approximately 60 minutes each

Phase 1: Engage

Materials Needed:

Science notebooks, one for each student

Procedure:

1. Have students create three columns in their science notebooks. Write Earth, moon, or sun at the top of each column. Ask students to write from memory at least three characteristics of each of these members of the solar system.

2. After the students have had a few minutes to reflect on their perceptions, compile a list on the board. Right or wrong answers are not important. These responses provide a starting place for the activities that follow. During the Explore activities, you can address any misconceptions revealed during this Engage activity.

Phase 2: Explore #1: Exploring the Moon through Literature

Materials Needed:

Sticky notes, one for each student

Poster paper

Transparency of a blank Meaning Grid tool

Meaning Grid tool, one copy for each student

The following books, which contain information about the Earth's moon (see the Teacher Resources section of this unit for more information on titles):

My First Book of Space by Rosanna Hansen and Robert A. Bell

Planets Around the Sun by Seymour Simon

Planets by Jennifer Dussling

Postcards from Pluto by Loreen Leedy

Solar System by Gregory Vogt

So That's How the Moon Changes Shape! by Allan Fowler

The Moon by Niki Walker

The Moon Seems to Change by Frankyn M. Branley

Procedure:

1. Explain to students that scientists often make predictions that need to be verified somehow. One way to verify predictions is to compare them with a reliable source. Today, we will use several books as reliable sources so that we can check our predictions for accuracy. We will need to locate established facts about the moon, then determine whether or not these characteristics support the information we recorded in our science notebooks.

2. Hold a brief discussion on the best ways to quickly find information. These may include: looking at the illustrations; using the table of contents, index, and glossary; reading boldface words, headings, and subheadings; and skim-read the paragraphs.

3. Model for students, by thinking aloud, the text features good readers use to locate specific information. Try to include a *prediction, a thought about a term, rereading, summarizing, asking a question, making a connection to prior knowledge*. Say things such as the following:

    "I wonder if this book has a table of contents or an index. Books of this length usually do because it helps the reader find information easily and quickly." (This makes a connection to prior knowledge.) If the book does, show students how you would go to the page referenced and begin reading the information on the page.

    "I predict this page will give me information on _____." (This models the making of a prediction.)

    Depending on the text chosen, it may be helpful to say:

    "I wonder if there are any boldfaced words or illustrations in here that would help me." (This models the use of target words and illustrations to locate information.) Or, "Hmmm, I bet I can use these headings and subheadings to help me locate what I need. I'm going to skim-read and find out."

4. When you have found a characteristic, use a sticky note to mark the page, and record the characteristic about the moon on the sticky note.

5. Pair students. Working with a partner, they should each find and record one characteristic about the moon. First, they will mark the page with a sticky note. Next, they will record the characteristics on the sticky note. Remind students to use the table of contents, the index, glossary, boldface words, and illustrations, as well as headings and subheadings, to locate the information they need.

6. When students are finished, go around the room and have each student share with the class what he or she has found. Record facts on the board, and omit duplicate information.

7. On poster paper, write the title "Characteristics of the Moon." Write the following categories under the title: Size, Appearance, Composition, Motion. Discuss with students what each category means and model placing one characteristic listed on the board under the appropriate label. Students will then sort the list of characteristics on the board into the four categories. If one category does not have a corresponding characteristic, tell students this is okay, since they will be collecting additional information throughout the unit. Sorting can be done as a class, in pairs, or individually, depending on teacher preference. Record the class sort on the "Characteristics of the Moon" poster.

8. Then, introduce the Meaning Grid tool. Tell them they will use this thinking tool to help them process and reflect on the information they will learn throughout this unit. Using a blank Meaning Grid tool, record the categories and a few of the moon's characteristics from the "Characteristics of the Moon" poster in the left column. Explain that when a relationship occurs between the characteristics in the left column and a label in the horizontal column, the intersecting box should be marked with an asterisk (*). If no relationship exists, the intersecting box should be marked with an X. For now, focus only on yes and no relationships, but tell students this is the first step for completing the Meaning Grid tool. See the Meaning Grid Tool #1 at the end of the unit as an example. The class will add to it as the unit progresses, and it can also be used throughout this unit as a means of formative assessment.

Phase 2: Explore #2: Comparing and Contrasting the Earth, Moon, and Sun

Materials Needed:

Earth, moon, and sun printed labels

Earth, moon, and sun characteristics, printed on index cards, one card for each student

Books about the sun and Earth (choose from those recommended in the Teacher Resources section of this unit)

Sticky notes, two per student

Meaning Grid Tool #1 begun in Explore #1

Thinker's Guide, one copy for each student

Poster paper, three to five sheets

Advanced Preparation:

Mount the labels for Earth, moon, and sun on the poster board, and place them in three different areas of the classroom. You will want considerable space between the labels. Print the characteristics and mount them on index cards. The purpose of this activity is for students to develop a better understanding of the Earth, moon, and sun by comparing the characteristics of each. The classroom will be used to model a Venn diagram. This phase of the lesson will also be used to encourage students to use the strategies you modeled to locate information quickly. It is designed to help them be metacognitively aware of how they are using literacy and thinking tools.

Procedure:

1. Explain to students that the class is going to create a huge graphic organizer with their bodies. However, before that can take place, they need to do additional fact checking on characteristics of the Earth and sun. Tell them that even though they most likely already know a lot about each, it is important to confirm or clarify their prior knowledge. Remind students this is a practice commonly used by scientists, and the reason scientists use a variety of sources is to verify their thinking to be sure it is accurate.

2. Distribute books on the Earth and sun to pairs of students. Explain to students their task is to find at least one characteristic about the Earth and one characteristic about the sun, so that they can add information to their Meaning Grid tool. They will also practice the strategies good readers use when they are locating information. Ask students to recall the thinking processes you used to find information about the moon. Distribute the Thinker's Guide to each student. Ask them to look at the thinking strategies listed on the left and recall the strategies you modeled when you located characteristics of the moon.

3. Explain that partners will observe and verbalize their thinking as they search for information on characteristics of the Earth and sun. As Partner 1 is searching for information and making his or her thinking explicit, Partner 2 documents what strategy or strategies the reader uses by putting a check in the appropriate box. When Partner 1 finds the information he or she is seeking, put a sticky note on the page. Switch roles so that Partner 1 observes Partner 2. Allow time for students to work in pairs to explore the books, looking for the necessary information. You may even want to group pairs of students so they become "experts" on one type of characteristic, such as Composition.

4. Remind students to use the same process they did when they looked for characteristics of the moon. After they have found a characteristic and marked the page with a sticky note, they will record either "Earth" or "sun" on the sticky note and the characteristic.

5. When students are finished locating their facts, go around the room and have students share the characteristics they found. When clarification is needed, encourage students to return to their sticky notes to locate specific information from the texts they used. Create two class charts, "Characteristics of the Sun" and "Characteristics of the Earth." Record facts, omitting duplicate information.

   Steps 6–10 guide your students in being reflective readers and thinkers. Students will explain what strategies they used when extracting information and justify their body placement in the class graphic organizer. They will critically evaluate the Meaning Grid tool and generate new questions for future research. These steps serve as an embedded assessment of their current state of knowledge.

6. To encourage students to be metacognitively aware of themselves while they are working, ask them which strategies and text aids they used, based on their Thinker's Guide. Remind students that good readers use a variety of text aids and strategies to help them. Ask students to reflect on and explain how the Thinker's Guide helped them locate information. Then, encourage students to reflect on their performance and create two goals for themselves. Ask:

   • How might you improve the next time we search for information?
   • What will you do differently?

7. Next, give each student an index card containing a characteristic. Use the ones included at the end of this unit, or create your own cards based on the lists your class generated. Then, have students physically move close to the station for Earth, moon, or sun, which is described by their card. Tell them it is okay to stand partway between the stations, if they think their characteristic describes more than one station. After students have positioned themselves around the room, have them read their characteristics. Ask the class if they agree with a classmate's location, or if this person needs to move closer to another station. Encourage the class to explain and verify their responses using the information they located in print.

8. Return to the Meaning Grid tool, and direct students' attention to the Descriptors column. (See the Meaning Grid Tool #2 at the end of this unit for an example, but it is not necessary to create a new, separate tool. You can simply add on to the original tool.) Review specific characteristics of

the moon that were written, such as "has many craters." Ask students to think about the information in the Descriptors column. Could it also apply to the Earth and sun? Discuss why or why not, based on the information they just located, and place the appropriate symbol in the cell. If students are uncertain of the relationship, record a question mark ("?") in the cell and tell them they will have the opportunity later to seek the answers to their questions. Ask students to think of other characteristics they might want to add to the Meaning Grid tool that would apply to the Earth and the sun. Guide them toward thinking about characteristics relating to appearance, composition, motion (orbit and rotation), size, and location in the solar system.

9. Add and sort additional characteristics to the Meaning Grid tool by taking from the posters created earlier. Encourage students to further process the information they are learning by writing reflective statements that help them interpret the symbols. For instance, if a characteristic has two of three rows with an X, we can conclude that this is one characteristic that the moon, Earth, and sun do not share, and we can write a statement to reflect our conclusion (see the Meaning Grid Tool #2 at the end of this unit for an example). This addition accomplishes the "process what we know" aspect of the Meaning Grid tool.

10. Look at the Meaning Grid tool one last time, and ask students to reflect on what they have recorded and learned. In what cells are there question marks? Get students to think of how they might reflect this uncertainty or lack of knowledge in the form of a question. For example, after looking at the Appearance category, we might ask, "Have the Earth, moon, and sun changed over their lifetimes, or have they always been like we see them now?" Have each student write one question about the Earth, sun, or moon that he or she would like answered. Other sample questions include:

- How do scientists know the age of Earth, moon, and sun?

- How does 1 day on the moon compare with 1 day on Earth?

- What would be needed for a moon colony to be self-sustaining?

Tell students they will have an opportunity to answer their own questions as they complete a Super Solar System activity later in this unit (Explore #4). See the Teacher Resources section at the end of this unit for model Venn diagrams. Diagram #1 compares and contrasts the Earth and sun; Diagram #2 compares and contrasts the Earth and moon; Diagram #3 compares and contrasts the Earth, sun, and moon.

Phase 2: Explore #3: Scale Model of the Sun, Earth, and Moon

Materials Needed:

Several sheets of yellow paper or one with a diameter of about 20 inches

One sheet of blue paper

A whole punch

Tape

Advanced Preparation:

Size is an important distinction between the sun, Earth, and moon. It is helpful to construct a scale model of the three members. Following is one way of constructing a scale model while students watch.

Draw a circle 19 ½ inches in diameter to represent the sun. Yellow art paper works well for this. Draw a circle 5 mm or about 3/16 inch to represent the Earth. Blue paper creates a nice Earth. If you use a paper punch, the circle of paper cut by the punch is close to the right size. Mount the blue circle on an index card so that it can be more easily seen. Using a pencil, draw a small circle 1.5 mm or about 1/16 inch in diameter on an index card to represent the moon (that's about the size of the "o" in the word "moon" in this sentence). To represent the distance from the sun to Earth, you will need a very long hallway or go outdoors. At this scale, the Earth will be approximately 176 feet from the sun. Measure and mark this distance. The moon will be about 5 ½ inches from the Earth. This scale model helps students conceptualize the immense distances and relative sizes of objects in the solar system.

The following represents some guiding questions you could ask as you demonstrate how to construct the model with your students. Tell students that scientists commonly use scale models to study different aspects of nature. In this case, we are dealing with very large objects (i.e., the sun, moon, and Earth), so we need to shrink them to fit in our classroom. Tell students the yellow circle represents the sun.

- If the sun was reduced to this size, how big would the Earth be? (The size of a tennis ball.)
- Hmmm…that seems a bit big. Think back to the research we did prior to making our Venn diagram. What did we learn about size? How can we figure it out? (Compare the diameters.)
- How big is the sun? The Earth? (The sun is 862,400 miles in diameter. Earth is 7,900 miles in diameter.)

Do a demonstration on the board and use approximation. Show students how to divide 800,000 by 8,000 to get the scale size of Earth. Explain how to create a ratio. Show how to cancel the thousands to create 800:8 or 100:1. Explain that the sun's diameter is about 100 times greater than the Earth, or the Earth is about 100 times smaller. Ask students to consider the size of a grape in this demonstration.

- Is the grape too big or too small? (Too big.)
- What is about the right size? (A pea. The eraser on my pencil.)

Yes, something about 5 mm, or about 3/16 of an inch. That's about the size of a "hole" from a hole punch.

- How big would the moon need to be in our scale model? (A speck, or tip of a pencil.)

We need a circle 1.5 mm or about 1/16 inch in diameter to represent the moon (about the size of an "o" on a printed page). Before class, I cut out a circle this size. Here it is for comparison. [Teacher holds up an "o" for comparison] Explain to students that the next step in creating the scale model is determining the distance between the Earth, moon, and sun. Go out into the hallway. Have one student hold the sun, one hold the Earth, and one hold the Moon. Tell the sun to stand in one place. Ask students:

- Approximate how far away the Earth should be. Walk down the hall and stop at the distance you think we should place the Earth. (Students will scatter down the hall. [*Note.* The correct distance, about 176 feet, should have been measured and marked prior to the activity.])
- Who is at the right place? How can we figure out who is right? (We need to know how big the sun is and the sun–Earth distance.)

Explain that the sun is 862,400 miles in diameter, and the sun–Earth distance is about 93,000,000 miles.

- Explain how we would solve this problem. (We can make this simple by looking at ratios. If we compare the diameter of the sun to the sun–Earth distance, the ratio is 93,000,000:862,400. We could simplify it to 90,000:900 for our estimate or 100:1. So, the sun–Earth distance is about 100 times the diameter of the sun.)

Discuss and model. Tell students the model sun is 19½ inches in diameter. So, 19.5 times 100 is 1,950 inches. If we divide by 12 inches per foot, that would be about 163 feet. So, based on a simple estimate, the Earth needs to be about 163 feet away. Point to the child who was closest to the correct distance. I wonder if, as scientists, you're ready for my next question? Ask something like:

- Predict where the moon should be. Explain how you figured that out. (Our research said the moon was about 240,000 miles away, and the diameter of the Earth was about 8,000 miles. If we make another ratio, it would be 240,000:8,000 or 30:1,… and the moon would be 30 Earth diameters away.)

Continue explaining. The model Earth is 3/16 inches in diameter. If we multiply that by 30, we get just over 5½ inches. You have just shrunk our solar neighborhood down inside the school!! Ask one final question before returning to your classroom:

- If the sun is so much larger, about 400 times the diameter of the moon, why do they appear to be approximately the same size in the sky? (The sun is so much farther away from the Earth than the moon is, so it appears the same size as the moon.)

- Why might a scientist ask these kinds of questions? (To better understand the nature and characteristics of the solar system.)

Phase 3: Explain

Materials Needed:

Completed Meaning Grid tool

Procedure:

Conduct a brief group discussion with your students to access their level of understanding regarding the Earth, sun, and moon. Encourage them to draw conclusions based on the information recorded on their Meaning Grid tool. Consider asking questions such as the following:

- Name ways a scientist might characterize the sun, the Earth, and the moon. (i.e., size, color, light, composition, life, position—there are numerous possible correct answers).

- Describe some characteristics of the sun. (The sun is much bigger and is the center of the solar system. It is the only body in our solar system that emits light. It is made of hydrogen and helium gas. It is too hot to sustain life.)

- How might we compare the Earth and the moon? (i.e., size, color, life, position. The Earth is bigger and is the foci of the moon's orbit. The Earth is blue, and the moon is gray. Earth's abundant liquid water and atmosphere make life possible. The Earth has active tectonics, such as earthquakes, volcanoes, and moving plates.)

- How are the sun, Earth, and moon similar? (They are spherical in shape. They are part of the solar system and the Milky Way galaxy. They are about the same age.)

- Are there new similarities or differences you want to add to your Meaning Grid? If so, record them now.

Phase 2: Explore #4: Super Solar System

Materials Needed:

Super Solar System graphic organizers, one per student

Super Solar System transparency and pen

The following books, which contain information on the solar system:

My First Book of Space by Rosanna Hansen and Robert A. Bell

My Picture Book of the Planets by Nancy E. Krulik

Planets by Jennifer Dussling

Planets Around the Sun by Seymour Simon

Solar System by Gregory Vogt

There's No Place Like Space by Tish Rabe

(Note. Do not use Postcards from Pluto for this activity.)

Chart paper

Sticky notes, five or six per student

Procedure:

1. Explain to students that they will now learn characteristics of other members of our solar system. Place students in pairs or small groups. Give each pair or group a book containing information about each planet.

2. Introduce the Super Solar System Graphic Organizer. Explain to students they will be recording information on the organizer as they work in their groups. Review criteria across the top of the organizer, such as size, location, appearance, composition, and motion. Be sure students understand what each term means. Define, if necessary. For instance, composition refers to what the planet is made of. Motion refers to the orbit and/or rotation of the planet.

3. Model how you would complete one row on the organizer by selecting a book, locating the information on the selected planet, and recording the information on the organizer. Be sure to verbalize the skills practiced earlier in this unit—using table of contents, index, headings, and boldface words, as well as the thought processes used.

4. Return to the Meaning Grid tool and remind students of the cells in which they may have indicated a question mark. Solicit students' questions and record them on poster paper. Tell the class that as they are searching for information on the planets, if they find any facts that may help answer these questions, they are to record it on a sticky note and stick it underneath the appropriate question. The information may also apply to the graphic organizer, in which case it should be recorded there as well.

5. Allow students time to complete their research and their graphic organizers.

Phase 2: Explore #5: Using *Postcards from Pluto*

Materials Needed:

Postcards from Pluto by Loreen Leedy, one copy for each student

Crayon for each student

Metacognitive Reader bookmarks, copied on cardstock, laminated, and cut apart

Advanced Preparation:

1. Determine who are your novice, average, and advanced readers. This is usually done with an informal reading inventory or other type of assessment.

Procedure:

1. Match bookmarks with individuals, and explain that to become a good reader, we need to practice good reading behaviors as we read.

2. Review what these good reading behaviors are: looking at the illustrations; predicting; thinking about our prior knowledge on the topic; skipping over words if they are too difficult; going back and rereading when something doesn't make sense; noticing the boldface words and captions; forming a picture or movie in our mind as we read; and summarizing as we are reading. Remind students that to become good readers, they need to practice these behaviors before and after they read. To become a great reader, we should also practice these behaviors *as* we read.

3. Have students look at the items on their respective bookmarks, and check for understanding. Tell students you want them to practice the good reading behaviors listed on their bookmark. When they complete an item, they should check it off with their crayon.

4. Introduce the book *Postcards from Pluto* and ask students, What is the first thing we should do? (Look at the illustrations.) Do a picture walk through the book. Ask: What else do good readers do? (They read the captions and notice boldface words.) Ask: What should we do if we come across a really tough word? (We should skip it, read ahead, make a guess about the unknown word, then go back and reread to see if it makes sense.) Remind students that their purpose for reading is to practice good reading behaviors.

5. When all students are finished reading, have them Summarize-Pair-Share. Pair students. Have students return to *Postcards from Pluto* and look at each 2-page spread, taking turns verbally summarizing the key ideas. Remind students that a summary answers the question, "What is the author telling me?" As pairs of students are summarizing, encourage them to add new information to their Super Solar System graphic organizers.

6. Have pairs of students share new information they have learned about the planets, as well as any answers they have learned about the questions raised on the Meaning Grid tool.

7. Hold a metacognitive discussion about the kinds of reading strategies students used as they completed this task. Have students refer to their Metacognitive Reader Bookmarks and give an example of each strategy they practiced.

8. End with an opportunity for student explanation and reflection. Ask a series of open-ended questions about the solar system, such as the ones below:

   - Compare the "inner planets" to the "outer planets." (The inner planets include Mercury, Venus, Earth, and Mars. These planets are rocky and solid. These planets are smaller that the outer planets. Their orbits are shorter than the outer planets.)

   - Predict why the Earth is the only planet that supports life as we know it. (Earth receives just the right amount of sunlight to maintain a temperature range that supports life. Earth has an atmosphere containing free oxygen. Earth's atmosphere has carbon dioxide for plants. Earth has water in the liquid phase, as well as ice and vapor.)

Phase 4: Elaborate

Materials Needed:

> Gym or playground
>
> Solar system labels
>
> 10 paint stirrers
>
> Construction paper, 10 sheets
>
> Package of index cards

Advanced Preparation:

This activity is designed to further familiarize students with the characteristics of the members of the solar system. The activity is best done in the gym or on the playground, as considerable space is needed. The distances between the members of the solar system are not to scale.

Print the labels for the solar system planets. Mount the labels on construction paper. It is advisable to make duplicate copies, and tape them together back to back or laminate the copies back to back. Cut a slit along the bottom of the construction paper, so that the label can slide over a support. A wooden paint stirrer works well. It is important that the labels are visible throughout the activity.

Select 10 students to hold the solar system labels. It works well to place the sun near the middle of the gym or playground. Place remaining planet labels accordingly, with Mercury being closest to the sun, and Neptune being the farthest away to mimic the relative orbits. The placement will not be to scale. Do not worry about scale distances for this activity.

Using the descriptions of each planet (see the Characteristics list for Elaborate #1 in the Teacher Resources section of this unit), create index cards for each planet. Mount one characteristic on one index card. It is a good idea to print a master sheet and number each characteristic. The index cards can also be numbered. This will provide a quick reference and answer key for the discussion and explanation phase.

Procedure:

1. Explain to students that they are going on an imaginary journey through the solar system, like the characters in *Postcards from Pluto* did. They are going to be given an index card with a descriptive characteristic. They are to "travel" through the solar system to the member that their card best describes.

2. Allow time for students to circulate.

3. After the students have found their locations, have each student read his or her description. Ask the class if they agree on the location for the space traveler. It may be necessary for the student to continue his or her journey until he or she is at the right location. (This is the reason for numbering each card and having a master copy to serve as a key. Many students may have to move from their original location.)

4. So that all students get to participate, you may have to repeat the process more than once. Then, return to the classroom.

Phase 5: Evaluate

Materials Needed:

Postcard-size card stock

Postcard stamps

Colored pencils, markers, and pens

Actual postcards you have received or collected

Procedure:

1. Tell students they will be creating and sending a postcard about one member of the solar system. Show them postcards you have received and discuss their components:

   • Picture face

   • Blank back for writing message

   • Area for address

2. Review the components in an address:

   • Line 1: person's name

   • Line 2: street address

   • Line 3: city, state, and postal code

   Ask students to decide which family member they want to send their postcard to.

3. Have students collect the necessary information they will need to complete the address. This may require help from home.

4. Next, ask students what kind of picture they might create to represent their planet. Encourage students to consult with one another and recall details about the planets, using their Meaning Grid tool and Super Solar System graphic organizers.

5. Have students record facts about their specific planet.

6. When all information has been collected, individuals will write their own message on the postcard to summarize the characteristics of their planet.

7. Mail.

Teacher Resources

Trade Books

Note. Most titles listed below still consider Pluto as one of the nine planets. Be sure to use the current definition when discussing "planets."

Berger, Melvin, & Berger, Gilda. (1993). *Where are the stars during the day?* [Blanche Sims, Illus.] Nashville, TN: Ideals Children's Books, 48 pp.; ISBN: 0-8249-5319-3 (paperback); $3.95.

> This book is a fascinating introduction to astronomy, written by two authors who have written hundreds of books for children. Part of the *Discovery Readers* series, this book is an easy-to-read introduction to constellations, the sun, and stars. The question raised in the title is answered in the text using a child-friendly analogy. The full-color drawings help simplify and explain complicated concepts.

Branley, Franklyn. (1987). *The moon seems to change.* [Barbara and Ed Emberley, Illus.) New York: HarperCollins, 31 pp.; ISBN: 0-06-445065-1 (paperback); $4.95.

> Part of the *Let's Read and Find Out* series, this book offers a complete description of the phases of the moon, how the moon orbits Earth, why we see the phases, and the rotation of the Earth and moon. Simple, effective, illustrated demonstrations help explain and clarify concepts within the text. This book would pair well with Fowler's *So That's How the Moon Changes Shape!*

Branley, Franklyn. (1986). *What makes day and night.* [Arthur Dorros, Illus.] New York: HarperCollins, 31 pp.; ISBN: 0-06-445050-3 (paperback); $4.99.

> Part of the *Let's Read and Find Out* series, this book provides a simple explanation of how the Earth's rotation causes day and night. Using illustrations, this book visually shows the spinning of the Earth, and a follow-up experiment clarifies the concept of rotation. One photograph of the Earth, taken from space, is included.

Bullock, Linda. (2003). *Looking through a telescope.* New York: Children's Press, 31 pp.; ISBN: 0-516-27906-8 (paperback); $4.95.

This delightful book begins with the nursery rhyme "Hey Diddle, Diddle" to introduce concepts such as the size of the moon and its distance from Earth. It is a good way to introduce the need for, and function of, a telescope. Part of the *Rookie Read About Science* series, colorful photographs and simple text explain how and why scientists use telescopes to learn more about space and our solar system.

Dickinson, Terence. (2002). *Exploring the night sky: The equinox astronomy guide for beginners.* Buffalo, NY: Firefly Books, 71 pp.; ISBN: 0-920656-66-8 (paperback); $9.95.

This enthusiastic book takes advanced readers on a tour of the galaxy and aims to encourage novice stargazers to expand their horizons beyond the Big Dipper. Dozens of colored, detailed paintings and diagrams clarify the text and focus on phenomenon viewable from North America. This book won the 2003 Children's Science Book Award given by the New York Academy of Sciences.

Dussling, Jennifer. (2000). *Planets.* New York: Grosset & Dunlap, 49 pp.; ISBN: 0-448-42406-1 (paperback); $3.99.

Written by a prolific science writer, this delightful book is part of the *All Aboard Reading* series for young readers. Using cut-paper collages and child-friendly examples and analogies, this text provides basic information about characteristics of the planets in our solar system. It even mentions historical beliefs and compares them to modern-day science.

Dussling, Jennifer. (1996). *Stars.* [Mavis Smith, Illus.] New York: Grosset & Dunlap, 32 pp.; ISBN: 0-448-41148-2 (paperback); $3.99.

This beginning reader, which is part of the *All Aboard Science Reader* series, is a simple introduction to stars and constellations. Topics include: number and size of stars, comparison of size of Earth and sun, solar eclipse, and a few constellations. The text contains excellent content, and its simple analysis makes concepts easier to understand.

Fowler, Alan. (1991). *So that's how the moon changes shape.* Chicago: Children's Press, 31 pp.; ISBN: 0-516-44917-6 (paperback); $4.95.

Lots of photos provide a simple introduction to the changing shape of the moon and its phases. Part of the *Rookie Read About Science* series, the text and accompanying diagrams describe the moon's orbit around Earth. This book is a good introduction to phases of the moon and would pair well with Branley's *The Moon Seems To Change.*

Hansen, Rosanna & Bell, Robert. (1985). *My first book of space.* New York: Simon & Schuster, 40 pp.; ISBN: 0-671-60262-4 (hardcover); $13.95.

> Developed in conjunction with NASA, this picture book describes features of the sun, planets, and satellites in our solar system. The large, full-color photographs, which were selected from NASA archives created by the Voyager mission of the early 1980s, provide graphic detail to illustrate the written text. The authors are very careful to also explain how the photos were taken (i.e., probe, telescope, or satellite) and whether or not details have been added. Thus, the reader is aware of actual photos versus photos representing phenomenon one might see. An excellent reference for any classroom library.

Krulik, Nancy. (1991). *My picture book of the planets.* New York: Scholastic, 33 pp.; ISBN: 0-590-43907-3 (paperback); $5.99.

> This picture book would make a nice companion to *My First Book of Space* (Hansen & Bell, 1985), since it, too, contains color photographs from NASA and gives a close-up view of all nine planets in our solar system. Each time a new planet is introduced, the same graphic is used to show the new planet's position in the solar system. Characteristics of planets are described by simple, yet accurate, explanations.

Leedy, Loreen. (1993). *Postcards from Pluto: A tour of the solar system.* New York: Holiday House, 30 pp.; ISBN: 0-8234-1237-7 (paperback); $6.95.

> Join Dr. Quasar, a robot guide, and his multicultural group of kids on a tour of the solar system. Information about each planet is conveyed through simple paintings of the planets and postcards the tourists send back to Earth. Additional information is provided in conversation call-outs between the space travelers. This book is sure to delight children of all ages.

Oleksy, Walter. (2002). *Mapping the skies.* New York: Franklin Watts, 63 pp.; ISBN: 0-531-16635-X (paperback); $8.95.

> This chapter book explores the tools and technologies that present and past scientists have used to map outer space. Topics include: competing theories of the universe, understanding telescopes, advanced telescope technology, and what we have learned about our closest celestial neighbors. The final chapter discusses mapping the skies of today and tomorrow. A timeline ranging from 3100 B.C. to A.D. 2003 and magnificent color photographs are included.

Rabe, Tish. (1999). *There's no place like space!* [Aristides Ruiz, Illus.] New York: Random House, 44 pp.; ISBN: 0-679-89115-3 (hardcover); $8.99.

This book is part of *The Cat in the Hat's Learning Library* and is designed to build basic concepts about our solar system in an easy-to-read format. Dr. Seuss–like characters are guided on a journey by the Cat in the Hat who explains facts about the planets using rhyming verse. Illustrations provide additional detail.

Rockwell, Anne. (1999). *Our stars.* New York: Harcourt, 22 pp.; ISBN: 0-216360-3 (paperback); $6.00.

In this simple text, Rockwell encourages the young reader to look into the night sky and wonder. Using beautiful illustrations and minimal text, this book describes stars, constellations, comets, and meteors. Given its length, this basic book takes on too many topics.

Simon, Seymour. (2002). *Planets around the sun.* New York: SeaStar Books, 30 pp.; ISBN: 1-58717-146-5 (paperback); $3.95.

Written by renowned science author Seymour Simon, this book is part of the *See More Readers* series. The black background, white text, and stunning color photographs are the perfect backdrop for the physical description, including a trivia tidbit, given for each planet. Simon also includes a perforated page of collectable planet cards and a chart that compares many facts about each planet.

Simon, Seymour. (1996). *The sun.* New York: Mulberry Books, 26 pp.; ISBN: 0-668-09236-5 (paperback); $6.99.

This book is part of a series written by Seymour Simon, each one focusing on a specific body within the solar system (the moon, the Earth, etc.). The dazzling photographs complement the brief text and provide a complete description of the sun, including its place in the solar system, size, source of energy, layers, solar eclipse, sunspots, prominences, and flares. Good diagrams, too. We recommend teachers number the pages for classroom use.

Sipiera, Paul. (1997). *Comets and meteor showers.* New York: Children's Press, 47 pp.; ISBN: 0-516-26166-5 (paperback); $6.95.

This detailed book, which is part of the *True Book* series, defines what a comet is, explains where comets come from, why they are important, how they travel, and why astronomers study them. There are even chapters on "did a comet kill the dinosaurs" and "are comets bad luck?" The colorful, captioned photos and drawings visually clarify the text.

Sipiera, Paul. (1997). *Constellations.* New York: Children's Press, 47 pp.; ISBN: 0-516-26167-3 (paperback); $6.95.

> Using the same format as *Comets and Meteor Showers*, this chapter book defines constellations, explains where constellations originate, how they were discovered and named, and why humans are fascinated with them. A glossary, index, and a Meet the Authors section complete the book. Colorful, captioned photos and drawings visually clarify the text.

Vogt, Gregory. (2001). *Solar system.* New York: Scholastic, 48 pp.; ISBN: 0-439-38247-5 (paperback); $3.99.

> Part of the *Scholastic Science Readers* series, this book has it all: colorful photographs, index, glossary, headings and subheadings, and charts to summarize facts about each planet. Learn all about the sun, planets, comets, and asteroids, as well as space exploration. This book is a wealth of information and would make a great addition to the classroom or school library.

Walker, Niki. (1998). *The moon.* New York: Crabtree Publishing, 32 pp.; ISBN: 0-86505-689-7 (paperback); $6.95

> *The Moon* is part of the *Eye on the Universe* series, designed with upper elementary students in mind. This book describes characteristics of the Moon, including how the moon was formed, its landscape, phases, and effects on Earth. There is even discussion of human exploration of Earth's nearest neighbor. Many color photographs and illustrations add detail to each page.

Wilson, Lynn. (1993). *What's out there?: A book about space.* New York: Grosset & Dunlap, 28 pp.; ISBN: 0-448-40517-2 (paperback); $3.49.

> This is a terrific little book that briefly covers many aspects of the solar system, including sun, terrestrial planets, gas planets, phases of the moon, day/night and constellations. The simple-to-read text make this book a great "first" book about space.

Web Sites

Note. The authors realize that Web site addresses are not guaranteed to work, as they change, move, or are removed from the Internet. Therefore, the authors have included the sponsoring organization of the Web site in the event the link provided here does not work. Simply type in the name of the organization in your search engine, and it will direct you to the appropriate URL.

National Aeronautic and Space Administration at:

http://solarsystem.nasa.gov/index.cfm

This Web site provides an interactive feature to explore the solar system. Other links include the top 10 images of planetary objects, information on NASA missions, and a kids' gallery of space artwork.

San Francisco's Palace of Fine Arts at:

http://www.exploratorium.edu/ronh/solar_system

The Exploratorium is a collage of hundreds of science, art, and human perception exhibits housed at the Palace of Fine Arts. Online since 1993, the Exploratorium was one of the first science museums to build a site on the World Wide Web. This Web site enables the user to build a scale model of the solar system.

Lawrence Hall of Science at:

http://seedsofscience.org/index.html

Developed at Berkeley's Graduate School of Education's Lawrence Hall of Science, this site is a link to a current National Science Foundation grant that is "working at the interface between science and literacy." Teachers can go to this site to field test materials, view curriculum as it is being developed, and read research papers written on this topic.

Dr. Philip Plait, the "Bad" Astronomer, personal Web site at:

http://www.badastronomy.com

This site contains an interesting compilation of common science misconceptions and offers great classroom activities and links for teaching astronomy. Philip Plait is an astronomer and faculty member in the Physics and Astronomy Department at Sonoma State University (Sonoma, CA).

The Thinker's Guide

Watch your partner search for information. What does your partner do? Put a checkmark in the box after you see or hear your partner doing that item.

STRATEGY	My partner's name	My name is
1. Looked for a word		
2. Made a prediction		
3. Asked a question		
4. Reread		
5. Made a connection to prior knowledge		
TEXT AIDS		
1. Used index		
2. Used glossary		
3. Used table of contents		
4. Used bold words		
5. Used headings		

AFTER READING, look at how well you did. List two things you will do tomorrow to help improve your searching skills:

1.

2.

Full size form available at www.Christopher-Gordon.com/authors/KingMattox-shtml

Index Cards for Explore #3: Comparing and Contrasting the Earth, Moon, and Sun

COLOR IS YELLOW	**COLOR IS MOSTLY YELLOW**
HAS AN ATMOSPHERE WITH OXYGEN	**SURFACE TEMPERATURE IS ABOUT 11,000 DEGREES**
IS A STAR	**IS A PLANET**
IS NOT A PLANET OR A STAR	**REVOLVES IN 1 MONTH**

Full size form available at www.Christopher-Gordon.com/authors/KingMattox-shtml

HAS SEAS MADE OF WATER	**DISTANCE ACROSS IS ABOUT 100 TIMES THE DISTANCE ACROSS EARTH**
DISTANCE ACROSS IS ABOUT ¼ THE DISTANCE ACROSS EARTH	**IMPOSSIBLE TO LAND ON**
COLOR IS GRAY	**HAS AN ATMOSPHERE**
CAN BE VERY COLD	**CAN BE VERY HOT**

SENDS OUT A WIND	**NOT A SOLID**
ROTATES IN ABOUT 24 HOURS	**ROTATES IN ABOUT 1 MONTH**
REVOLVES IN 1 YEAR	**PRODUCES INTENSE HEAT**
HAS MANY CRATERS	**HAS "SEAS" MADE OF LAVA**

IS MOSTLY COVERED BY WATER	**SUPPORTS PLANTS**
SUPPORTS ANIMALS	**SEEMS TO CHANGE OVER SEVERAL DAYS**
HAS NO ATMOSPHERE	**HAS MANY ACTIVE VOLCANOES**
HAS AN ATMOSPHERE	

Full size form available at www.Christopher-Gordon.com/authors/KingMattox-shtml

Labels for Explore #3: Comparing and Contrasting the Earth, Moon, and Sun

Earth

Moon

Sun

Full size form available at www.Christopher-Gordon.com/authors/KingMattox-shtml

Meaning Grid Tool Template

Topic: _____

Key:
* = Yes   X = No   Δ = Yes and No   ? = Don't Know

Descriptors	Item #1	Item #2	Item #3	Processing what we know All, some, none, few, most . . . statements

Processing What We Know Statements:
(Write statements to compare/contrast items on the grid. Use words like "contrast" or "similar" in your statements.)

Meaning Grid Tool #1
The Moon, Sun, and Earth

Key:
* = Yes   X = No   Δ = Yes and No   ? = Don't Know

Descriptors	Moon	Earth	Sun	Processing what we know All, some, none, few, most . . . statements
MOTION • orbits a planet	*			
COMPOSITION • made of rock	*			
APPEARANCE • has many craters • lots of water	* X			
SIZE • diameter of 2,160 miles	*			

Full size form available at www.Christopher-Gordon.com/authors/KingMattox-shtml

Meaning Grid Tool #2: The Moon, Sun, and Earth

Key: * = Yes   X = No   Δ = Yes and No   ? = Don't Know

Descriptors	Moon	Earth	Sun	Processing what we know All, some, none, few, most . . . statements
MOTION				
• orbits a planet	*	X	X	
• orbits the sun	X	*	X	*Most* bodies in our solar system orbit the Sun.
• rotates in about 24 hours	?	*	X	
• rotates in about 600 hours	?	X	*	
COMPOSITION				
• has an atmosphere	?	*	X	
• has atmosphere with oxygen	?	*	X	*Few* planets in our solar system have an atmosphere with oxygen.
• made mostly of hydrogen gas	X	X	*	
APPEARANCE				The Earth has *some* craters caused by meteors striking it.
• has many craters	*	Δ	X	
• has lots of water				
• color is mostly blue	X	*	X	
• color is yellow	X	*	X	
	Δ	X	*	At *some* times, the harvest moon is yellow in the early evening sky.

Processing What We Know Statements:

In contrast to the moon and Earth, the sun appears yellow in the sky. OR
In contrast to the moon and Earth, the sun is the center of our solar system.

The Earth, moon, and sun are all similar because they are approximately the same age.

Super Solar System Graphic Organizer

Planet	Size	Location	Appearance	Composition	Motion
Mercury					
Venus					
Earth					
Mars					
Jupiter					
Saturn					
Uranus					
Neptune					

Full size form available at www.Christopher-Gordon.com/authors/KingMattox-shtml

Metacognitive Reader Bookmarks

Level 1: Novice Readers	Level 2: Average Readers	Level 3: Advanced Readers
As you read, ask: does it make sense? If it does not, check which comprehension strategies you used to help you understand. BEFORE READING: _____I looked at the pictures. _____I made predictions. _____I thought about what I already know about this topic. AFTER READING: _____I checked my predictions to see if they were right. _____I reread when my predictions didn't agree with the author.	As you read, ask: does it make sense? If it does not, check which comprehension strategies you used to help you understand. BEFORE READING: _____I looked at the pictures and made predictions. _____I thought about what I already know about this topic. DURING READING: _____I created a picture in my head. _____I skipped over hard words. AFTER READING: _____I checked my predictions to see if they were right. _____I reread when my predictions didn't agree with the author.	As you read, ask: does it make sense? If it does not, check which comprehension strategies you used to help you understand. BEFORE READING: _____I looked at the pictures and made predictions. _____I thought about what I already know about this topic. _____I read and understood the bold words and captions. DURING READING: _____I made a movie in my head. _____I skipped over hard words. _____I summarized as I read. AFTER READING: _____I checked my predictions to see if they were right. _____I reread to find new information.

Full size form available at www.Christopher-Gordon.com/authors/KingMattox-shtml

Labels for Elaborate #1: Journey through the Solar System

Sun

Mercury

Venus

Earth

Mars

Jupiter

Saturn

Uranus

Neptune

Full size form available at www.Christopher-Gordon.com/authors/KingMattox-shtml

Characteristics for Elaborate #1: Journey Through the Solar System

Sun

Sends out a wind

Contains 98.86% of the mass of the entire solar system

Surface temperature of about 11,000 degrees (F)

Surface known as photosphere

Diameter is about 100 times that of the Earth

Has an atmosphere called the corona

Atmospheric temperature approaches 2 million degrees (F)

Known for spots and flares

Mercury

Is closest planet to the sun

Orbits the sun every 88 days

Diameter is about 2/5 that of Earth

Has greatest range of temperature between day and night

Surface is scattered with thousands of craters

Rotates in 59 days

Has a very thin atmosphere made of atoms blasted off the surface by the solar wind

Has no moons

Venus

Is the second planet from the sun

Brightest of all planets

Has no moons

Is 7,500 miles in diameter

Is covered by thick, rapidly spinning clouds

Atmosphere consists of mainly carbon dioxide

Rotates on its axis every 243 Earth days

Orbits the sun every 224 days

Diameter is slightly smaller than Earth (.95)

Surface atmospheric pressure is 92 times greater than on Earth

Full size form available at www.Christopher-Gordon.com/authors/KingMattox-shtml

Earth

Only planet known to harbor life

Fresh water exists in three phases

Its land surfaces are also in motion

Has one moon or natural satellite

Third planet from the sun

Rotates on its axis every 24 hours

Orbits the sun in 365¼ days

Has an atmosphere of mostly nitrogen

Has an atmosphere with oxygen

Moon

Rotates at the same rate that it revolves

Lacks a magnetic field

Is not a planet or a star

Has "seas" made of lava

Has many craters

Appears gray in color

Has a diameter of about 2,083 miles

Mars

Known as the red planet

Has the largest volcanic mountain in the solar system,
but no evidence of current volcanic activity

Has two moons: Phobos and Deimos

Is the fourth planet from the sun

There is evidence of water on this planet.

Has polar ice caps made of water and solid carbon dioxide

Rotates every 24.6 Earth hours

Orbits the sun every 1.9 Earth years

Has a diameter about half that of Earth

Full size form available at www.Christopher-Gordon.com/authors/KingMattox-shtml

Jupiter

Has 63 known moons, as of 2004

Is the most massive planet

Is the fifth planet from the sun

Is considered a gas giant

Has a mass 318 times that of Earth

Its moon, Io, has active volcanoes.

Is a gas giant made mostly of hydrogen and helium

Rotates about every 10 hours

Orbits the sun every 11.9 Earth years

Has faint, dark rings

Has a diameter about 11 times that of Earth

Saturn

Is the sixth planet from the sun

Is a gas giant made mostly of hydrogen and helium

Its rings are made mostly of water ice

Has a density less than that of water

Has 34 named natural satellites or moons

Rotates every 10 hours

Orbits the sun every 29 Earth years

Has a diameter about nine times that of Earth

Uranus

Orbits the sun every 84 Earth years

Rotates about every 17 Earth hours

Seventh planet from the sun

Has a blue-green color caused by methane gas

Rotational axis is nearly horizontal

Has faint, dark rings

Has 21 named moons and 6 un-named moons

Has a diameter of about four times that of Earth

Full size form available at www.Christopher-Gordon.com/authors/KingMattox-shtml

Neptune

Orbits the sun every 165 Earth years

Rotates about every 16 Earth hours

Has 13 known moons

Eighth planet from the sun (usually)

Has the fastest winds in the solar system, reaching 1,200 mph

Has dark rings of unknown composition

Has a diameter of about four times that of Earth

Full size form available at www.Christopher-Gordon.com/authors/KingMattox-shtml

Teacher's Shopping List for The Earth in the Solar System

☐ Science notebooks, one for each student

☐ Sticky notes, one for each student

☐ Poster paper

☐ Transparency of a blank Meaning Grid tool

☐ The following books, which contain information about the Earth's moon (see the Teacher Resources section of this unit for more information on titles):

   My First Book of Space by Rosanna Hansen and Robert A. Bell

   Planets Around the Sun by Seymour Simon

   Planets by Jennifer Dussling

   Postcards from Pluto by Loreen Leedy, one copy for each student

   Solar System by Gregory Vogt

   So That's How the Moon Changes Shape! by Allan Fowler

   The Moon by Niki Walker

   The Moon Seems to Change by Frankyn M. Branley

☐ Earth, moon, and sun printed labels

☐ Earth, moon, and sun characteristics, printed on index cards, one card for each student

☐ Books about the sun and Earth (choose from those recommended in the Teacher Resources section of this unit)

☐ Thinker's Guide, one copy for each student

☐ Poster paper, three to five sheets

☐ Sticky notes, 10 per student

(Continued on next page)

- ☐ Meaning Grid tool, one copy for each student

- ☐ Several sheets of yellow paper or one with a diameter of about 20 inches

- ☐ One sheet of blue paper, 8.5 x 11 inch

- ☐ A whole punch

- ☐ Tape

- ☐ Super Solar System graphic organizers, one per student

- ☐ Super Solar System transparency and pen

- ☐ *My First Book of Space* by Rosanna Hansen and Robert A. Bell

- ☐ *My Picture Book of the Planets* by Nancy E. Krulik

- ☐ *Planets* by Jennifer Dussling

- ☐ *Planets Around the Sun* by Seymour Simon

- ☐ *Solar System* by Gregory Vogt

- ☐ *There's No Place Like Space* by Tish Rabe

- ☐ Chart paper

- ☐ Gym or playground

- ☐ Solar system labels

- ☐ 10 paint stirrers

- ☐ Construction paper, 10 sheets

- ☐ Package of index cards

- ☐ Postcard-size card stock

- ☐ Postcard stamps

- ☐ Colored pencils, markers, and pens

- ☐ Actual postcards you have received or collected

References

American Association for the Advancement of Science (AAAS). (2001). *Atlas of science literacy.* Washington, DC: Author.

American Association for the Advancement of Science (AAAS). (1990). *Science for all Americans: Project 2061.* New York: Oxford University Press.

Anderson, R. C., & Pearson, P. D. (1984). A schema-theoretic view of basic processes in reading. In P. D. Pearson, R. Barr, M. Kamil, & P. Mosenthal (Eds.), *Handbook of reading research* (pp. 255–291). New York: Longman.

Armbruster, B. B. (1984). The problems of inconsiderate text. In G. Duffy, L. Roehler, & J. Mason (Eds.), *Comprehension instruction: Perspectives and suggestions* (pp. 202–217). New York: Longman.

Baker, L., & Brown, A. (1984). Cognitive skills and reading. In P. D. Pearson, R. Barr, M. Kamil, & P. Mosenthal (Eds.), *Handbook of reading research* (pp. 352–394). New York: Longman.

Bar, V. (1989). Children's views about the water cycle. *Science Education, 73,* 481–500.

Baxter, J. (1989). Children's understandings of familiar astronomical events. *International Journal of Science Education, 11,* 502–513.

Beck, I. L., & McKeown, M. G. (1991). Conditions of vocabulary acquisition. In R. Barr, M. Kamil, P. Mosenthal, & P. D. Pearson (Eds.), *Handbook of reading research* (Vol. II, pp. 789–814). White Plains, NY: Longman.

Beck., I. L., McKeown, M. G., Hamilton, R. L., & Kucan, L. (1998). Getting at the meaning: How to help students unpack difficult text. *American Educator, 22*(1), 66–71.

Blachowicz, A., & Fisher, P. J. (2002). *Teaching vocabulary in all classrooms* (2nd ed.). Upper Saddle River, NJ: Merrill Prentice Hall.

Bloom, B. (1956). *Taxonomy of educational objectives.* New York: Longman, Green and Co.

Britton, B. K., & Gulgoz, S. (1991). Using Kintsch's computational model to improve instructional text: Effects of repairing inference calls on recall and cognitive structures. *Journal of Educational Psychology, 83*(3), 329–345.

Bybee, R. W. (1997). *Achieving scientific literacy: From purposes to practices.* Portsmouth, NH: Heinemann.

Calkins, L., Montgomery, K., Santman, D., & Falk, B. (1998). *A reader's guide to standardized reading tests: Knowledge is power.* Portsmouth, NH: Heinemann.

Caswell, L. J., & Duke, N. L. (1998). Non-narrative as a catalyst for literacy development. *Language Arts, 75,* 108–117.

Chapman, M. (1999). The sociocognitive construction of written genres in first grade. *Research in the Teaching of English, 29,* 164–191.

Coiro, J. (2005). Making sense of online text. *Educational Leadership, 63*(2), 30–35.

Collins, A., & Loftus, E. (1975). A spreading activation theory of semantic processing. *Psychological Review, 82,* 407–428.

Collins Block, C., Schaller, J. L., Joy, J. A., & Gaine, P. (2002). Process-based comprehension instruction: Prespectives of four reading educators. In C. Collins Block & M. Pressley (Eds.), *Comprehension instruction: Research-based best practices* (pp. 42–61). New York: Guilford Press.

Donovan, C. A., & Smolkin, L. B. (2002). Considering genre, content, and visual features in the selection of trade books for science instruction. *Reading Teacher, 55,* 502–522.

Dreher, M. J. (2002). Children searching and using informational text: A critical part of comprehension. In C. Collins Block & M. Pressley (Eds.), *Comprehension instruction: Research-based best practices* (pp. 289–304). New York: Guilford Press.

Duffy, G. (1993). Teachers' progress toward becoming expert strategy teachers. *Elementary School Journal, 93*(3), 231–247.

Duke, N. K. (2000). 3.6 minutes per day: The scarcity of informational texts in first grade. *Reading Research Quarterly, 35,* 202–224.

Duke, N. K., & Pearson, P. D. (2002). Effective practices for developing reading comprehension. In A. E. Farstrup & S. J. Samuels (Eds.), *What research has to say about reading instruction* (3rd ed., pp. 205–242). Newark, DE: International Reading Association.

Farah, M. (1989). The neural basis of mental imagery. *Trends in Neurosciences, 12,* 395–399.

Farah, M. J., & McClelland, J. L. (1991). A computational model of semantic memory impairment: Modality specificity and emergent category specificity. *Journal of Experimental Psychology: General, 120,* 339–357.

Ford, D. J. (2004). Highly recommended trade books: Can they be used in inquiry science? In E. Wendy Saul (Ed.), *Crossing borders in literacy and science instruction* (pp. 277–290). Newark, DE & Arlington, VA: International Reading Association & National Science Teachers Association.

Ford, C., Yore, L. D., & Anthony, R. J. (1997, March 21). *Reforms, visions, and standards: A cross-curricular view from an elementary school perspective.* Paper presented at the annual meeting of the National Association for Research in Science Teaching, Oak Brook, IL. [ERIC Document Reproduction Service No. ED406168]

Freyberg, P. (1985). Implications across the curriculum. In R. Osborne & P. Freyberg (Eds.), *Learning in science* (pp. 125–135). Auckland, NZ: Heinemann.

Galda, L., & Cullinan, B. E. (1991). Literature for literacy: What research says about the benefits of using trade books in the classroom. In J. Flood, J. M. Jensen, D. Lapp, & J. R. Squire (Eds.), *Handbook of research on teaching the English language arts* (pp. 529–535). New York: Macmillan.

Goodwin, A. (2000). *Concept cartoons in science education (ConCISE): An evaluation.* Manchester: The Institute of Education: The Manchester Metropolitan University.

Guthrie, J., & Ozgungor, S. (2002). Instructional contexts for reading engagement. In C. C. Block & M. Pressley (Eds.), *Comprehension instruction: Research-based best practices* (pp. 28–41). New York: Guilford Press.

Guzzetti, B., Hynd, C., Williams, W., & Skeels, S. (1995). What students have to say about their science texts. *Journal of Reading, 38,* 656–665.

Hermann, R., & Lewis, B. F. (2003). Moon misconceptions. *The Science Teacher, 70,* 51–55.

Hyerle, D. (1996). *Visual tools for constructing knowledge.* Alexandria, VA: Association for Supervision and Curriculum Development.

International Reading Association & National Council of Teachers of English (IRA & NCTE). (1996). *Standards for the English language arts.* Newark, DE & Urbana, IL: Author.

Klentschy, M. P., & Molina-De La Torre, E. (2004). Students' science notebooks and the inquiry process. In E. Wendy Saul (Ed.), *Crossing borders in literacy and science instruction* (pp. 340–354). Newark, DE & Arlington, VA: International Reading Association & National Science Teachers Association.

Kosslyn, S. M., Ganis, G., & Thompson, W. L. (2001). Neural foundations of imagery. *Neuroscience, 2,* 635–642.

Leu, D. J., Jr. (2002). The new literacies: Research on reading instruction with the Internet. In A. E. Farstrup & S. J. Samuels (Eds.), *What research has to say about reading instruction* (3rd ed., pp. 310–336). Newark, DE: International Reading Association.

Leu, D. J., Jr., Leu, D. D., & Coiro, J. (2004). *Teaching with the Internet K–12: New literacies for new times* (4th ed.). Norwood, MA: Christopher-Gordon.

Martin A., Haxby, J. V., Lalonde, F. M., Wiggs, C. L., & Ungerleider, L. G. (1995). Discrete cortical regions associated with knowledge of color and knowledge of action. *Science, 270,* 102–105.

Matthewson, G. C. (1985). Toward a comprehensive model of affect in the reading process. In H. Singer & R. Ruddell (Eds.), *Theoretical models and processes of reading* (3rd ed., pp. 841–856). Newark, DE: International Reading Association.

McRae, K., de Sa, V. R., & Seidenberg, M. S. (1997). On the nature and scope of featural representations of word meaning. *Journal of Experimental Psychology: General, 126,* 99–130.

Meyer, B. J. F., & Poon, L. W. (2004). Effects of structure strategy training and signaling on recall of text. In R. B. Ruddell & N. J. Unrau (Eds.), *Theoretical models and processes of reading* (5th ed., pp. 810–850). Newark, DE: International Reading Association.

National Reading Panel. (2000). *Teaching children to read: An evidence-based assessment of the scientific research literature on reading and its implications for reading instruction.* Washington, DC: National Institute of Child Health and Human Development.

National Research Council. (1996). *National science education standards.* Washington, DC: National Academy Press.

National Research Council. (2000). *Inquiry and the national science standards.* Washington, DC: National Academy Press.

Naylor, S., & Keogh, B. (2000). *Concept cartoons in science education.* Sandbach, Cheshire: Millgate House.

Ogle, D. (1986). KWL: A teaching model that develops active reading of expository text. *The Reading Teacher, 40,* 564–570.

Paris, S. G., Wasik, B. A., & Turner, J. C. (1991). The development of strategic readers. In R. Barr, M. Kamil, P. Mosenthal, & P. D. Pearson (Eds.), *Handbook of reading research* (Vol. II, pp. 609–640). White Plains, NY: Longman.

Pearson, D. P., & Duke, N. K. (2002). Comprehension instruction in the primary grades. In C. C. Block, & M. Pressley, (Eds.), *Comprehension instruction: Research-based best practices* (pp. 247–258). New York: Guilford Press.

Pressley, M., El-Dinary, P. B., Gaskins, I., Schuder, T., Bergman, J., Almasi, L., & Brown, R. (1992). Beyond direct explanation: Transactional instruction of reading comprehension strategies. *Elementary School Journal, 92,* 511–554.

Pressley, M. (2002). Comprehension strategies instruction. In C. C. Block & M. Pressley (Eds.), *Comprehension instruction: Research-based best practices* (pp. 11–27). New York: Guilford Press.

Reardon, J. (1992). *Vital connections: Children, science, and books.* Portsmouth, NH: Heinemann.

Reutzel, D. R., Smith, J. A., & Fawson, P. C. (2005). An evaluation of two approaches for teaching reading comprehension strategies in the primary years using science information texts. *Early Childhood Research Quarterly, 20,* 276–305.

Ryan, A., & Aikenhead, G. (1992). Student's preconceptions about the epistemology of science. *Science Education, 76,* 559–580.

Sadoski, M., & Paivio, A. (2001). *Imagery and text*. Mahwah, NJ: Lawrence Erlbaum.

Saul, E. W. (2004). Introduction. In E. W. Saul (Ed.), *Crossing borders in literacy and science instruction* (pp. 1–9). Newark, DE & Arlington, VA: International Reading Association & National Science Teachers Association.

Saul, E. W., & Dieckman, D. (2005). Choosing and using informational trade books. *Reading Research Quarterly, 40*(4), 502–513.

Saul, W., Reardon, J., Pearce, C., Dieckman, D., & Neutze, D. (2002). *Science workshop: Reading, writing, and thinking like a scientist*. Portsmouth, NH: Heinemann.

Tomasino, B., Borroni, P., Isaja, A., Rumiati, R., & Farah, M, (2005). The role of the primary motor cortex in mental rotation: A TMS study. *Cognitive Neuropsychology, 22*(3–4), 348–363.

Vacca, R. T. (2002). Making a difference in adolescents' school lives: Visible and invisible aspects of content area reading. In A. E. Farstrup & S. J. Samuels (Eds.), *What research has to say about reading instruction* (3rd ed., pp. 184–204). Newark, DE: International Reading Association.

Whitehead, D. (2001). *Top tools for literacy and learning*. Auckland: Pearson Education.

Whitehead, D. (2004). *Top tools for teaching thinking*. Auckland: Pearson Education.

Wolfe, P. (2001). *Brain matters: Translating the research to classroom practice*. Alexandria, VA: Association of Supervision and Curriculum Development.

Yore, L. D., Hand, B. M., Goldman, S. R., Hildebrand, G. M., Osborne, J. F., Treagust, D. F., & Wallace, C. S. (2004). New directions in language and science education research. *Reading Research Quarterly, 39*, 347–352.

A Short Annotated Explanation Text about Erosion

The "Engagement" Section

When we look up at the Rocky Mountains, it's hard to imagine they were almost twice the height they are today. But they were, and today they are shorter because of a process called erosion.

The "What I'm Going to Explain" Section

Erosion is the process of transporting worn-down rock and washing away dirt and rocks. It is happening all the time, and it is caused by <u>water</u>, <u>wind</u>, <u>ice</u>, <u>gravity</u>, <u>animals</u>, and <u>humans</u>.

The "Body of Explanation" Section

Water <u>dissolves minerals</u> in rock and is powerful enough during a <u>flood</u> to sweep away the <u>dirt and rocks</u> that form river banks. <u>Glaciers</u>, frozen rivers of ice, <u>grind</u> over rocks and turn them into fine "<u>rock flour</u>." <u>Earthquakes</u> can cause <u>land-slides</u>, and when <u>animals</u> eat the vegetation off a hillside, or when <u>humans</u> remove the trees and carve roads into a hillside, there is a risk of erosion, especially if the ground becomes heavy with water. Finally, when the <u>wind</u> picks up <u>sand</u> and blasts it against rocks, they are slowly eroding, sometimes into interesting shapes.

The "Conclusion and Comment" Section

So, the next time you see a big mountain or a smooth, old, hard rock, remember that there is a process that is continuously wearing them down—a process called erosion.

Note. <u>Underlined</u> words are from the Multi-Flow tool about erosion (see Figure 2:3).

A Short Annotated
Description Text about Birds

The "Engagement" Section

Our <u>parakeet</u>, Wally, <u>squawks</u> and his cage sometimes smells. Wally is a bird and has a curved <u>beak</u> and beautiful <u>feathers</u>.

The "Classification of the Thing I'm Writing about" Section

Most birds are <u>animals that can fly</u>. But there are some birds, such as <u>emus</u> and <u>kiwis</u>, that don't fly. All birds have <u>feathers</u>. Some birds, such as <u>parakeets</u>, have colorful feathers, and some, such as the bald eagle, are mostly dark in color. All birds belong to the class of animals called <u>avian</u>.

The "Body" Section

Feathers, Beaks, and Wings

All birds have <u>feathers</u>. Some feathers are long like the tail feathers of a peacock. Some feathers are colorful and others black like a crow. Feathers are hollow inside, which makes them light.

All birds have <u>beaks</u>. Some are curved, others are long and curved, others are short and strong, and others are flat and wide. The type of beak a bird has and what it eats are related.

All birds have <u>wings</u>, but not all birds can fly. Some sea birds have wings up to 2 yards long. The <u>emu</u> has stumpy wings and cannot fly.

Fly, Chirp, and Eat

Most birds can <u>fly</u>. Some birds, such as the <u>hummingbird</u>, fly very fast. Other birds, such as the <u>eagle</u>, soar and <u>glide</u> and don't flap their wings as fast as a <u>hummingbird</u>.

You might think that all birds can chirp, but the <u>parakeet</u> we have at home makes a loud squawking noise that doesn't sound like a chirp. Many small birds chirp, especially the ones with short, strong beaks for <u>eating grain</u>.

But not all birds eat grain. Birds with different-shaped beaks eat different things. For example, <u>hummingbirds</u> <u>eat nectar</u> from flowers and the eagle can eat meat and fish.

Note. <u>Underlined</u> words are from the simple Concept Frame about birds (see Figure 2:4).

Supplemental Lesson on Properties of Minerals

Introduction

Mineralogists have identified over 3,000 different minerals, but the task of mineral identification does not need to be overwhelming. For elementary students, simply learning to conduct some simple tests and asking the right questions is the goal. The following simple activities are designed to use the best common minerals to illustrate key characteristics. It is not intended to be comprehensive but provides a concrete foundation. Placing correct names on minerals is not critical early in the unit, since students will revisit the samples in the Elaborate phase. Once mastered, the skills can be applied to other common minerals to assist in identification.

Big Idea: Earth is made of a limited number of common materials. By learning the basics of identification, we can classify most of the Earth materials encountered.

Key Science Questions: What types of materials make up the Earth? What are the origins of the different types of materials?

Materials Needed:

This list is only a recommendation and is by no means all-inclusive. The materials chosen may vary according to your geographic location. The varieties listed below represent economically important and common minerals. Using white-out and a fine-tip pen, number each sample prior to instruction.

Quartz	Calcite	Orthoclase	Galena
Hematite	Olivine	Biotite	Gypsum

Sediment samples may be collected or purchased at local pet stores, home improvement stores, or hardware stores. Silt is included in the description of particles, but pure samples are difficult to obtain. The term is included because silt will be encountered as students observe different soils.

Materials may be purchased at:

DJ Minerals at: http://www.djminerals.com/

Explore # 1: Color and Luster of Minerals

Materials Needed:

Mineral samples

Carpet samples

Background:

The color of a mineral is controlled mostly by composition and the arrangement of atoms. For example, graphite and diamond are both made of carbon, yet graphite is gray and diamond is colorless. Greater amounts of iron and magnesium tend to make minerals dark in color. Even trace amounts of different elements can cause differences in color. For example, quartz is made of silicon and oxygen and is commonly colorless or white. With trace amounts of other elements, it turns purple (amethyst, caused by iron), pinkish (rose quartz, caused by titanium), or citrine (light yellow).

Procedure:

1. Place all the mineral specimens on a table for the students to see and touch. Guide students' exploration by asking questions such as the following:

    -   What colors are most common? (Colorless or whitish.)

    -   Are there any other colors that seem a bit more common? (Grayish.)

    -   Which specimens have distinctive colors? (One is pink. One is green. One is black.)

- Do you think you can identify all minerals just by using color itself? (No.)

- Why not? (Because some minerals have the same color.)

- Right, so we have to look for at least two or more characteristics. Do you think using just color is useful for identifying some minerals? (Yes. Maybe the pink and green one.)

2. Next, tell students that *luster* refers to the general appearance of a mineral in reflected light. The two most common types of luster are vitreous, where minerals have a glass-like appearance, and metallic, where minerals look like they are made of metal.

3. Have students place the minerals into two groups: those that look like colored or clear glass and those that look like metal (shiny, metallic). Ask the following questions:

- What luster is most common in your set? (Glassy.)

- Do you have any that look like metal? (One or two.)

- What colors are your glassy ones? (Mostly white or colorless but also pink, green, and black.)

- What colors are your metal ones? (Grayish.)

Explore #2: Hardness and Cleavage of Minerals

Materials Needed:

Mineral samples

Mineral testing kits that include plate for scratch test, weak acid, eye dropper, scale, and magnifying lenses

Carpet samples

Background:

The strength of the chemical bond and the arrangement of the atoms influence the hardness of a mineral. Hardness is defined as the resistance of a mineral to scratching. Soft minerals scratch easily. Hard minerals are more difficult to scratch.

Procedure:

1. Have students remove the specimens of gypsum, calcite, and quartz by referring to the sample numbers. Names are not important at this stage.

2. Next, have the students separate the minerals into two groups: those that can be scratched by their fingernail and those that cannot be scratched. Guide their exploration of minerals by asking the following questions:

   - How many are softer than your fingernail? (One.)

   - Of the two remaining, which one is harder? Can you develop a test? (We could scratch something else.)

   - Geologists commonly use a glass plate to test hardness. Do both your minerals scratch the plate? (No, just one.)

   - Describe the relative hardness of your samples compared to your fingernail and the glass plate. (Mineral #1 is softer than my fingernail. Mineral #2 is harder than my fingernail but softer than glass. Mineral #3 is harder than the glass.)

   - So even though a mineral might be the same color and luster, we can use hardness as an additional characteristic to help with identification.

3. Explain to students that cleavage is how a mineral breaks. It is controlled by planes of weak bonds within the mineral. Cleavage appears in good mineral samples as flat faces on the crystal that reflect light. Geologists commonly describe the number of cleavage faces (1, 2, or 3) and the angle between them (90 degrees, not 90, 60, or 120 degrees).

4. Have students remove the specimens of biotite, potassium feldspar, calcite, halite, and galena. Remember to refer to them by the sample numbers.

5. Have them separate the minerals into groups based on their shapes: sheets (flat), boxy or squarish, or rhombs (boxes pushed over on their sides). Guide their exploration by asking the following questions:

   - How many of your minerals are flat sheets? (One.)

   - What color is it? (Black.)

   - Geologists say that a mineral has one direction on cleavage because it always breaks into these sheets. Can you find any minerals that tend to break into squares? If so, how many? (Yes, two.)

   - What color are they? (One is colorless, or white, and the other is gray.)

   - You have a few minerals left. Describe their cleavage. (Well, one is sort of squarish but not really.)

   - What do you mean? (Well, it has six sides, so I guess that means three directions of cleavage, but the angles are not straight [not right angles].)

- What do you mean by not straight? (It looks like the box got pushed over on its side.)

- It (i.e., calcite) has three directions of cleavage, making it like a box or rectangle, but the sides are not at 90 degrees. What about the last one (i.e., potassium feldspar)? (I can see some right angles but not like the other one.)

- Right, it has two directions of cleavage at 90 degrees. Think of a box but one with raggedy, poorly defined ends.

Explore #3: Other Properties of Minerals: Density, Streak, Reaction to Acid

Materials Needed:

Mineral samples

Mineral testing kits that include plate for scratch test, weak acid, eye dropper, scale, and magnifying lenses

A beaker with 100 mL of water added

Carpet samples

Background:

Other characteristics are useful for mineral identification. Density is the weight of a mineral per unit volume. For minerals, the units are grams per cubic centimeter (g/cc).

Procedure:

1. Have students remove the specimens of quartz and galena and refer to them by the sample numbers.

2. Have students weigh each mineral on a scale or balance.

3. Determine the volume of each specimen. An easy way to determine the volume is to measure the amount of water displaced by each specimen. For example, fill a beaker to 100 mL and gently drop in the sample. The amount of water displaced is equal to the volume of the mineral. Divide the weight in grams by volume in milliliters (a milliliter is equal to a cubic centimeter). For example, the density of quartz is 2.7 g/cc and galena is 7.5 g/cc.

4. Explain to students that *streak* is the color of the powdered mineral. It is another characteristic that is useful in identifying minerals. Demonstrate

how to hold the porcelain plate from the mineral testing kit against the table and firmly drag a mineral across the plate.

5. Using the calcite and hematite samples (remember to refer to them by the sample numbers), have students complete the streak test. Ask them:

    • What color is the streak for mineral #1 (calcite)? (White.)

    • What color is the streak for mineral #2 (hematite)? (Red.)

6. Conduct an experiment. One of the most common minerals, calcite, reacts with diluted acid. Vinegar is a safe, appropriate acid to use in this experiment. Have students remove the calcite and quartz. Remember to refer to them by the sample numbers. Place one or two drops of acid on sample #1 (quartz). Ask the following guiding questions:

    • Does vinegar make the mineral bubble or fizz? (No, it does not.) Now, place one or two drops of acid on sample #2 (calcite), and repeat the question.

    • Does vinegar make the mineral bubble or fizz? (Yes, it does.)

    This sample is the only mineral in the set that will react with acid. This mineral is common in two rocks used in chapter 9, The Earth Beneath Our Feet.

Phase 3: Explain

Materials Needed:

    Mineral sets

    Carpet samples

Procedure:

1. Have a discussion about the previous Explores, and lead a discussion in which you clarify concepts, help students understand why they did the experiments, introduce scientific vocabulary, and correct any misconceptions. Ask questions such as:

    • We started off by looking at minerals. What were some of the characteristics you described? (Color, luster, hardness, and reaction to acid.)

    • Which is easier to determine, color or luster? (Color.)

    • Why is color easier to determine? (Well, we have known our colors for a long time.)

    • What color was most common? (Whitish or colorless.)

    • Were any of the colors distinctive? (Maybe the pink one or the green one.)

- Those two minerals have really distinctive colors. [The pink one is potassium feldspar. The green one is olivine.] So, color is a useful way to help identify those materials. Was luster useful? (Yes, we could make two groups. The glassy ones and the metal ones.)

- Geologists call the glassy minerals *vitreous*. The ones that look like metal are said to have a *metallic luster*. Vitreous and metallic luster are the two most common.

- Did all the minerals have the same hardness? (No.)

- How did you determine which were harder and which were softer? (We scratched our fingernails and the glass plates and the other minerals.)

- Okay, could you put them in order of softest to hardest? (Yes.)

- What did our reading book say about hardness? (Some guy made a scale from 1 to 10. A diamond is the hardest.)

- Your fingernail has a hardness of 3 on the scale. The glass plate has a hardness of 7. So, you can actually determine a number for hardness. What about the acid? Did all your samples fizz? (No, only one.)

- Do you think it was a useful test? (It's fun. And it helped us find that one mineral out of the three or four that were whitish in color.)

- What other characteristics on minerals did we determine? (Cleavage, density, and streak.)

- How did the minerals break? (Some were flat and some were squares.)

- Right, we looked at the shiny faces on the crystals and counted how many and at what angles. Geologists call how a mineral breaks *cleavage*. It is controlled by how the atoms are arranged inside the mineral. What was the shape of the mineral that fizzed? [Calcite] (Sort of like pushed-over boxes.)

- Right, those are called rhombs. There are three different planes at but not at right ("└") angles. Did all the minerals have the same weight in your hand? (Well, some were heavy and some were light.)

- Okay, but you need to be careful. Remember what we did to determine a number? (Oh, we weighed it and then put it in water.)

- Right, that's called *density*. So, for density, we are determining the weight for the same amount of mineral. Were your numbers all the same? (No, we found some minerals with lower density and some with higher density.)

- What did we use the white porcelain squares for? (To smash up some of the mineral.)

- Right, geologists call that *streak*. Streak is the color of the powdered mineral. Did you have any surprises? (Yes, one of the metallic gray minerals had a red streak.)

- Right. That is the mineral hematite. One of its key characteristics is a red streak. Great, you are well on your way to being able to identify the most common minerals on Earth!

Phase 4: Elaborate

Materials Needed:

Investigating Minerals booklet, one copy for each student

Variety of trade books, Web sites on minerals

Procedure:

1. Have students go to the "Investigating Minerals" booklet and complete the cover, and direct students' attention to the "Investigating Earth Materials: Minerals" page.

2. Place students in a group of four. Have each group list their samples by number in the left column, and notice their task for the right column, where they are going to list descriptions of each sample. Distribute trade books and/or have Web sites bookmarked for student use. Encourage students to use specific terminology, so instead of saying a sample is "light" in color, encourage students to say it is "variable white." Likewise, when describing the mineral's hardness, encourage students to record descriptions that say "harder than ——" or "softer than ——." Encourage students to use the resources as needed for the correct use of scientific vocabulary.

3. Allow a few minutes for students to record, in the right-hand column, words to describe each sample. Tell them this is the first step actual geologists take when they are making observations about minerals.

4. Using the same materials, have students complete the "Classifying Earth Materials: Minerals" *or* the "Minerals Note-Taking Guide" page in their booklet. Allow time for small-group discussion and collaboration.

Investigating Minerals

Name _____

Date_____

Full size form available at www.Christopher-Gordon.com/authors/KingMattox-shtml

Investigating Earth Materials: Minerals

Name:_____

Date:_____

You have been given common minerals found on Earth. Your job is to describe and classify them. You may use your own words or the words geologists use. Record your observations by writing the sample number and a description of the sample.

Sample numbers:	Description:

Full size form available at www.Christopher-Gordon.com/authors/KingMattox-shtml

Classifying Earth Materials: Minerals

Observe the samples on your table. Use the chart below to help you classify the samples. Write a description of the mineral using the information.

Mineral Set:

Mineral	Color/Streak	Hardness	Luster	Cleavage

Notes:

Full size form available at www.Christopher-Gordon.com/authors/KingMattox-shtml

Key to Mineral Descriptions

(Optional challenge specimens denoted by *)

Mineral	Color/Streak	Hardness	Luster	Cleavage
Quartz	variable/white	harder than glass 7.0	nonmetallic, vitreous, glassy	no cleavage, has fracture
Orthoclase Feldspar	pink, white, or gray/white	harder than glass 6.0	nonmetallic	yes
Calcite	variable/white	softer than penny 3.0	nonmetallic	yes
Galena	color is gray, streak is lead gray	about as hard as a fingernail 2.5	metallic	yes
Hematite	gray, streak is rust colored	about as hard as glass 5.5 – 6.5	metallic	no
Olivine	green, whitish streak	harder than glass 6.5 - 7	nonmetallic	no
Biotite Mica	color is black, streak is greenish black	softer than penny 2.5	nonmetallic, very shiny	yes
Magnetite*	black, streak is black	a little harder than glass 6	metallic	no
Muscovite Mica*	color is white, streak is white	softer than penny 2.5	nonmetallic, very shiny	yes
Amphibole* (Hornblende)	black	about as hard as glass 5.5	nonmetallic	yes
Pyrite*	brassy yellow, streak is greenish black	a little harder than glass 6	metallic	no

Full size form available at www.Christopher-Gordon.com/authors/KingMattox-shtml

Minerals Note-Taking Guide

Geologist Name: _____

1) Name of mineral: _____

2) What does this mineral look like? What is its color, streak, luster?

_____

_____

_____

3) Where can we find this mineral? _____

_____

_____

4) What makes this mineral unique? _____

_____

5) How is this mineral used? _____

_____

6) A picture or photo of this mineral here can be found (list source):

_____

_____

Now write a sentence or two that combines the information from questions 1–5 above. Write your summary below:

Full size form available at www.Christopher-Gordon.com/authors/KingMattox-shtml

SAMPLE
Minerals Note-Taking Guide

Geologist Name: Irah

1) Name of mineral: sulfur

2) What does this mineral look like? What is its color, streak, luster?
it is bright yellow with a yellow streak and an earthy luster.

3) Where can we find this mineral? near a volcano

4) What makes this mineral unique? sulfur smells like rotten
eggs!

5) How is this mineral used? it is used in fertilizer and in
making rubber

6) A picture or photo of this mineral here can be found (list source):

"Looking at Rocks" by Jennifer Dussling, page 17.

Now write a sentence or two that combines the information from
questions 1–5 above. Write your summary below:

Sulfur is a yellow mineral found close to volcanoes. It smells

like rotten eggs, but we use it to make fertilizer.

Full size form available at www.Christopher-Gordon.com/authors/KingMattox-shtml

Supplemental Lesson on Supporting Life and Phases of the Moon

Introduction

Supporting Life

In this appendix, we provide additional information and activities on supporting life and the phases of the moon. Central to our exploration of the solar system and the universe is the possibility of life on other planets and moons. As humans explore space, we need oxygen, water, and food, and protection from the environment. An ideal planet would have enough oxygen in the atmosphere for us to breathe, abundant water (preferably as a liquid), and means to grow food (soil and light). Environmental threats include temperature extremes and too much radiation. The atmosphere is commonly a moderator of both temperature and radiation. Earth is the only known planet with the unique combination of factors to allow life to originate and evolve.

Phases of the Moon

From Earth, the moon is observed to undergo a monthly pattern of changes called phases. This apparent change in the amount of the moon that is illuminated is caused by the moon's changing position relative to the sun and the Earth. For example, when the moon is opposite the sun, relative to Earth, all of the moon facing the Earth is illuminated and we see a full moon. When the moon is between the sun and the moon, the illuminated face of the moon is facing away from us and we do not see the moon (the new moon phase).

Big Ideas: (1) Life on earth is possible because of the presence of liquid water, a protective atmosphere that includes oxygen, moderate temperatures, and abundant carbon; (2) The observed phase of the moon is the result of the position of the moon relative to the Earth and sun.

Key Science Questions: What factors contribute to make life possible on Earth? Why does the phase of the moon change in an observable pattern?

National Science Standards: (1) Organisms have basic needs. Animals need air, water, and food. Organisms can only survive in environments in which their needs can be met; (2) The sun and moon have properties, locations, and movements that can be observed and described. The observable shape of the moon changes from day to day in a cycle that lasts about a month.

Materials Needed:

    Solar System by Gregory Vogt

    Mapping of the Skies by Walter Oleksy

    "Wrecked on the Moon" ranking sheets, one per student

    A transparency of "Wrecked on the Moon" ranking sheet

    "Wrecked on the Moon" key

    Transparency pen

    Poster paper

    Marvelous Moon journal, one for each student

    The Moon Seems to Change Shape by Franklyn M. Branley

    Styrofoam ball

    Wooden meat skewer or pencil

    Light source for group

    Moon on a Stick Observations sheets, one for each student

    Diagram #1, on overhead transparency

    Diagram #2, on overhead transparency

    North, South, East, West labels printed on chart paper

    Tape

Engage #1: Surviving on the Moon

Show a photograph of an astronaut on the moon. Consider using the photo of astronaut Buzz Aldrin on page 20 of *Solar System* (2001) by Gregory Vogt or the one on page 35 of *Mapping the Skies* (2002) by Walter Oleksy (see the Teacher Resources section of chapter 11 for more details on these books). Or, use Images at Google (http://www.google.com) and search under "astronaut." Ask students to predict what this astronaut would need to survive on the moon.

Explore #1: Wrecked on the Moon

Materials Needed:

> "Wrecked on the Moon" ranking sheets, one per student
>
> A transparency of "Wrecked on the Moon" ranking sheet
>
> Transparency pen

Procedure:

1. This activity is based on a NASA activity, Astro-Venture Astronomy Training, which is addressed in http://astroventure.arc.nasa.gov/teachers/astron_train.html. Begin by stating the purpose of the activity, which is to prioritize the needs of humans when they visit other planets or moons. Have students imagine they are astronauts on an exploration trip to the moon. While on an expedition, their lunar rover breaks down. They must walk back to their base camp if they are to survive.

2. Give them the "Wrecked on the Moon Ranking Sheet," which contains a list of items found on their rover. Have them rank each item in terms of importance for survival. The most important item would be ranked #1. Ask students to individually record their personal ranking of the items on their activity sheets in the column marked Personal. One option to make this more challenging is to tell students they can only use 10 items on their list.

3. Have students discuss their rankings in small groups, including their rationale, and indicate the group's response for each item on their individual sheet.

4. After the groups have shared their responses, record the range of student responses on the transparency, again requesting that students verbalize their rationale for ranking the items.

Explain #1: Surviving on Other Worlds

Materials Needed:

"Wrecked on the Moon" key

Poster paper

Procedure:

1. After the students have compiled their group's rankings, discuss the items as a whole class and provide NASA's rationale. Compare and contrast student rankings with those of actual astronauts. In making these comparisons, draw students' attention to the characteristics of the moon that influences ranking. For instance, since there is no air on the moon, the matches will not ignite, so they are not essential to survival in that environment. Likewise, the compass will not work on the moon because of the lack of polarized magnetic fields. Thus, the compass is ranked low in terms of survival on the moon. Look at the hypothetical dialogue between a teacher and students that models how the Explain portion of a 5E lesson should operate at this point in the unit.

    • Okay everyone, your lunar rover is dead. It's going to be a long walk back to base. Based on your study, what items are most important to your survival? (Water, oxygen, pistol, and a heater.)

    • That's an interesting list. Which of those two items are most important and why? (Water and oxygen. You need to breathe and it gets hot in your spacesuit so you need water. The pistol is heavy and not very useful. The heater would only be useful on the dark side of the moon.)

    • Of those two items, which is most important? (The oxygen. We could go minutes or hours without a drink, but we need to be breathing all the time.)

    • I agree the oxygen and water are essential. What else do you think is important? (Food, constellation map, raft, and the compass.)

    • Which of those two items are most important and why? (We think the food and the compass are most important. You need to eat and know which way to go.)

    • Are you sure about the compass? Does the moon have a magnetic field like the Earth? (No, the moon doesn't have a magnetic field. So, the compass wouldn't work. We should use the constellation map.)

Engage #2: Observing The Moon

Materials Needed:

Marvelous Moon journal, one for each student

Procedure:

Like real scientists, students need to construct their knowledge based on their own observations. Therefore, for this Engage activity, have the students make observations of the moon in the evening for 14 days. Even a few observations over this period will demonstrate that the moon changes in a systematic way, and that the students can make meaningful observations. It is a good idea for them to start their observations when the moon is in its waxing crescent phase. Have the students make their observations just after sunset and record them in their Marvelous Moon journals. They will make a sketch of the moon and note the time of their observation. They should also describe the change in the location of the moon in respect to the western horizon. The U.S. Naval Observatory (http://aa.usno.navy.mil/) provides data on moon phases.

Explore #2: Moon on a Stick

The goal of this activity is for students to see that the position of the sun and moon, relative to an observer on Earth, plays a key role in generating the phases of the moon. Research by Hermann and Lewis (2003) found that most students thought phases of the moon were caused by the shadow of the Earth falling on the moon. This activity is designed to overturn this common misconception by allowing students to make their own direct observations. The activity will help them develop a conceptual model to explain their own observations.

The "Moon on a Stick" activity is described in *The Moon Seems to Change Shape* by Franklyn M. Branley or in other books. If these books are not available, use the process described below. Similar versions of this activity are online at Moon Madness at:

(http://starchild.gsfc.nasa.gov/docs/StarChild/solar_system_level2/Moonlight.html)

Materials Needed:

The Moon Seems to Change Shape by Franklyn M. Branley

Styrofoam ball

Wooden meat skewer or pencil

Light source for group

Moon on a Stick Observations sheets, one for each student

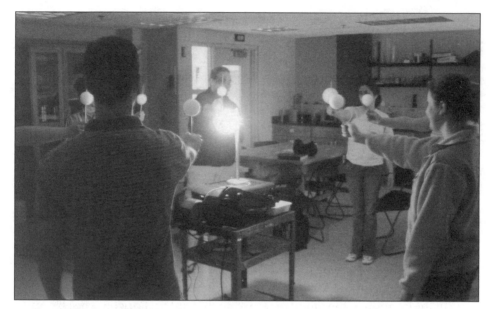

Figure D:1. Preservice teachers demonstrate the Moon on a Stick activity. The students' heads represent the Earth, the ball is the moon, and the lamp is the sun. All students are modeling the arrangement of the Earth, moon, and the sun that generates the new noon phase. Note. From the camera's perspective, different amounts of each ball are illuminated, making different phases on each "moon."

Procedure:

1. Give each student a Moon on a Stick Observations sheet. Place the light bulb in the middle of the classroom. Students stand around the room facing the light and at arm's length from each other. The light bulb represents the sun, the styrofoam ball represents the moon, and the student's head represents the Earth. Place the ball on the skewer to make it easier to handle. The student will hold the "moon" at arm's length. Ask students to record their observation under item #1.

2. Starting with the "moon" between the student and the "sun" have each student rotate and turn in place to the left while watching the "moon." Have them describe and record what they see on their Moon on a Stick Observations sheet, item #2. The following are hypothetical observations, but your students' responses should be close to these:

    • The light is so bright, it is hard to see the moon. My side of the moon is in shadow.

    • As the moon moves out of alignment with the sun, I can see the edge of it illuminated by the light/Sun. It makes a very thin crescent on the right side of the moon.

- As the moon keeps moving to the left, more and more of it gets illuminated until the right half is all in light. I think this is the first quarter phase.

3. Continue to move the ball until it is straight out to the right. Ask students to record their observation on their Moon on a Stick Observations sheet, item #3.

    - As I keep moving, more and more of the moon is illuminated until is as all lit up. It is a full moon. The sun, Earth, and moon are in a line. It is a full moon. Then, as the moon keeps moving, less and less is lit up. When the moon is perpendicular to the Earth and the sun, I see the moon half lit up again, but this time it is the other half in light. This must be a third quarter moon.

4. Continue to move the ball until it returns to its original position. Ask students to record their observation on their Moon on a Stick Observations sheet, item #4. Student observations should say something like:

    As I sweep through the last bit, there is a crescent that gets smaller and smaller but, again, it is the other side of the moon lit up compared to when I started. Then, the moon is near the sun again and I can't see it. It must be a new moon again.

5. For a challenge, briefly discuss eclipses with students. Start by offering a simple explanation of a lunar eclipse. For instance, say something like "When the sun shines on the Earth, the Earth creates a shadow. Once in a while, the moon moves into the Earth's shadow, and when this occurs, a lunar eclipse happens." Ask students to create a "lunar eclipse" and record their observation on their Moon on a Stick Observations sheet, item #5. Student observations should say something like:

    For a lunar eclipse I need to put the ball in the shadow of my head. So, it's like a full moon with the sun, Earth, and moon in a line. The eclipse is due to shadows but not the phases.

6. To continue challenging students, say something such as, "During a solar eclipse, the moon moves between the Earth and the sun." Ask students to create a "solar eclipse" and record their observation on their Moon on a Stick Observations sheet, item #5. Student observations should say something like:

    For a solar eclipse, I need the ball to block the light. So, it all makes a line but this time the order is sun, moon, then Earth. The moon blocks out the sun.

Explain #2: Earth, Sun, and Moon

Materials Needed:

>   Diagram #1, on overhead transparency

>   Diagram #2, on overhead transparency

Procedure:

1.   Hold a discussion to help students understand and articulate their observations. Remind students they began by being scientists and made observations in their Marvelous Moon journals. Then, they explored the phases of the moon using a simulation. Discuss these activities using questions such as the following:

     •   What did you observe and record? (The moon got bigger.) Bigger? Do you mean it actually increased in size? (No. Just the part with the light on it.)

     •   How did it change? (It started as a skinny crescent and got fatter until it was a full moon.)

     •   Did you see the moon at the same time each night? (No, it would come up later and later each night.)

     •   Good observation. The moon rises later and later each night as it goes through its phases. Did anyone note the time when the full moon came up? (9:00 p.m.)

     •   Did you see the phases on clear nights, nights with no clouds? (Yes. The phases changed even when there are no clouds.)

     •   What did you see on cloudy nights? (I didn't see the moon at all.)

     •   What did you see on nights when it was partly cloudy? (I could see the moon, but the phase stayed the same.)

     •   What were the clouds doing? (They just moved through the sky.)

     •   Did the moon's phase change as they moved? (No.)

     •   Why not? (Because the phase depends on where the moon is as it goes around the Earth.)

     •   In class, we used a model to explore position of the moon, relative to the Earth and sun, as the moon orbited the Earth. What objects represented the sun, Earth, and moon? (The light bulb was the sun. My head was the Earth. The styrofoam ball was the moon.)

     •   How were these arranged? (The sun stayed in the center. We faced it and the moon went around our heads.)

- Is this very realistic? (Yes, the Earth slowly goes around the sun, and the moon goes around the Earth.)

- Describe what you saw as you moved the ball around your head. (The ball acted like the phases we observed in the Moon on a Stick activity and in our Moon journal.)

- Now describe it using scientific terms, and be specific. (It started as a thin crescent when it was just away from the sun. Then, it was a first quarter moon when the moon was perpendicular to the sun-Earth line. Then full when the moon was in line with the sun and the Earth. Then it was a third quarter moon when the moon was perpendicular to the sun-Earth line on the other side. Then, crescent again as the moon got close to the sun again.)

- Was the moon really getting closer to the sun? (No, just a tiny bit as it moved through its orbit.)

- So, do clouds have anything to do with causing the phases to change? (No.)

- What does? (It depends on where the moon is compared to the Earth and sun.)

- Right. Did any of you make an eclipse with your model? How? (We put the ball in the shadow we made with our head.)

- What kind of eclipse was that? (It was a lunar eclipse because the light on the moon got blocked out.)

- What phase was the moon in just before and after the eclipse? (It was a full moon.)

- Did anyone else create an eclipse? What kind? (We made a solar eclipse by blocking out the light bulb with our ball.)

- Yes, a solar eclipse occurs because the sun is blocked by the moon. What phase was the moon in just before and after the eclipse? (It was a new Moon.)

- Why don't solar eclipses happen all the time? (Because everything needs to line up just right.)

- Do you think this was a good model to use? (Yes.)

- Why did we use a model to explore phases? (Because the sun, Earth, and moon are too big to fit in our classroom.)

- Yes, some things that scientists study are too big or too small to fit in their labs, so they make smaller or bigger representations that are easier to manipulate and see. Can you give me another example of a model we used in class? (Answers will vary.)

• So, when we use models, we are using a method scientists use to understand how some systems work.

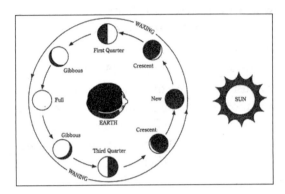

Figure D:2. The moon as seen from Earth. Reprinted with permission from Astro Adventures II, by Dennis Schatz and Paul Allan, copyright 2003 by Pacific Science Center.

2. Place Figure D:2 on the overhead and explain it to the class. Say something like:

"This diagram is a type of model. We use diagrams and models in science to represent real life. In this case, since we can't literally bring part of the solar system into our classroom to help explain what we've just observed, we will use this diagram. The diagram shows the relative position of the sun (the lamp), moon (the ball), and Earth (the student) during the moon on a Stick activity. The view is from above. Each phase shows what you observed when the moon is at a specific position in its orbit relative to the Sun and Earth. For example, a new moon is observed when the ball is between you and the light. A full moon is observed when the ball is on the opposite side of you relative to the light."

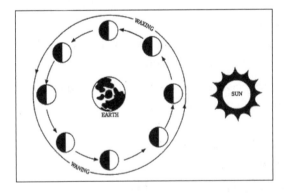

Figure D:3. The moon's position relative to the Earth and sun as viewed from above our solar system. Reprinted with permission from Astro Adventures II, by Dennis Schatz and Paul Allan, copyright 2003 by Pacific Science Center.

3. Show students Figure D:3 and explain it. "This diagram represents the actual position of the sun, moon, and Earth as the moon passes through its monthly phases. Again, this view is from above the solar system. Note that one half of the moon is always illuminated by the sun. The amount of the moon illuminated, as seen from Earth, varies with the position of the moon, relative to the Earth and sun. For example, a new moon is observed when the illuminated side of the moon faces away from Earth. [Point to the part of

the diagram that shows a new moon.] A full moon is observed when the fully illuminated face of the moon is seen from Earth. [Point to the part of the diagram that shows a full moon.] The reason we are reviewing this diagram is to help us explain why the moon looked the way it did when we recorded our observations in our Marvelous Moon journals."

Elaborate #1: The Moon Dance

Materials Needed:

North, South, East, West labels printed on chart paper

Tape

Background:

This dance is adapted from an Operation Physics Astronomy Unit. Although moon phases and the position of the sun can become apparent with other models, the Moon Dance, which is a type of lunar aerobics, can put it all into perspective. Whereas all participants will do this activity at the same time, it is best described as a demonstration where you, the teacher, will provide instructions orally. We recommend this activity be done in the gym or other large room where there is ample room to move around. Label the walls: North, South, East, and West. All participants should face south during this activity.

The purpose of the activity is to help participants understand why the moon is sometimes visible during the day. Be sure to state this purpose before you begin. With the Moon Dance, they see that the full moon rises as the sun sets, and sets as the sun rises, so it will never be visible during the day. However, the first quarter moon, whose separation is 90 degrees to the left, is visible during the day. When the sun is at high noon, the moon is rising in the east. Therefore, the first quarter moon will be up with the sun from noon until sunset. The last quarter moon will be high in the south when the sun is rising and the moon sets at noon. This activity challenges the misconception that some students hold that the moon is only out at night. After each step in the dance, we include hypothetical dialogue between the teacher and students to help solidify their discovery.

Procedure:

1. To begin the dance, the teacher stands at the front of the class facing south, the same direction as all the participants. Using an outspread right hand as the sun, everyone reaches out with their right arm and traces the motion of the sun from sunrise in the east to sunset in the west

with the sun reaching its highest point at noon. Because the sun rises due east and sets due west only on the equinoxes, you may want to indicate that the sun is rising and setting farther north in the summer and farther south during the winter. At night, the sun drops below the horizon, indicated by moving the hand northward and low, 180 degrees from the noontime position. Discuss:

- Where does the sun come up in the morning? (In the east.)

- Show me its path across the sky. [Students use their open hand to trace an arc in the southern sky.]

- Place your hand where you think the sun is at noon. [Students point their open hand to the south.]

- Why are your arms are at different angles above the horizon? (We're showing where the sun is at different times of the year. It's higher above the horizon in summer than in the winter.)

- What is going on as you drop your open hand below the western horizon? (The sun goes down, and it is night.)

2. Next, make a fist with your left hand. This represents the moon. Remind students they have already learned that a new moon rises and sets with the sun. Bring the two hands up together and have them move across the sky at the same rate setting together in the west. Discuss.

Figure D:4. Preservice teachers demonstrate the Moon Dance activity. Students' right hands represent the sun and their left hands represent the moon. The students are facing south. In this photograph, the students are showing the moon nearly aligned with the sun, producing a new moon phase at about noontime.

- Why do you have your two hands together? (Because, during the new moon, the moon and the sun are in a line and they travel across the sky together.)

- Are we going to see the new moon? (No. The illuminated side is facing away from us.)

- Is it in the day or night sky? (It's with the sun, so it has to be in the daytime sky.)

3.   Next, bring the right hand up just ahead of the moon. Have your sun and moon move across the sky at the same rate. The sun will set a little ahead of the moon. This is the waxing crescent moon. Discuss.

   • Which sets first, the sun or the moon? (The sun, followed by the moon.)

   • Right, and what phase is the moon? (It would be a waxing crescent.)

4.   Next, bring the sun up and move it to the south before you raise the moon. Move your sun and moon both across the sky; when the sun sets, the moon will be to the south. This is the first quarter. Discuss.

   • What is the angle between the sun and the moon? (Sort of a right angle.)

   • Right, and your head is in one corner of the triangle.

5.   Bringing the sun up and moving it to the southwest before the moon rises models a waxing gibbous moon. Bringing the sun up, moving it across the sky, and having it set as the moon rises models a full moon. The waning phases can best be shown by having the right hand represent the moon and the left hand representing the sun. During the waning phases, the moon rises before the sun. If students get confused during this activity, return to either of the moon diagrams and use the illustration to clarify their misunderstanding. Discuss.

Figure D:5. Preservice teachers demonstrate the Moon Dance activity. In this photograph, the students are showing the moon nearly opposite with the sun producing a full moon phase at about noontime.

   • During the full moon, which comes up first, the sun or the moon? (The sun.)

   • When does the moon come up? (It comes up just as the sun sets.)

   • Is the full moon part of the day or night sky? (We only see it at night.)

   • When does it set? (At sunrise.)

6.   The waning phases can best be shown by having the right hand represent the moon and the left hand representing the sun. During the waning phases, the moon rises before the sun. Discuss.

- During the third quarter moon, which comes up first, the sun or the moon? (The moon.)

- When does the moon come up? (It comes up hours after the sun sets.)

- Is the third quarter moon part of the day or night sky? (Well, sort of both.)

- Explain what you mean. (It must come up late at night. Then, I see it in the day sky on my way to school. It sets during the day while I'm at school.)

Wrecked On The Moon Ranking Sheet

Name _____

You are a member of a space crew and have experienced mechanical difficulty about 100 miles from your base camp. In order to survive, you must reach the base camp. Listed below are 15 items that were on your rover when it broke down. Decide what items are important for you to survive walking to base camp. Rank them in order of importance with #1 being most important. First, rank them personally, then discuss the ranking with your small group and determine your group's ranking. Compare your rankings with NASA's.

Item	Personal	Group	NASA
Box of matches	_____	_____	_____
Food concentrate	_____	_____	_____
50 feet of nylon rope	_____	_____	_____
Parachute	_____	_____	_____
.45 caliber pistol	_____	_____	_____
Case of dehydrated milk	_____	_____	_____
Two 100-lb tanks of oxygen	_____	_____	_____
Moon constellation map	_____	_____	_____
Self-inflating life raft	_____	_____	_____
Magnetic compass	_____	_____	_____
Five gallons of water	_____	_____	_____
Self-igniting signal flares	_____	_____	_____
First aid kit w/hypodermic needle	_____	_____	_____
Solar powered FM transmitter	_____	_____	_____
Portable heating unit	_____	_____	_____

Full size form available at www.Christopher-Gordon.com/authors/KingMattox-shtml

Wrecked on the Moon Key: NASA's Ranking

Item	Ranking	Reason
Box of matches	15	No air on the moon, matches will not burn
Food concentrate	4	Efficient means of providing energy requirements
50 feet of nylon rope	6	Useful in scaling cliffs or in case of injury
Parachute	8	Possible use as a sun shield
.45 caliber pistol	11	Possible means of self-propulsion
Case of dehydrated milk source	12	Bulkier duplication of energy
Two 100-lb tanks of oxygen	1	Most pressing survival requirement
Moon constellation map	3	Primary means of navigation
Self-inflating life raft	9	CO_2 bottle may serve as a propulsion source
Magnetic compass	14	There are no polarized magnetic fields on the moon, so the compass is useless.
Five gallons of water	2	Replacement of tremendous liquid loss
Self-igniting signal flares	10	Distress signal if mother ship is sighted
First aid kit	7	Needles for medicines and vitamins fit with special hypodermic needle and spacesuit
Solar powered FM transmitter mothership	5	For communication with
Portable heating unit	13	Not needed during moon's daylight

Full size form available at www.Christopher-Gordon.com/authors/KingMattox-shtml

Name_____

Marvelous Moon Journal

Go outside just after sunset and face west. Observe the following things about our marvelous moon, and record your observations below.

DATE	TIME	WEATHER (Clear, Partly Cloudy, Mostly Cloudy, Foggy)	MY SKETCH OF THE MOON

Name_____

Moon on a Stick Observations

The light bulb represents the sun. The styrofoam ball represents the moon. Your head represents the Earth. Stick the "moon" on the skewer. Hold the skewer in your hand and turn so that the "moon" is between you and the "sun." It may be necessary for you to raise the "moon" just a little so that you can just see the "sun" under the moon.

1. Describe the appearance of the moon:

_____

_____

_____

_____

2. Hold the skewer in your left hand, and slowly move the moon around your head to the left. You are moving the "moon" in a counter-clockwise direction. This imitates the direction in which the moon orbits the Earth. Describe what happens to the appearance of the "moon" as you move it until it is opposite the "sun":

_____

_____

_____

_____

3. Continue to move the ball until it is straight out to your right. Describe what happened to the lighted portion of the "moon":

_____

_____

_____

Full size form available at www.Christopher-Gordon.com/authors/KingMattox-shtml

4. Now bring the "moon" back to its original position. Describe the changes of the "moons" appearance you observed during this last motion:

_____

_____

_____

_____

5. Challenge questions:

• Where would you need to place the "moon" to simulate a lunar eclipse?

_____

_____

_____

• Where would you need to place the "moon" to simulate a solar eclipse?

Full size form available at www.Christopher-Gordon.com/authors/KingMattox-shtml

Index

About the Authors

Caryn M. King is a Professor in the College of Education at Grand Valley State University, Grand Rapids, MI. She received her Ph.D. from the University of Pittsburgh.

In addition to preparing M.Ed. Reading Specialist candidates, Caryn has begun teaching in an exploratatory research project known as Target Inquiry. This three year program, funded by the National Science Foundation, is an innovative, coherent, inquiry-focused professional development program for high school chemistry teachers who work with economically disadvantaged and limited English proficient students. The program is designed to meet the national need to move high school science instruction from traditional lecture toward actively engaging students in scientific inquiry as outlined by the National Science Education Standards.

Stephen R. Mattox is an Associate Professor in the Department of Geology at Grand Valley State University. He received his Ph.D. from Northern Illinois University. Current research projects include looking at the quality of content in children's Earth science trade books, gender and race in children's Earth science trade books, and gender and race in college introductory geology books.